Beyond

Policy

Analysis

PUBLIC ISSUE

MANAGEMENT

IN TURBULENT

TIMES

P9-DEG-064

Beyond

Policy

Analysis

PUBLIC ISSUE

MANAGEMENT

IN TURBULENT

TIMES

Leslie A. Pal

CARLETON UNIVERSITY

I**T**P® International Thomson Publishing
The ITP logo is a trademark under licence

Published in 1997 by
I**T**P® **Nelson**

A division of Thomson Canada Limited
1120 Birchmount Road
Scarborough, Ontario M1K 5G4

Visit our Web site at **http://www.nelson.com/nelson.html**

All rights reserved. No part of this work covered by the copyrights hereon may be reproduced or used in any form or by any means—graphic, electronic, or mechanical, including photocopying, recording, taping, or information storage and retrieval systems—without prior written permission of the publisher.

To show your appreciation for the time and effort that the authors and publisher have invested in this book, please choose **not** to photocopy it. Choose instead to add it to your own personal library. The investment will be well worth it.

Every effort has been made to trace ownership of all copyrighted material and to secure permission from copyright holders. In the event of any question arising as to the use of any material, we will be pleased to make the necessary corrections in future printings.

Copyright notices: The text quoted on page 198 is from *Advising West European Governments: Inquiries, Expertise and Public Policy,* B. Guy Peters and Anthony Barker, eds., ©1993. Reprinted by permission of the University of Pittsburgh Press. The text quoted on pages 256 and 258 is from *Annual Report May 1996,* Auditor General of Canada. Reproduced with the permission of the Minister of Public Works and Government Services Canada, 1997.

Canadian Cataloguing in Publication Data

Pal, Leslie A. (Leslie Alexander), 1954–
Beyond policy analysis: public issue management in turbulent times
Includes bibliographical references and index.
ISBN 0-17-604946-0
1. Policy sciences.   2. Political planning—Canada.
I. Title.
H97.P33   1997   361.6'1   C97–930087–9

Publisher and Team Leader   Michael Young
Acquisitions Editors   Andrew Livingston, Michael Young
Production Editor   Marcia Miron
Project Editors   Dianne Horton, Joanne Scattolon
Production Coordinator   Brad Horning
Art Director   Angela Cluer
Cover Design   Liz Harasymchuk
Interior Design   Sylvia Vander Schee
Senior Composition Analyst   Alicja Jamorski

Printed and bound in Canada

1 2 3 4 (WC) 00 99 98 97

Contents

List of Boxes

List of Figures

List of Tables

Preface

Readers of my previous book, *Public Policy Analysis: An Introduction,* should be warned. This is not a third edition, though it does pick up some key themes and develops some similar arguments. When Andrew Livingston of ITP Nelson approached me to write another edition, I hesitated. Drawing from the same well yet another time seemed unexciting, and no one should attempt to write a book unless the prospect of sitting in front of a screen for several hours a day promises some intellectual adventure. More importantly, however, the contents of the well have changed. My ideas about public policy and policy analysis have evolved since the second edition, and the discipline (and the world of governance it occupies) has changed considerably as well. I finally agreed to the project because it offered the opportunity for fresh reflections on the field, at a particularly important juncture for the discipline.

I am firmly convinced that it is time to go beyond the conventional categories of policy analysis, and no introduction to the field should presume that the shibboleths of the past will be adequate to deal with public problems in the future. This pronouncement may sound apocalyptic, but consider the coincidence of three broad factors and their combined effect on what we think of as public policy analysis. First, the world of governance is changing in fundamental and irreversible ways. Not everyone likes the changes or their effects, but globalization, information technologies, smaller and leaner (or meaner) governments, and deeply diverse societies are the marks of a new age. Second, while this new age is largely defined by smaller governments that do less by letting markets do more, the demand for governance is, if anything, increasing. Global systems are incredibly complex, and they need guidance mechanisms. Those mechanisms may involve new hybrids of government–private collaboration, but some sort of policy framework is required in everything from peace in Bosnia to porn on the Internet and international capital flows. Moreover, this new world of governance has a price that many are not willing to pay: communities corroded by the weirdly modern combination of hyper-commercialism, chronic unemployment, and social despair; public institutions plastered with happy-face commercial logos; and an emphasis on individualism, chronic competition, and ceaseless change. Government is the only weapon big enough to deal with these forces. Thus the demand for protective public policies is not likely to disappear, and neither is the idea that government can be a proactive instrument to improve competitive abilities in a global market.

The third factor relates to the field of policy analysis itself. As a mode of inquiry and of practice, policy analysis is a postwar phenomenon that was built up around the hope that the rational application of social science techniques would help solve public problems. This mandate has come on rather hard times recently, despite the continued need for good policies. Intellectually, the policy sciences have been criticized for being hyper-rational—that is, for being preoccupied with narrow quantitative techniques and with formal procedures. Policy-making is always embedded in politics, and democratic politics require citizen participation as well as expert guidance. The political process is also messy, and marked by extra-rational (*not* irrational) factors. At the practical level, policy analysis has often been driven by the political process, and often appears as nothing more than a weapon in the struggle for political advantage. As well, the public often questions the results of policies: Is education better or worse? Are more poor people on welfare or are fewer? Is unemployment ever going to go down? In short, policy analysis as a field has been rocked by growing criticism of its intellectual foundations and of its practical accomplishments.

Together, these three factors—technological and economic constraints on the traditional forms of governance, continued demands for government action through public policy, and a policy discipline that is in some disarray—require a rethinking of what policy analysis is all about. Policies will be demanded, proposed, and made, but not in the same mould as in the past. The challenge is to understand the difference these new circumstances make to the ways in which we think about public policy.

The core assumption of this book is that part of what is needed is available in the policy analysis literature, but that it must be revised and rethought in light of the radically new context of governance that has swept most industrialized countries in the last twenty years. Most of the features of this new context are quite familiar: globalization and the loss of sovereignty; the information and communications revolution; the rise of social movements and of demands for direct political participation; factionalism and group conflict; and the decline of public resources and of respect for the capacities of the public sector. Practising policy analysts realize how important these forces are, but have had little sense of how they might be incorporated into a workable analytical paradigm. Unlike *Public Policy Analysis,* which tried to balance both applied and academic orientations, this book tilts slightly more toward the challenges of application. To that end, I interviewed senior policy analysts from inside and outside government, to get a "reality check" on the ideas and arguments I was presenting in this book. They kindly agreed to interviews on a nonattributable basis; quotations from these transcripts are set in italics, and the policy analysts' names and affiliations are listed in the Appendix. I would never pretend that this was a systematic survey, but it was fascinatingly rich in perspectives.

Chapter 1 introduces basic concepts and outlines some of the problems in the field. This chapter argues that while many of the criticisms of the traditional paradigm are well founded, the rational paradigm—with its emphasis on determining goals, developing options, selecting and designing a preferred option, implementing, and evaluating—is a useful guide, providing its limitations are acknowledged. The first part of Chapter 1 offers a condensed review of the basic concepts associated with public policy and policy analysis. Experienced hands may want to skip over it (I'm a realist!), but students new to the field should read it carefully, as the rest of the book will make more sense if the basic concepts are well absorbed. Whereas Chapter 1 argues that the basic intellectual apparatus of policy analysis is still useful, Chapter 2 sketches the key changes that promise to make governance, as well as policy analysis, fundamentally different in the new millennium. Chapters 3 to 7 revisit the standard categories of the analytical paradigm (problem definition, design, implementation, policy communities, and evaluation), quickly review the current literature in each of the fields, and then consider the impact of the forces outlined in Chapter 2. Chapter 8 pulls together the previous chapters and demonstrates the range of possibilities embedded in a fresh approach to policy analysis. Readers should note that each of Chapters 3 to 7 is divided into two broad sections. The first section provides an overview of the existing policy literature on that chapter's subject, while the second goes beyond and looks at some of the major changes taking place. The latter sections are written in a more provocative style, drawing on the interviews I conducted, as well as on a wide variety of examples. As personal judgment is more prevalent here than in the literature reviews, these sections should generate more discussion and debate.

ABOUT THE WEB SITE
http://www.carleton.ca/~lpal/beyond

If it is time, as this book argues, to go beyond conventional policy analysis, then it is also time to go beyond conventional textbook publishing. Therefore, I have designed a Web site, at the address listed above, to complement and extend the content of *Beyond Policy Analysis*.

The site will be updated and amended regularly, but its constant features will include:

- a unified bibliography of all citations in the book

- a complete list of all URLs (with links) cited in the book

- a list of additional links to both Canadian and international sites with policy-relevant information

- an Afterthoughts section with detailed reflections on issues discussed in the book

- a Current Readings section that will list the most recent publications on policy analysis

- an E-mail link, so that readers may contact me directly

- a Readers' Response section with comments and suggestions on a variety of topics

Eventually, the site may post discussion threads, sample course outlines, paper topics, and approaches to using the book. I am no wide-eyed technophile, but I am convinced that the Web provides unique opportunities to dramatically extend the teaching potential of books such as *Beyond Policy Analysis*. Given the experimental nature of the Internet, as well as its interactive potential, I hope that readers and instructors will feel free to contact me and to make suggestions about both the Web site and the book.

ACKNOWLEDGMENTS

It takes courage to display one's limitations in a book like this. Many friends and colleagues have helped reduce my inhibitions. In particular, the School of Public Administration at Carleton University indulged me with a seminar (on Friday the 13th!), where some of these ideas were first floated. Other colleagues who have read and commented on various parts of the manuscript saved me from many errors of fact and interpretation, and helped me see connections that otherwise would have been invisible: Frances Abele, Bruce Doern, Katherine Graham, Roberto Gualtieri, Susan Phillips, Saul Schwartz, Geoffrey Reid, Phil Ryan, Mark Seasons, and Glen Toner. I wish to thank the following reviewers for their comments: Paul Barker, University of Western Ontario; Stephen Brooks, University of Windsor; Kenneth M. Gibbons, University of Winnipeg; Evert Lindquist, University of Toronto; and Anthony Perl, University of Calgary. I owe a special debt to Evert Lindquist, who not only suffered through the entire manuscript and made very precise and detailed suggestions, but who also helped set up some of the interviews with provincial officials. His collegiality was in the best traditions of scholarly fellowship. I also extend thanks to the interviewees who gave generously of their very limited time. Project Editor Joanne Scattalon cheerfully fulfilled her title by getting me to produce, tolerating a variety of small delays and large bursts of enthusiasm. She had to leave the book in August 1996 to look after a project of her own (an impending baby!), and passed on her responsibilities to Dianne Horton and Marcia Miron, who shepherded the manuscript through its final stages. My thanks as well to Hisham El-Leithy and Alia Tayyeb for their research assistance. Research for some parts of this manuscript was supported by a Social Sciences and Humanities Research Council Award.

Public Policy Analysis was my first published book, written when our first child was two years old. Now blessed with three children, but with uncanny symmetry and not a little déjà vu, I once again had a two-year-old toddling about as I pecked at the keyboard. Miraculously, I have the same supportive, if somewhat bemused, wife. Ultimately, when I look beyond policy analysis, it is them I see. This book is theirs.

Leslie A. Pal
Carleton University

Chapter 1 Policy Analysis: Concepts and Criticisms

Public policy analysis, as part of a broad alliance of disciplines sometimes termed the policy sciences, is in trouble. In practical terms, many of our key policy problems (unemployment, poverty, education) are actually getting worse, not a good recommendation for a set of skills dedicated to making things better. Intellectually, the traditional paradigm of the policy sciences—rationalism—has been under assault from a variety of directions for at least a quarter century. The alternatives, however, are not especially workable either. This chapter introduces the key concepts of public policy and policy analysis, and explores their limitations. It concludes with a cautious defence of the traditional model, but one that urges greater attention to major contextual factors that are revolutionizing modern forms of governance. These factors are taken up in Chapter 2.

WHAT IS PUBLIC POLICY?

Citizens expect many things from their governments, but at the very least they expect intelligent decision-making. Perhaps even more importantly, however, they expect those decisions to flow from some general position, or vision. Governments can be very decisive without being terribly intelligent. Intelligent decisions come from operating within some consistent framework, however general. We will return to this issue of consistency below, but for the moment it should be clear that the very nature of intelligent governance in a democracy demands more than mere decision-making, it demands decision-making within a framework or pattern. In short, we demand that our governments have policies.

For the purposes of this book, public policy will be defined as a course of action or inaction chosen by public authorities to address a given

problem or an interrelated set of problems. Several aspects of this definition bear some emphasis. First, note that it refers to a *course* of action.
This picks up on the idea of frameworks or patterns—policies are guides
to a range of related actions in a given field. A policy-maker is someone
who develops these guides, a policy-taker is someone who operates within
that policy framework, applying it to new situations. Immigration policy,
for example, is a broad framework that structures the actions of a host of
different organizations, from the passport office to the foreign embassy.
When political parties differ over their immigration policies, we know that
they differ over first principles (e.g., open versus closed immigration;
admission based on family considerations or economic contributions).
When a policy is changed, the actions that take place within its framework
are reconfigured to yield different results.

Another aspect of the definition is that it refers to action as well as inaction, as long as it has been chosen by public authorities. Consider the issue
of recognizing same-sex marriages. Up until a few years ago, it never
would have entered the minds of most policy-makers that this was a policy
issue that had to be addressed, and so inaction cannot be seen as a
policy decision. On the other hand, once the issue was raised directly, and
governments did face the choice of amending human rights acts and other
legislation and did not, then the failure to act can indeed be ascribed to a
policy stance. Not everything that governments do is policy driven, of
course. Indeed, the definition of a "crisis situation" is that governments
have little option but to react. As deLeon (1988) points out, a crisis is a
surprise; crises are "unpredictable and unavoidable" (p. 116). Rochefort
and Cobb (1994, 21) note that decision-making in crisis situations is
synonymous with an emergency mentality that enables "quick responses
but also tended to produce temporary band-aid solutions" to major public
problems. As well, some actions taken by government agencies are so far
down the chain of implementation that they are properly seen as reflections of organizational routine rather than policy per se. The municipal
bus driver's route is a function of policy; changes in routes due to road
construction or seasonal weather are just administrative decisions.

Finally, note that the definition refers to problems and interrelated sets
of problems. Public policy, whatever its symbolic dimensions, is seen by
policy-makers and citizens as a means of dealing with problems. In this
sense, policies are largely instrumental; that is, they are not ends in themselves, or even good in themselves, but are instruments or tools to tackle
issues of concern to the political community. But the instrumental character of public policy does not remove it from the realm of values. For one

thing, problems are only defined as such in relation to goals or things we value. For another, means and ends are not so easily separated. In public policy-making, to use the right tool means both using the tool best suited (in an instrumental sense) to the task, but also the tool that is consistent with a morally acceptable range of government behaviour. There is of course the dirty hands problem—that policy-makers will have to weigh costs and benefits in a utilitarian fashion and sometimes do bad things to achieve good ends. As Sutherland (1995) points out in a finely crafted essay, however, the dirty hands model of political life understates the importance of constitutionalism, which is the "belief in the rule of law and the belief that ideals and rules about how deliberation is realized and how the mechanisms of democratic procedure will operate are important enough to be summarized and expressed in normative documents that should and usually do guide the processes of government ..." (p. 490).

The complicated nature of problem definition in public policy-making is nicely illustrated in the final report of the Information Highway Advisory Council (1995). On the one hand, the council noted that public involvement with the information highway was inevitable because of growing fiscal pressures to use the technology to save money and improve productivity. It would also provide an opportunity to "modernize and reform the critical social infrastructure of education, learning and training, and health care" (p. 7). In the very next paragraph, however, the council noted that the policy challenge is not merely to facilitate market forces in this area: "Canadians have worked hard over the generations to give expression to equality and opportunity—values that must be preserved" (p. 7). This shows the complex entanglement of values with the more instrumental aspects of policy-making. The report also shows the way in which policy problems present themselves in clusters: the council was asked by the government to address fifteen "public policy issues" in the area of information technologies and communication. They ranged from building infrastructure and dealing with privacy and copyright, to business competitiveness, R&D and government services (Information Highway Advisory Council 1995, viii).

Policies rarely tackle single problems; rather, they face clusters of entangled problems that may have contradictory solutions. Many policy problems are complex "because of their size and breadth; they comprise *sets* of other, perhaps smaller problems whose very interconnectedness makes them difficult to comprehend, and whose boundaries are difficult to define across issues and over time" (Desveaux, Lindquist, & Toner 1994, 497). In 1993, for example, the federal government faced the problem of cigarette smuggling across the Québec and Ontario border. High Canadian cigarette taxes (designed in part to raise money and in part to dissuade smoking) had made it lucrative to smuggle cigarettes in from the United States and sell them substantially below the cost of the Canadian equivalent. Owners of stores in Québec, especially the *dépanneurs*, fueled the crisis by organizing a public "duty-free" sale of cigarettes at St. Eustache, north of Montréal (Pross & Stewart 1994, 150). A nasty cluster of problems was presented in this case. First, most of the smugglers were Aboriginals on the reserves that overlap the borders of these two provinces and New York State. After the Oka incident in 1990 (York & Pindera 1990), Ottawa was very leery of challenging Aboriginals, even if they were involved in criminal activity. Second, both levels of government levy cigarette taxes, and so while Québec was willing to reduce its taxes, Ontario was not. In the absence of coordinated federal efforts, Ontario feared that this would simply drive smokers across the border to Québec for cheaper cigarettes. Third, the smuggling problem was local to Québec and Ontario, but irrelevant in the rest of the country. Anything Ottawa did to appease the two central provinces would not necessarily have support elsewhere. Finally, it was clear that in order to deal with smuggling, the government would have to reduce taxes in one way or another. This would make Canadian cigarettes cheaper, but would presumably also increase the number of smokers. What worked for smuggling would hurt health. Eventually, Ottawa decided to reduce taxes and spend more on health promotion (up to $185 million from a planned $18–$20 million), proclaimed the Tobacco Sales to Young Persons Act (which raised the legal smoking age to 18), banned "kiddie packs" of less than twenty cigarettes, strengthened health warnings on packages, and restricted vending machines. When these many initiatives are bundled in one policy, it clearly shows a daunting cluster of problems.

The general character of a public policy therefore is that it is a guide to action, a plan, a framework, a course of action or inaction designed to deal with problems. This fits with the classic definitions of public policy in the field. Thomas Dye (1984) simply defined policy as "whatever governments choose to do or not to do" (p. 1), and Harold Lasswell (1951), arguably the originator of the modern policy sciences, defined it as "the most important choices" (p. 5). All of these definitions are grounded in a rational model of what it means to make decisions and respond to problems: "policy or strategy is formulated consciously, preferably analytically, and made explicit, and then implemented formally" (Mintzberg & Jørgensen, 1987, 216). The intentional aspect, as we noted above, is important in this classic approach to what policy is. Another approach is to de-emphasize intention in favour of action: organizations can engage in consistent patterns of behaviour that emerge or form rather than being planned. Mintzberg and Jørgensen refer to this as "emergent strategies" that bubble up from all corners of an organization. In this perspective, policy is what governments do, not what they say or intend (Burt 1995). As they point out, however, this concept is at most a corrective, since no organization could survive through the "hothouse" generation of uncoordinated strategies.

The definitional exercise does not end there, however. Of what does this guide or framework consist? If someone asked you to search out the government's policy on X and summarize it, what would you look for, and where? Let's begin with the "where" since it takes us to yet another aspect of the definition that seems so natural that it is easily overlooked. Policies emanate from public authorities, but that is not to say that every public servant has the power to articulate policy. Since policy is a guide, it has a normative or coercive dimension: if the policy says you must do X, then you must (should) do X. Not everyone is empowered to make these sorts of statements. Policies get made in organizations all the time, and typically they are made by management. When we speak of public policy, we are referring to policies that deal with public problems, not organizational routines or structure. Policy, to put it simply, comes from those who have the legitimate authority to impose normative guidelines for action. In a democracy, policy is made by elected officials in concert with advisors from the higher levels of the administration. In strongly hierarchical systems of government like Canada's, public servants often ruefully joke that policy is whatever the minister says it is. The hard truth behind the humour is that since the minister is the elected official at the apex of the government department, only he or she has the right to enunciate policy. If the written documents say one thing, and the minister says something else, then that something else (at least temporarily) is the policy.

Not everyone, therefore, is empowered to articulate policy. But for those who are, what is it that they are saying in a policy statement? Every policy has three key elements. The first is the definition of the problem, the second is the goals that are to be achieved, and the third is the instruments or means whereby the problem is to be addressed and the goals achieved.

Problem definition will be considered the central element of a policy statement. If there is no perceived problem, or a problem is seen to be insoluble, one would hardly expect a public policy to solve it. In Chapter 3 we will consider the nature of problem definition more closely, but several points should be noted here. First, problems have to be recognized and defined. Recognition might be nothing more than a sense that something is wrong or that some new situation is looming. This often happens as a result of changes in some fairly systematic indicator that suggests a problem: "Such indicators abound in the political world because both governmental and nongovernmental agencies routinely monitor various activities and events: highway deaths, disease rates, immunization rates, consumer prices, commuter and intercity ridership, costs of entitlement programs, infant mortality rates, and many others" (Kingdon 1995, 90). Second, the process of problem definition can either be exhaustive or casual. The Royal Commission on Aboriginal Peoples (1991), for example, spent five years and over $50 million dealing with a two-page mandate calling for it to "investigate the evolution of the relationship among Aboriginal peoples (Indian, Inuit, and Métis), the Canadian government, and Canadian society as a whole" (P.C. 1991-1597). On the other hand, the editorial pages overflow with instant experts on every conceivable public problem, and the policy positions of many groups are quite predictable since they base those positions less on analysis than on ideology. Third, as noted above, problems usually come in clusters, and so problem definitions typically operate across a range of dimensions. The cigarette smuggling issue mentioned above, cut across fiscal as well as health concerns. Fourth, problems can sometimes appear in the guise of a substantially changed context or situation, more like new realities or opportunities to which we have to adapt. An arresting example of this aspect comes from our foreign policy. Consider the opening words of the government's 1995 White Paper on Foreign Policy, entitled *Canada in the World*: "The international community must increasingly navigate in uncharted waters. The peaceful triumph of democracy destroyed the Soviet bloc and with it, the bipolar world. Many of the old certainties that guided foreign policy through the Cold War have collapsed ... This is therefore a time of great uncertainty, but also of great opportunity" (Government of Canada 1995, 1). Fifth, all problem definitions have a causal character: they indicate what the problem or issue is, and bundle that with some indication of the factors that created it. Without this causal connection, it would be difficult to figure out what to do about the problem.

The irony of problem definition is that while it is central to understanding public policy, it rarely is articulated in great detail in a policy statement itself. Interest groups and the media spend a great deal of time debating problem definitions and causal factors, and governments cannot avoid rooting their policy reactions in the often exhaustive analyses undertaken by their departments or other agencies. However, the policy statement in itself will rarely reflect this level of detail. As the definitions cited earlier suggest, policy is about action or deliberate inaction. It is the framework or guide, and while problem definition is crucial to understanding the rationale for policy, it is not in itself crucial to the statement of what that guide is to be. From a purely practical point of view as well, the rationale for an action is often considerably more complex than the action (or statement of what that action will be). The importance of this is simply that doing policy analysis, trying to make sense of a policy statement, involves a fair amount of detective work in tracking down both the policy statement and the supporting rationale in terms of problem definition.

Problem definitions are inextricably bound to policy goals. A key distinction, however, is between general goals and policy-specific goals. Health care policy, for example, has as its most general goal the maintenance and improvement of good health among the Canadian population. At this level, almost no one disagrees about goals. The same is true of general goals in foreign policy, education policy, social policy, and so on. As policies get more specific, however, so do their goals. Those goals are still related to the broader ones, but they are contributory rather than final. A provincial health care policy to improve services for at-risk youth will have goals that are directly tied or related to those youth (e.g., safer pregnancies, reduced substance abuse). If achieved, those goals will contribute to the larger goals in the health care field.

As with problem definitions, intermediate policy goals sometimes have to be inferred since they are not always clearly stated. The federal Liberal party's 1993 election "Red Book," for example, promised to "reduce the federal deficit to 3 percent of gross domestic product by the end of its third year in office" (Liberal Party of Canada 1993, 20). This had an admirable clarity that would enforce accountability. The same is true of the Progressive Conservative Party of Ontario document entitled *The Common Sense Revolution*. Its section on "Finding the Savings" listed nine specific areas, from welfare to legal aid, where government policy would be clearly changed. Not all of these provided numerical indicators (e.g., the promise to reduce welfare payments to 10 percent above the national average), but the proposals for the most part would permit fairly unambiguous assessment (Progressive Conservative Party of Ontario 1995, 8–13). However, most policy goals are fuzzy: in cases like these, the mere fact that the problem is not getting worse is sometimes used as proof that the policy goals are being met. Another problem, of course, is that the real goals of the policy might be quite different from the stated goals. Policy-makers may decide that they want to send a message rather than solve a specific problem—the introduction of Bill C-37, for example, to shift the emphasis of the Young Offenders Act from treatment to "protection of society." Most scholarly opinion agrees that "harsher measures would not only be ineffective, but would in fact exacerbate the situation in the long run" (Lithwick & Lithwick 1995, 290), but harsh measures send a message that the government is tough on crime.

The third key component of a public policy statement is some indication of the nature of the instruments or means whereby the problem is to be addressed and the goals achieved. Defining a policy problem and determining a solution are frequently overshadowed in the policy-making process by the question of how. The choice of instruments is also entangled with a choice of the means of implementing those instruments. A government might choose, for example, to dissuade substance abuse through advertising. But who will do the advertising and how? The first is a choice of instrument issue, the second is an implementation issue. In principle, governments have a wide range of instruments that they might choose to tackle a policy problem and achieve their goals. They can rely on information (the advertising example), they can spend or tax, they can regulate, or in some instances they can set up agencies that combine these instruments under public auspices and address the problem directly. Linder and Peters (1989, 56) list as many as twenty-three types of instruments (see Box 4.1 in Chapter 4).

The theoretically wide range of choices over instruments is actually quite constrained in the real world. For one thing, even as policies change from time to time, they take for granted the instruments to achieve their goals. Canadian broadcasting policy, for example, has evolved substantially since the 1960s, but the key instruments of achieving its policy goals, the Canadian Radio-television and Telecommunications Commission (CRTC) and the Canadian Broadcasting Corporation (CBC), have remained. Health policy has changed marginally from time to time, and yet the key delivery mechanisms of hospitals, health care professions, and public expenditures have been quite stable since the 1960s. Recent restructuring, however, with the closure of hospitals and the possible use of private clinics, does represent a fundamental shift (Boase 1995). Sometimes, of course, policy changes so radically in terms of problem definition and goals that instruments get reconfigured quite dramatically as well. In educational policy, for example, Alberta, New Brunswick, and Ontario have dramatically reduced the number of school boards (New Brunswick eventually did away with them altogether), suggesting a major change in direction.

Instrument choice can also be significantly constrained by perceptions of legitimacy. In only rare cases, for example, are Canadians prepared to accept government coercion over matters of sexual behaviour. Therefore, government action to deal with problems such as sexually transmitted diseases has had to rely primarily on informational instruments. Legitimacy is elastic, and it will change with circumstances (e.g., an epidemic of sexually transmitted diseases would lead to stronger action), and also culturally contingent. For example, most Western European states have postal monopolies that also control telecommunications. These authorities have made access to the Internet expensive and difficult, something that North Americans would not tolerate (Neubarth 1995).

Finally, instrument choice can be limited by legal restrictions—a constitutional division of powers or international agreements that prohibit the use of some policy tools—or by practical constraints. Both of these are important. In the Canadian case, federalism divides sovereignty among two levels of government, so that the provinces, for example, have control over health and education, whereas Ottawa has exclusive powers over unemployment insurance (now called "employment insurance") and banking. Governments can still use some instruments to effect policy changes in fields outside their jurisdiction; the classic Canadian case is Ottawa's use of its spending power in the health care and postsecondary education fields (Banting 1987, chap. 4). The North American Free Trade Agreement (NAFTA) is a good example of an international agreement that limits the trade policy instruments governments can use. Canada, the United States, and Mexico cannot give preferential treatment to their own national firms over those from the other two countries. Consequently, a host of traditional economic policy tools to help one's own companies against their competitors are simply not available by agreement, though this should not be taken to mean that governments won't try to find ways around the rules. Human rights conventions do much the same thing in fields as diverse as language and the treatment of children. These legal constraints can be joined by more practical ones. Examples include limits on spending programs due to high deficit levels, or limits to taxation and regulatory policies in a global environment where investors and capital are increasingly mobile and can go anywhere they please. Also, instrument choice is often constrained by organizational routines and preferences: regulatory departments reach first for regulatory instruments; finance departments reach first for fiscal instruments, and so on.

Figure 1.1 summarizes the preceding discussion of policy content. If one were asked to find out the government's policy on X, one would (1) seek an authoritative source for the policy statement, and (2) search relevant documents for clues on problem definition, goals, and instruments. All of these concepts and some of their nuances will be explored in greater detail in subsequent chapters. Note that Figure 1.1 connects these elements in a loop. While problem definition is central to an understanding of policy in a logical sense, in reality the three elements are inextricably entwined. Policy-makers' goals orient them toward certain problems they think need solving; expertise with a set of policy tools encourages one to seek out problems and goals that are consistent with what is achievable with the tools. Moreover, it is virtually impossible to understand any one of these elements without considering the others. In this sense, policy analysis is usually iterative: it moves through the loop several times, refining an understanding of any one element in light of the others.

The loop also suggests that there will be consistency between the different elements. A definition of a problem should "fit" somehow with the instruments and goals. Policy consistency is an important concept to appreciate, since it underpins both what we do as policy analysts and how we perceive public policies as citizens. Policies are expected to be consistent in several interrelated ways (see Figure 1.2). First, as noted above, we expect policies to have an internal consistency among the three elements of problem definition, goals, and instruments. Second, we expect a policy to be vertically consistent, in the sense that the programs and activities that are undertaken in its name are logically related to it. This is in part the nub of implementation. Policy statements are normally fairly abstract and general. They must be actualized through an implementation process that elaborates programs and activities to give the policy effect. A municipal policy to maintain the livability of the downtown core assumes programs and initiatives that support business and residential developments in that area. If the municipality simultaneously had programs to disproportionately encourage suburban development, these would on their face appear inconsistent with the larger policy framework.

A third type of consistency is horizontal consistency, or consistency across policy fields, not just within them. This is an expectation that what governments do in one field will not contradict what they do in another. A fiscal policy of restraint coupled with high spending in a wide variety of areas makes no sense. An open trade policy would be inconsistent with an industrial policy to encourage domestic producers and limit competition.

Figure 1.1   **Elements of Policy Content**

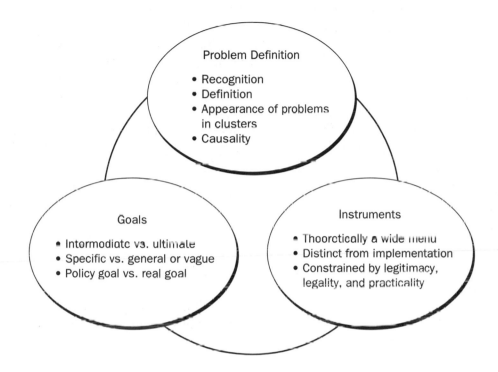

This type of consistency is quite important in democratic politics, since it implies that there is an underlying philosophy of government that cuts across all policy fields. From a policy perspective, when people vote, they vote less for specific policies than the whole package. It is a way of ensuring a degree of accountability, since every part of the government is expected to follow a broadly consistent line of policy. Horizontal consistency varies considerably in the real world, both because of the sheer sprawl of government and the existence of multiple jurisdictions. There are so many actors with some influence over the policy process, and so many agencies with relatively autonomous control of their policy fields, that it is not unusual to have quite widely disparate policy frameworks operating simultaneously. In systems like Canada's, where the executive has greater control over the policy agenda and is internally more coherent for reasons having to do with the role of the prime minister and the governing party, there is a higher degree of policy consistency. Even here, however, where strong ministers can control their own departments, horizontal consistency is never perfect. Nonetheless, the concept (if not the term) seems to be gaining favour. Both the federal Liberals and Ontario Tories issued pre-election policy booklets that clearly tried to articulate a consistent policy vision across a range of fields. The same was true of the American Republican party with its "Contract with America." It is tempting to speculate that budgets have become the great engines of horizontal policy consistency for many governments. In the old days, when fiscal constraints did not matter, or were ignored, the budget was little more than a compendium of spending initiatives undertaken by departments. Now that money is tight, everything gets measured against the bottom line, which, in turn, becomes a compelling reference point for all departments (more on this in later chapters).

A final note. In reflecting on the nature of public policy, we also have to realize what it is not. It is not the implemented programs, the behaviours of public servants who put it into effect, or indeed the reactions of citizens affected by it. If we take the definition developed above, we are forced to realize that public policy, as a course of action, is not the action itself, in the same way that a map is different from travelling. Policies are mental constructs, strings of phrases and ideas. The text of a policy statement and the programs and actions that follow it are simply evidence for the mental construct. Analyzing policy is akin to trying to recreate the maps people used on a journey by studying the paths they took to get to their destination. The fact that there was both a journey and a destination is not proof that maps were, in fact, used, as anyone who has taken a pleasant ramble in the woods can attest. But we presume that our governments do more than ramble, that they have a plan, that their journeys and their destinations are guided by policy. This presumption will often be proven wrong; government actions may be the result of accident, instinct, or habit, rather than of policy. Once we understand this, we understand the challenge of doing policy analysis. It is nothing less than an attempt to grasp an underlying structure of ideas that supposedly guide action.

WHAT IS PUBLIC POLICY ANALYSIS?

In this book, policy analysis will be defined as the disciplined application of intellect to public problems. Apropos of the last point in the previous section, policy analysis is in large part a cognitive activity—a thinking game, if you will—a large part of which focuses on public policy outputs

Figure 1.2   **Policy Consistency**

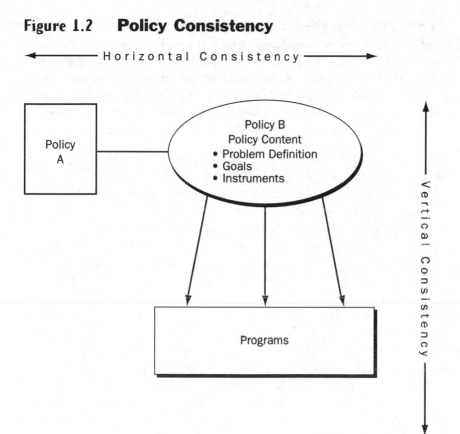

in terms of their problem definition, goals, and instruments. As Wildavsky (1979, 11) pointed out, it is not exclusively a matter of "cogitation" but of "interaction" as well—of letting problems get solved through experiment, bargaining, and exchange rather than exclusively through planning—but the reflective, cognitive aspect is central. Ours is a broad definition, and is complemented by a thicket of other conceptual terms such as policy studies, policy science, and policy evaluation. The central distinction to keep in mind is between a style of policy analysis that is more explanatory and descriptive and a style that is more applied or prescriptive, or between what Harold Lasswell (1970, 3) called "knowledge *of* the policy process" and "knowledge *in* the policy process." Hogwood & Gunn (1984, 29) point out that the broad term "policy studies" is often used to indicate "an essentially descriptive or explanatory set of concerns" while "policy analysis" is usually reserved "for prescriptive activities." The distinctions among these terms are less important than what they have in common:

Obviously, the conceptual distinction between these terms is rather indistinct. It would appear that, when the word *policy* appears as a prefix to the words *science, studies,* and *analysis*, we are talking about activity that investigates some form of government problem or output. This includes studies that examine the policy-making process to determine how it affects the output of that process. (McCool 1995, 10; *emphasis in original*)

Or, as George Graham argues: "The policy orientation provides a means for dealing with human purposes in the best scientific framework possible to aid those who will make social choices. The instrumental end is better intelligence" (1988, 152; quoted in McCool 1995, 10).

All these definitions stress the degree to which this reflection is more than just casual observation. The idea that analysis is disciplined implies that it is both grounded in some method and that it is systematic. The methodological basis can vary from a generic (and usually multidisciplinary) approach to one that is grounded in either natural or social sciences. Policy analysis of environmental issues, for example, will be informed by several natural sciences, but this is not to say that only natural scientists can analyze environmental policy. Economics offers an intellectual apparatus that is broadly applicable to a wide range of policy issues, but once again the central concerns of the policy analyst have less to do with the disciplines that seem to be naturally aligned to the policy issue than with the larger issues discussed in the previous section: how well is the problem defined, what are its characteristics, what goals are being pursued, and are the instruments adequate and likely to produce results? In fact, as we will see in a moment, there are a host of supplementary issues that also are well within the scope of policy analysis per se, rather than separate disciplines. The other aspect of policy analysis is that it is systematic; it proceeds logically through a series of clearly defined stages to come to its conclusions. It should be possible, in other words, to see how someone arrived at his or her conclusions.

All this may seem self-evident, but it holds three implications of great importance to the way that we view contemporary policy analysis. The first is that, at least insofar as policy analysis seems to be allied with scientific disciplines, not just anyone can do it properly. Ordinary citizens have opinions about public policy, but their views may be determined by prejudice or what happened to be on that morning's front page. Sometimes people have extraordinarily strong views about policy that they cannot explain. Once again, this would seem to fall short of policy analysis. The issue this raises, of course, is the division between citizens and experts. Can policy analysis only be performed by those trained to do it? Put another way, do citizens, when they contemplate public policy issues, engage in "real" policy analysis or merely in fuzzy thinking?

The second implication, given that policy analysis should be disciplined and systematic, is that there will be good and bad analysis. More disciplined and systematic analysis will be superior to the less disciplined and systematic. As one interviewee put it, good policy analysis is

> *a way of thinking, an ability to sift the extraneous from the essential, to get to the bottom, to see patterns and connections such as historical or international comparisons. It's the ability to think ahead a few moves, about the consequences downstream. It's the ability to organize information.*

This implies some intersubjective standard of judgment that will act as a benchmark for all participants in the analytical process. Once again this implies some training. However, the idea of valid intersubjective standards has come under sustained criticism in recent years from a number of quarters: the familiar refrain is that everything is relative and depends on perspective. But even if, as Burt (1995, 357) rightly argues, traditional public policy analysis has excluded the interests of women because of the "early adoption of rational, self-interested man as the reference point for both policy development and policy studies," feminist and other perspectives on public policy still share fundamental assumptions about what constitutes quality (not that this excludes vigorous controversy).

A good practical example of policy work that had to grapple with different cultural perspectives is the Royal Commission on Aboriginal Peoples. Hundreds of researchers from across Canada were invited to participate, but the commission was well aware of the problem that Aboriginal peoples had been "studied" for generations and felt very much like the objects of policy rather than its agents. Moreover, the research directors were sensitive to the issue that Aboriginal peoples themselves might see their problems through a different cultural lens.

> The Research Directorate, both in its staffing and commissioning, strives to achieve a balance between Aboriginal and non-Aboriginal researchers, and among Indian, Inuit and Métis. Much of our work will take place outside universities in Aboriginal cultural institutes and communities. We hope that this innovative approach will allow our research to speak in two voices—and be heard by both Aboriginal and non-Aboriginal people in Canada. (Hawkes & Castellano 1993, 7)

The commission's ethical guidelines for research were even more clear about this juggling act. All commission research would have to display respect for "the cultures, languages, knowledge and values of Aboriginal peoples, and to the standards used by Aboriginal peoples to legitimate knowledge" (Royal Commission on Aboriginal Peoples n.d., 1).

The third implication is that policy analysis, however much it may draw on other scientific disciplines, is itself a specific form of inquiry. Policy analysis, for example, has a unique focus of inquiry: public policies themselves and the several elements that comprise them, along with the processes that produce them and the impacts they ultimately have. It has its own traditions of debate (some of which will be explored in the last section of this chapter), its journals, its schools, and its characteristic intellectual paradigms and issues.

It is important not to paint too rigid a picture of policy analysis. Taking the two elements of the definition—(1) the disciplined application of intellect, and (2) public problems—it is easy to see that if we break each one down into its possible elements, there are a wide variety of possibilities and permutations that might come under the broad rubric of policy analysis. The first category is really about styles of reasoning, as long as these styles are disciplined and systematic in some recognizable sense. The second is about the various aspects of process, content, and outcome that are relevant to policy. As Figure 1.3 shows, one can analyze policy using several equally legitimate methods: normative, legal, logical, and empirical analysis.

Normative analysis measures some aspect of policy against an ethical standard: secular morality, the Bible, the Koran, the Canadian Charter of Rights and Freedoms, the UN Universal Declaration of Human Rights. This type of analysis is remarkably important in today's world, but is rarely acknowledged in the literature on policy analysis. It is included here, however, both for its importance and because it fits the definition of disciplined and systematic—while one may not agree with the conclusions, at least one can see how they were arrived at.

Legal analysis looks at public policy through the prism of law: constitutionality, consistency with statute, the practices of legal convention. This overlaps slightly with the previous category, in that a prime measure of contemporary morality is human rights, and hence constitutional provisions on human rights. But this category also contains questions about jurisdiction and legality in the more technical sense.

Logical analysis deals with questions of consistency such as were raised earlier in this chapter: is the policy internally consistent, is it vertically consistent, is it horizontally consistent? This kind of analysis can be done without extensive empirical research, and so is a favourite of media pundits. The fact that these pundits shape the opinion of millions of people should underscore how important a form of analysis it is.

Empirical analysis takes logical analysis one step further by actually posing the same questions in the light of empirical evidence; not what might the *likely* effect of policy X be, but what was its actual effect? Impact questions can be about the direct intended impact, or about unintended consequences on other targets—what, in the Gulf War, was called "collateral damage."

Figure 1.3 also highlights some of the dimensions of policy that can be analyzed: process (the various determinants of a policy, the actors and institutions that shaped it), content (problem definition, goals, instruments), and outcomes (legislation, regulations, actual impact or effect).

Defining policy analysis in this way, as the disciplined application of intellect to public problems, deliberately excludes some other ways of knowing. It does so because it is itself based on a certain epistemology, or system of knowledge. That system is rationalism, the characteristic form of

Figure 1.3 **Policy Analysis: Types of Reasoning**

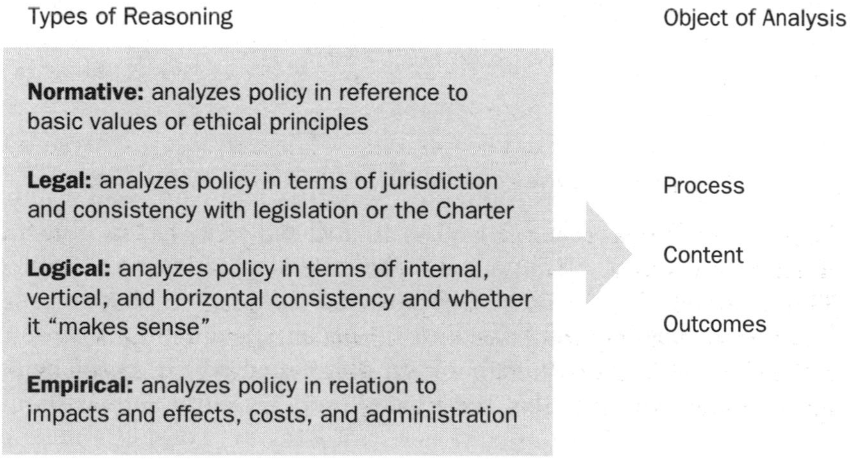

Types of Reasoning	Object of Analysis
Normative: analyzes policy in reference to basic values or ethical principles	
Legal: analyzes policy in terms of jurisdiction and consistency with legislation or the Charter	Process
Logical: analyzes policy in terms of internal, vertical, and horizontal consistency and whether it "makes sense"	Content
Empirical: analyzes policy in relation to impacts and effects, costs, and administration	Outcomes

---

Box 1.1   THE RATIONAL DECISION-MAKING MODEL

Choose Objectives: The first step in making a decision is knowing what one wishes to do or accomplish. This necessarily involves a statement of the problem as well as of goals.

Considering Alternatives: Once the problem and goals are identified, the second step is to identify the means by which the objectives may be attained.

Outline Impacts: Each alternative will consist of a bundle of costs and benefits, positive and negative impacts on the problem. Measure them.

Determine Criteria: A fourth step is to rank all of the alternatives in order of desirability, but this requires some explicit criterion, such as least cost, for a given objective.

Apply Models: The final step before actual implementation is the construction of a model or models to help predict the empirical consequences of the chosen alternative.

Implement Preferred Options: Put the preferred option into effect.

Evaluate Consequences: What happened, and how well do the real impacts fit with predicted outcomes?

---

knowing in the West that is rooted in the Greek and European civilizations (Saul 1992). This is hardly the place to discuss the intellectual history of Western civilization, but it is important to understand what this form of reason implies about how we come to decisions, and what counts as knowledge and what does not. The rational decision-making paradigm, a feature of virtually every introductory textbook on policy analysis on the planet, is outlined in Box 1.1. Note that the procedure is a generic one: it should apply as well to deciding public policy as it does to choosing a mate or picking one's wardrobe for the day.

Few of us are this systematic when we make everyday decisions, but the more important a decision, the more likely that we will think about it carefully and perhaps approximate this model. Will this make for a better decision? Maybe. But making decisions rationally is not the same as making reasonable decisions. A reasonable or good decision is defined less by the process that produced it than by its appropriateness as a solution to the initial problem. While the rational model could in principle be used to choose a mate, most people would argue that it is more reasonable to make this type of decision with the heart or one's emotions. By the same token, non-Western cultures are much more comfortable with decision-making processes that rely less on systematic analysis than on wisdom, intuition, or even signs (Suzuki & Knudtson 1992).

It is worth taking a moment to consider the implications of the rational model for policy analysis and decision-making, if only because rational seems synonymous with reason, and the opposition of rationality and intuition seems to give preference to the former. For one thing, the rational model has embedded in it a strong concern with efficiency, which Herbert Simon (the most important proponent of rational decision-making models) defined as choosing alternatives which provide the greatest results for the least cost (Simon, Smithburg, & Thompson 1958, 60). Simon was convinced throughout his long and distinguished career (he was born in 1916, won the Nobel Prize for Economics in 1978, and was still publishing in 1987) that social betterment would come from the application of rational techniques to complex decisions. In 1957 he was excited about the use of the "digital computer and the tools of mathematics and the behavioral sciences on the very core of managerial activity—on the exercise of judgment and intuition; on the process of making complex decisions" (Simon & Newell 1957, 382). Mintzberg (1994, 310–311) has noted how, for Simon, "the fundamental assumption is that continuous knowledge can be broken down into discrete elements, that is, decomposed for the purposes of analysis ... intuition gets reduced to analysis." The rational model presumes certain patterns of thought: it is linear, systematic, self-conscious, purposive, and efficient.

The standard definition of policy analysis therefore clearly carries with it some cultural baggage. Even if we substantially relax the definition to include a wider variety of ways of knowing and thinking, it is hard to escape the core assumptions that analysis will demand, at minimum, (1) expertise, (2) reliance on Western science, (3) deductive logic, (4) measurement, and (5) clear and replicable steps or stages. For the last fifty years, this model of rationality has been at the heart of what people do when conducting policy analysis. For almost as long, that model has been challenged and criticized for what it leaves out.

So what's wrong with being rational? It may seem a bit mechanical and plodding, but hardly sinful or dangerous. The challenges and criticisms have come under two guises. The first is a debate internal to the discipline about the rational model itself, and has had two variants: incrementalism and postpositivism. The second is more of an external challenge, and also has two dimensions: utilization (does analysis ever get used?), and negative impact (when it is used, does it do more harm than good?).

POLICY ANALYSIS: CHALLENGES AND CRITICISMS

Internal Challenges

One of the earliest salvos in the debate on rational models of policy-making was that the model was rarely applied in the real world. In a famous 1959 article, Charles Lindblom argued that the unforgiving strictures of rational decision-making were so unrealistic in terms of the cognitive and political situation faced by most decision-makers that in fact they made choices by "muddling through." In later work, Lindblom (1979) refined the model, both as a normative and a descriptive framework. In other words, incrementalism better described what really went on. Moreover, it had certain advantages over its apparently superior rival. Rational decision-making models work best, if they work at all, when there is a single decision-maker with a clear and ordered set of priorities and objectives, plentiful information, and comfortable time lines. In the real world of politics and administration, of course, there are multiple decision-makers with conflicting perspectives and priorities, information is in short supply or contradictory, and everything has to be done immediately. In this situation, Lindblom and others argued, decisions get made on the basis of "successive limited comparisons." In this method, goals and values are not neatly separated from each other or from the process of choice. In making decisions, we often only really clarify what we want and what we believe through the process of concrete choices in specific situations. As well, we usually make choices against a backdrop of what has been done before. We move in usually small increments from one situation to the next. Incrementalism seems a sorry standard in many respects—slow, halting, without clear vision or conviction—but it probably captures routine, day-to-day public policy-making in most organizations (Weiss & Woodhouse 1992). At least it once did. We will come back to this in Chapter 2.

So, the rational decision-making model, which in any event was offered less as a description than a standard to shoot for, was attacked as early as the 1950s for its unreality. But the rational model of policy analysis retained its preeminence, perhaps because it reflected a logical standard. We might not be able to attain that standard, but this is what it meant to think logically and rationally (if all our limitations could be overcome). It is this association that contemporary critics have seized upon. It is an association with a rich complex of ideas about politics, reason, science, values, and methods, too rich to give anything but a taste here. The rational model, for example, presumes that there are such things as "facts," but critics point out that facts are always constructed through values and perceptions, or more accurately, through deep theories that structure our cognition of reality. These theories are chosen rationally in the sense of deliberation among a range of alternatives according to multiple criteria, but "however exhaustive the arguments advanced in support of one position, considered judgments concerning the best theory will remain contentious and tentative ... " (Hawkesworth 1988, 87).

Stone (1988) makes a similar postpositivist critique to Hawkesworth's, though less in terms of methodology and science than in terms of the implications of the traditional approach for our understanding of politics and the policy-making process. Stone notes that what she calls the "rationality project" necessarily holds out science, facts, and reason as the means for arriving at policy choices. But policy-making takes place in the political community—the polis:

> My central argument is that the categories of thought behind reasoned analysis are themselves constructed in political struggle, and nonviolent political conflict is conducted primarily through reasoned analysis. It is not simply, therefore, a matter that sometimes analysis is used in partisan fashion or for political purposes. Reasoned analysis is necessarily political. It always involves choices to include some things and exclude others and to view the world in a particular way when other visions are possible. Policy analysis *is* political argument, and vice versa. (Stone 1988, 306; *emphasis in original*)

Frank Fischer and John Forester (1993) have termed this emphasis the "argumentative turn" in policy analysis and planning. For them, policy-making is a "struggle over the criteria of social classification, the boundaries of problem categories, the intersubjective interpretation of common experiences, the conceptual framing of problems, and the definitions of ideas that guide the ways people create the shared meanings which motivate them to act" (p. 2). The argumentative turn entails, among other things, the critical study of the structure of argument in policy analysis (Fischer 1980); the role of values (Fischer & Forester 1987); the deep impact of positivism through its associated logic of technocratic mastery (Fischer 1990). This has been complemented by work such as Dryzek's (1990), exploring the epistemological foundations of policy analysis.

As a species of postmodern criticism, the postpositivist approach to policy analysis makes several powerful claims against the traditional model. However, it has problems of its own. As Dryzek and Torgerson (1993) remarked recently, a "difficulty with postmodern policy analysis and postmodern democracy alike is that they suggest no clear criteria for reaching and implementing a legitimate policy decision" (p. 133). An otherwise fine book such as Deborah Stone's *Policy Paradox and Political Reason* (1988) is brilliant at dissecting the ways in which we use narratives, metaphors, numbers, facts, and rules in constructing policy arguments and programs themselves. Its conclusion, however, recognizes that the strong claim in favour of the social construction of reality leads to the view that the search for criteria and justification of choices is pointless.

> The sport, it seems to me, is worth the candle. Equity, efficiency, liberty, security, democracy, justice and other such goals are only aspirations for a community, into which people read contradictory interpretations. But while the interpretations divide people, the aspirations unite us. The process of trying to imagine the meaning of a common goal and fitting one's own interpretation to that image is a centripetal force. (p. 310)

Really? The logic could cut the other way: the social construction of reality implies that every construction is equally valid, from science to witchcraft, and what works or is instrumental depends on one's worldview. The only way out is through process, through the development of intersubjectively competent communication among relevant actors who will eventually construct a set of shared understandings that will be valid for them. This reduces policy analysis to, as Fischer notes, "facilitation." But without some standards to uphold, analysis becomes largely empty, except in the sense of being acutely skilled at the deconstruction of language and arguments (Durning 1995; Sabatier 1995).

It is important not to caricature postpositivist policy analysis. For one thing, its critique of the limits of rationalism, or more precisely, what should be termed hyper-rationalism (Elster 1989), is largely correct. For another, the analysis of language and arguments is by no means useless; in fact it is a powerful tool in the early stages of analysis as one tries to come to grips with the foundations and structure of conflicting recommendations and problem definitions. As well, postpositivist critics are not without a normative agenda. The emphasis on participation and active citizenship is joined with a clear suspicion of systems of power emanating from the corporate sector and government. A final feature of postpositivism to keep in mind is that it does refer to reason—Fischer (1993), for example, clearly understands that there is a role for science, evidence, and logic. He is perhaps clearest in showing how the real issue is the privileged position that a scientific view of the world has claimed for itself, and the damage this does to democracy. As an antidote, he offers a model which he terms participatory research:

> Participatory research is primarily an effort to gear expert practices to the requirements of democratic empowerment. Rather than providing technical answers designed to resolve or close off political discussion, the task is to assist citizens in their efforts to examine their own interests and to make their own decision ... This process includes coming to grips with the basic languages of public normative argumentation, as well as gaining knowledge about the kinds of environmental and intellectual conditions under which citizens can formulate their own ideas. (p. 171)

Though the preceding has simply been a brief overview of the debates within the field, it should be clear that the internal challenges to policy analysis are quite substantial. One strategy has been to simply ignore these challenges, or highlight the weaknesses of the postpositivist approach. Another strategy has been to try to incorporate some of the elements of this new paradigm in emphasizing the role of ideas and interests in policy-making. A leading text on evaluation, for example, notes that it is important to "acknowledge that the potential contributions of the evaluation enterprise are constrained by the range of competencies and self-interests of both the persons who undertake evaluations and the consumers of them, the diversity in styles of work and organizational arrangements in the field of evaluation, and the political contradictions and economic constraints that mitigate all efforts at planned social change" (Rossi & Freeman 1989, 419). Weimer and Vining (1992) also note that policy analysis is a client-driven process undertaken within an institutional context. Along with a heavy emphasis on standard rationalist analytical techniques like cost-benefit analysis, they also have chapters on "professional ethics" and "landing on your feet."

But this simply papers over the cracks in the discipline. A recent review of some leading books in the field reveals the schizophrenia. On the one hand, "the jurisdictional boundaries are murky and ill-defined; there is neither consensus about nor hegemony over the core intellectual turf;" but on the other, "Postpositivism and so-called postmodernism in policy analysis is a swamp of ambiguity, relativism, and self-doubt" (Lawlor 1996, 110 & 120).

External Challenges

The preceding section dealt with challenges within the discipline, or intellectual debates that suggest that while the traditional paradigm of rationalism that underpins policy analysis is attacked from various quarters, there is nothing viable to replace it. The challenges discussed in this section are external in the sense of raising questions about the application of policy analysis in the real world. Even if the internal challenges could in some way be resolved in an intellectually satisfactory manner, would it matter much if policy-makers ignored the advice, or if that coherent discipline were only randomly applied?

The rational model that underlies policy analysis assumes that decisions will be driven by information and by the careful and systematic comparisons of alternatives and consequences. Indeed, the history of the policy sciences began with the hope that new social science and mathematical tools would improve decision-making. This assumes, of course, that decision-makers choose on the basis of rational information as opposed to political calculation, experience, instinct, or habit. The high point in the fortunes of policy analysis and scientific decision-making was in the 1960s, when the United States decided to adopt the Planning-Programming-Budgeting System (PPBS), which was later adopted in Canada as well, and then made program evaluation mandatory, thus setting off a boom in the industry in the 1970s. A natural question was whether all this activity was having any effect on the policy process. Carol Weiss and her colleagues began a series of studies through the 1970s to answer this question. Their conclusion was that the "implications of explanatory studies and the recommendations from policy-oriented studies seemed to have little effect on either the day-to-day operations of program management or the long-term directions of public policy" (Weiss 1983, 217).

If it was clear that policy analysis did not influence the policy process directly, then what contributions did it make? One early argument was that policy analysis and the rest of the social sciences have a broad "enlightenment" function, providing broad ideas, concepts, insights, and theoretical perspectives (Janowitz 1972). Another version of this image is the "limestone" metaphor, to capture how science enters politics:

> It relies on indirect or cumulative interest and requires no action other than the research itself and the presentation of the findings in a readable way. If circumstances permit (and the research has no control over many of them) the work may, in combination with other work with a similar theme and message, seep into the public consciousness. If this happens, people's views are subtly altered and the parameters within which the public and policy-makers conduct debates on or discussions of the issues are changed. (Thomas 1987, 57)

Weiss (1990) accepts that this accretion or "enlightenment" indeed goes on, but develops a continuum of impact stretching from information that is used simply to warn, guide, enlighten, and finally to mobilize support (pp. 106–108).

If this sounds like whistling in the dark, it is. It suggests that the practical influence of policy analysis—and it has made a case for itself in terms of practical influence—is quite slight or at best murky. As one would expect, since the usefulness of analytical functions in government could not be proved clearly, units that performed these functions began to decline in importance and numbers. A review of analytical units in the Canadian federal government, however, found that by the end of the 1980s, these analytical units still existed. This study discerned three general trends in the 1980s, and into the early 1990s.

> The first was the increasing influence of the auditors and comptrollers general, and the tendency toward restraint in government spending, which resulted in a relatively (though perhaps unevenly) increased emphasis on analysis related to ongoing operational activities and on matters related to efficiency and effectiveness ... As a second trend, these pressures appear to be leading to an increased emphasis on environmental scanning as a response to the increasing use of the media by lobby groups, and by others involved in collective action, to put forward their points of view ... A third trend is that

traditional, in-house research activities continue to be in decline, owing to government downsizing measures and perhaps a diminution of the credibility of in-house analysis among the public and special interest groups. (Hollander & Prince 1993, 196–197)

CONCLUSION

The paradox of the policy sciences is that while they have a reasonably clear foundation and intellectual apparatus (as sketched out in the first part of this chapter), that foundation has come under attack, both internally from other students of policy analysis, and externally from practitioners and the public who wonder what effect all this high-priced talent actually has on policy-making. What are we to make of this paradox? The starting point is to recognize that policy analysis is—whatever its internal and external challenges—both necessary and in demand. As a senior policy advisor put it: *"good policy officers are one of the rarest resources in this town and much in demand."* Most of that demand is generated in light of the need to deal with public problems, and the task for policy analysis is, at minimum, to clarify those public problems. At its best it may offer some alternative solutions, based on careful reflection. In both instances—clarification and problem-solving—the touchstone for the enterprise is the rational model, not because it can stand on its own, but because it provides a powerful heuristic tool, or guide, to thinking through problems and trying to come to grips with solutions. Of course, the role of ideas, symbols, political institutions, and interests, have to be addressed. But as long as policy-making is in large part about solving problems (e.g., lowering unemployment rates, providing child care, helping people make provision for their retirement), the standards of rational discussion and analysis will figure prominently in any effort.

Ironically, the argument that policy analysis does not have much impact on the policy process has turned back on itself. In an age of major policy transformations, there are increasing worries that the capacity of governments to make policy has reached a dangerous low. In short, if policy analysis does not have much impact, then it should. The Task Force on Strengthening the Policy Capacity of the Federal Government (1995), for example, noted:

Within the federal government, the emphasis on improved management in the 1980s may have caused a de-emphasis on policy work. Indeed, there is a widespread sense that senior officials were for several years actually discouraged from engaging in active or structured policy dialogues across departments ... However, the need for policy work has not diminished. Internationally, the world has been transformed by the end of the Cold War, the rise of Asia, the internationalization of capital markets, the new information technologies and the decline of many barriers to trade ... The process of policy-making has changed as well. Public participation in the policy process is undoubtedly greater and media scrutiny arguably tougher than a generation ago. There has been increasing scepticism of the contribution of experts given their evident failure or befuddlement in relation to key social and economic problems. Finally, new technologies offer possibilities for interesting innovations in policy-making methods (pp 1–2)

So policy analysis is needed more than ever in a turbulently changing world. But if the changes are truly fundamental, then the kind of policy analysis we do, and the tools and the intellectual apparatus we use, will have to adapt as well. That is what this book is about. Before we trace out the nature of these new tools and perspectives, however, let us look at the nature of the challenges to our domestic and international policy-making environment.

SUMMARY

What Is Public Policy?

- definition of public policy: a course of action or inaction chosen by public authorities to address a given problem or interrelated set of problems

- the definition of public policy emphasizes action as well as deliberate inaction

- policies aim to solve problems, or clusters of complex problems

- public policy emanates only from those individuals or organizations with the requisite authority

- key elements of a public policy statement are: problem definition, a statement of goals, and instruments

- policy problems: (1) have to be recognized and defined; (2) definitions can be complex or casual; (3) definitions, like problems, come in clusters or sets; (4) problems sometimes imply radically new situations or contexts; (5) problem definitions contain some causal links

- policy consistency: (1) internal, among the elements of policy; (2) vertical, between the policy and its implementation and programs; and (3) horizontal, across policy fields

What Is Policy Analysis?

- definition of policy analysis: the disciplined application of intellect to public problems

- styles of policy reasoning: normative, legal, logical, and empirical (see Figure 1.3)

Policy Analysis: Challenges and Criticisms

- rational model: the intellectual foundation of the policy sciences; presumes that we move through a logical, systematic sequence of choosing objectives, considering alternatives, outlining impacts, determining criteria, applying models, implementing, and evaluating

- incremental model: assumes the rational model is unrealistic; policy is made in small steps, with limited information, through interaction among a vast number of players

- postpositivist/postmodern policy analysis: critical of rational model and its emphasis on a distinction between facts and values; emphasizes the importance of conceptual frameworks, language, and the construction of reality

REFERENCES

Auditor General of Canada. (1993). *1993 Annual Report*. Ottawa: Minister of Supply and Services.

Banting, K. (1987). *The welfare state and Canadian federalism*. Kingston: McGill-Queen's University Press.

Boase, J. (1995, September). *Rationing medical care: A cross-national and institutional comparison.* Paper presented at the annual meeting of the American Political Science Association, Chicago.

Burt, S. (1995). The several worlds of policy analysis: Traditional approaches and feminist critiques. In S. Burt and L. Code (Eds.), *Changing methods: Feminists transforming practice* (pp. 357–378). Peterborough, ON: Broadview Press.

deLeon, P. (1988). *Advice and consent: The development of the policy sciences.* New York: Russell Sage.

deLeon, P. (1994). Reinventing the policy sciences: Three steps back to the future. *Policy Sciences, 27,* 77–95.

Desveaux, J. A., Lindquist, E. A., & Toner, G. (1994). Organizing for policy innovation in public bureaucracy: AIDS, energy and environmental policy in Canada. *Canadian Journal of Political Science, 27,* 493–528.

Dryzek, J. S. (1990). *Discursive democracy. Politics, policy and political science.* Cambridge, England: Cambridge University Press.

Dryzek, J., & Torgerson, D. (1993). Democracy and the policy sciences: A progress report. *Policy Sciences, 26,* 165–187.

Durning, D. (1995). [Review of the book *The argumentative turn in policy analysis and planning*]. *Policy Sciences, 28,* 103–107.

Dye, T. R. (1984). *Understanding public policy* (5th ed.). Englewood Cliffs, NJ: Prentice-Hall.

Elster, J. (1989). *Solomonic judgements: Studies in the limits of rationality.* Cambridge, England: Cambridge University Press.

Fischer, F. (1980). *Politics, values, and public policy: The problem of methodology.* Boulder, CO: Westview Press.

Fischer, F. (1990). *Technocracy and the politics of expertise.* Newbury Park, CA: Sage.

Fischer, F. (1993). Citizen participation and the democratization of policy expertise: From theoretical inquiry to practical cases. *Policy Sciences, 26,* 165–187.

Fischer, F., & Forester, J. (Eds.). (1987). *Confronting values in policy analysis: The politics of criteria.* Newbury Park, CA: Sage.

Fischer, F., & Forester, J. (Eds.). (1993). *The argumentative turn in policy analysis and planning.* Durham, NC: Duke University Press.

Government of Canada. (1995). *Canada in the world.* Ottawa: Foreign Affairs and International Trade.

Graham, G. (1988). The "policy orientation" and the theoretical development of political science. In E. Portis & M. Levy (Eds.), *Handbook of political theory and policy science* (pp. 150–161). New York: Greenwood Press.

Hawkes, D. C., & Castellano, M. B. (1993). Research: A challenging agenda. *The Circle (Royal Commission on Aboriginal Peoples)*, 2(January), 1, 7.

Hawkesworth, M. E. (1988). *Theoretical issues in policy analysis*. New York: State University of New York.

Hogwood, B. W., & Gunn, L. A. (1984). *Policy analysis for the real world.* Oxford, England: Oxford University Press.

Hollander, M. J., & Prince, M. J. (1993). Analytical units in federal and provincial governments: Origins, functions and suggestions for effectiveness. *Canadian Public Administration, 36*(Summer), 190–224.

Information Highway Advisory Council. (1995). *Connection, community, content: The challenge of the information highway.* Ottawa: Minister of Supply and Services Canada.

Janowitz, M. (1972). Professionalization of sociology. *American Journal of Sociology, 78*, 105–135.

Kingdon, J. W. (1995). *Agendas, alternatives, and public policies* (2nd ed.). New York: HarperCollins.

Lasswell, H. (1951). The policy orientation. In D. Lerner & H. Lasswell (Eds.), *The policy sciences* (pp. 3–15). Stanford, CA: Stanford University Press.

Lasswell, H. (1970). The emerging conception of the policy sciences. *Policy Sciences, 1*, 3–13.

Lawlor, E. F. (1996). [Review of the books *The argumentative turn in policy analysis and planning* and *Narrative policy analysis: Theory and practice* and *Policy change* and *learning: An advocacy coalition approach*]. *Journal of Policy Analysis and Management, 15*(1), 110–121.

Liberal Party of Canada. (1993). *Creating opportunity: The Liberal plan for Canada.* Ottawa: Liberal Party of Canada.

Lindblom, C. E. (1959). The science of muddling through. *Public Administration Review, 19*, 79–88.

Lindblom, C. (1979). Still muddling, not yet through. *Public Administration Review, 39*(November–December), 517–526.

Linder, S., & Peters, B. G. (1989). Instruments of government: Perceptions and contexts. *Journal of Public Policy, 9*, 35–58.

Lithwick, N. H., & Lithwick, D. (1995). The "Liberal" treatment of violent young offenders. In S. D. Phillips (Ed.), *How Ottawa spends, 1995–96: Midlife crises* (pp. 287–322). Ottawa: Carleton University Press.

McCool, D. C. (Ed.). (1995). *Public policy theories, models, and concepts: An anthology.* Englewood Cliffs, NJ: Prentice-Hall.

Mintzberg, H. (1994). *The rise and fall of strategic planning: Reconceiving roles for planning, plans, planners.* New York: The Free Press.

Mintzberg, H., & Jørgensen, J. (1987). Emergent strategy for public policy. *Canadian Public Administration, 30*(Summer), 214–229.

Neubarth, M. (1995). The Internet: A global look. *Internet World, 6*(November), 94–101.

Prince, M. J., & Chenier, J. (1980). The rise and fall of policy planning and research units: An organizational perspective. *Canadian Public Administration, 23*, 519–541.

Progressive Conservative Party of Ontario. (1995). *The common sense revolution.* Toronto: Progressive Conservative Party of Ontario.

Pross, A. P., & Stewart, I. S. (1994). Breaking the habit: Attentive publics and tobacco regulation. In S. D. Phillips (Ed.), *How Ottawa spends, 1994–1995: Making change* (pp. 128–164). Ottawa: Carleton University Press.

Rochefort, D. A., & Cobb, R. W. (1994). Problem definition: An emerging perspective. In D. A. Rochefort & R. W. Cobb (Eds.), *The politics of problem definition: Shaping the policy agenda* (pp. 1–31). Lawrence, KS: University of Kansas Press.

Rossi, P. H., & Freeman, H. (1989). *Evaluation: A systematic approach* (4th ed.). Newbury Park, CA: Sage.

Royal Commission on Aboriginal Peoples (Canada). (1991). *The mandate: Royal Commission on Aboriginal Peoples, background documents.* Ottawa: Royal Commission on Aboriginal Peoples.

Royal Commission on Aboriginal Peoples (Canada). (n.d.). *Ethical guidelines for research.* Ottawa: Royal Commission on Aboriginal Peoples.

Sabatier, P. A. (1995). [Review of the book *The argumentative turn in policy analysis*]. *American Political Science Review, 89*(March), 201–203.

Saul, J. R. (1992). *Voltaire's bastards: The dictatorship of reason in the West.* Toronto: Viking.

Saul, J. R. (1995). *The unconscious civilization.* Toronto: Anansi.

Simon, H., & Newell, A. (1982). Heuristic problem solving: The next advance in operations research. In H. A. Simon, *Models of bounded rationality: Volume 1. Economic analysis and public policy* (pp. 380–389). Cambridge, MA: MIT Press.

Simon, H., Smithburg, D. W., & Thompson, V. A. (1958). *Public administration.* New York: Alfred A. Knopf.

Stone, D. A. (1988). *Policy paradox and political reason.* New York: HarperCollins.

Sutherland, S. (1995). The problem of dirty hands in politics: Peace in the vegetable trade. *Canadian Journal of Political Science, 28*(September), 479–507.

Suzuki, D. T., & Knudtson, P. (1992.) *Wisdom of the elders: Sacred native stories of nature.* New York: Bantam.

Task Force on Strengthening the Policy Capacity of the Federal Government (Canada). (1995). *Strengthening our policy capacity.* Ottawa: April.

Thomas, P. (1987). The use of social research: Myths and models. In M. Bulmer (Ed.), *Social science research and government: Comparative essays on Britain and the United States* (pp. 51–60). Cambridge, England: Cambridge University Press.

Throgmorton, J. A. (1991). The rhetorics of policy analysis. *Policy Sciences, 24,* 153–179.

Weimer, D. L., & Vining, A. R. (1992). *Policy analysis: Concepts and practice* (2nd ed.). Englewood Cliffs, NJ: Prentice-Hall.

Weiss, A., & Woodhouse, E. (1992). Reframing incrementalism: A constructive response to critics. *Policy Sciences, 25,* 255–273.

Weiss, C. H. (1983). Ideology, interest, and information: The basis of policy positions. In D. Callahan & B. Jennings (Eds.), *Ethics, the social sciences, and policy analysis* (pp. 213–245). New York: Plenum Press.

Weiss, C. H. (1990). The uneasy partnership endures: Social science and government. In S. Brooks & A. G. Gagnon (Eds.), *Social scientists, policy, and the state* (pp. 97–112). New York: Praeger.

Wildavsky, A. (1979). *Speaking truth to power: The art and craft of policy analysis.* Boston: Little, Brown & Co.

York, G., & Pindera, L. (1991). *People of the pines: The warriors and the legacy of Oka.* Toronto: Little, Brown & Co.

Chapter 2 Modern
Governance:
The Challenges
for Policy
Analysis

The critiques of policy analysis discussed in Chapter 1 are symptoms of major social, economic, and political changes in the industrialized world. In order to reclaim its contributions to policy-making, analysis has to come to terms with this changed context. This chapter reviews the key forces underpinning this change: globalization, political culture, and governance. They are closely entangled, and sometimes conflicting, but with broad consequences that make a big difference to the nature of policy-making and analysis. Globalization involves deeper and more intense economic and political interdependencies, and challenges fundamental assumptions about sovereignty and the role of the nation-state. In Canada and other industrialized countries, political culture is less deferential and more individualist and participatory. Changing notions of governance reflect these forces but also have their own dynamic that stresses smaller government and new forms of public management. Subsequent chapters take up the detailed implications of these forces for problem definition, policy design, implementation, agenda-setting, and evaluation.

In Chapter 1, public policy was defined as a course of action or inaction undertaken by public authorities to address a problem or an interrelated set of problems. Policy analysis was defined as the disciplined application of intellect to public problems. If the nature of public problems changes, if the broad context within which problems arise and are addressed is altered, then both public policy and policy analysis should change as well.

This is precisely what has been happening in the past decade in industrialized countries, Canada included, and a revitalized policy analysis has to come to terms with what is different about modern governance. It is a cliché, of course, that our times (like all times!) are marked by change. But it is in the nature of clichés to expose obvious truths, and no truth is more obvious on the eve of the next millennium than that we are surrounded and affected by changes of unparalleled magnitude and scope. On a global level, the last ten years have seen the collapse of the Soviet empire, of apartheid in South Africa, and the emergence of some measure of peace in the Middle East. In 1993, few people had heard of the Internet; by 1996 school children were routinely researching their projects on-line. Closer to home, in the last five years Canadians have gone through a national referendum on constitutional change, a Québec referendum on sovereignty, massive cuts in government expenditures by Alberta, Ontario, and Ottawa, accompanied by a solid swing toward conservative economic and social policies.

These changes are more than merely numerous, they have altered key social and political systems in the West. As Simeon (1994) puts it, "the fundamental challenge we face is that social and economic change has deeply eroded the worldview or social contract that shaped postwar Canadian politics" (p. 15). Christopher Hood (1995) has come to much the same conclusion in surveying a host of "policy reversals" that even a decade ago would have seemed unimaginable:

> Hype may have far exceeded the substance of change, as often happens in the world of public policy. Nevertheless, the policy changes that did occur are hard to dismiss as trivial: the doubling or trebling of unemployment rates across most of the OECD world to levels which would have been considered politically intolerable in the 1950s and 1960s; the widespread abandonment of "classical" regulation in areas like telecommunications and finance which were once considered central to economic and military sovereignty; dramatic cuts in top income tax rates in many countries; the privatization of public enterprises in some countries on a scale unprecedented in normal peacetime conditions this century; the fairly general slowdown in government expenditure growth; and the move in several countries to overturn the PPA [Progressive-era public administration] public administration style which had been carefully built up over a century. (p. 144)

Everyone knows that these changes are "non-trivial," but the trick is to try to make some sense of the broad pattern and to tease out the implications for policy analysis and governance. This chapter argues that there are three powerful undercurrents beneath the waves of political turmoil and policy reversal evident in Canada and throughout the industrialized world. They are globalization, shifts in political culture, and new ideas about governance and public management. Each of these is multifaceted, of course, and connected intimately to the others. Nonetheless, it is possible to outline at least a few of their most important features. They have been building for over twenty-five years, and in some respects are so natural a part of our political, economic, and social environment that we take them for granted. A policy analysis that fails to come to grips with these forces and their implications for policy and governance is doomed to irrelevance.

GLOBALIZATION

Economic Globalization

The modern phenomenon of globalization has to be carefully distinguished from the mere fact of international connectedness. The British Empire was global in scope, and other imperial systems, such as Rome's, covered enormous tracts of territory. The Moors extended their empire as far as Spain, and the Portuguese in turn established outposts as far away as Goa, India. Marco Polo travelled from the Mediterranean to China in the late 1200s. The city states of medieval Europe had extensive trade connections of their own to the Orient, and vast, complex systems of trade that were virtually global developed by the 1700s around sugar, spices, and slaves. In short, human history in the last thousand years has been clearly marked by internationalism that sometimes came close to embracing the entire planet. What is different about the present situation?

Modern globalization is driven by unprecedented technological factors. These have accelerated and deepened the tendency toward international connections, so that what distinguishes the contemporary form of globalization from its predecessors is a scope and intensity that together amount to a qualitative change, a "substantial discontinuity in our economic experience" (de la Mothe & Paquet 1996, 4). The key technological change have occurred in information processing, communications, and tra portation. In communications the obvious interrelated developments h been TV, satellites, phone, fax, and computers. Underpinning the marriage of these technologies has been the development of the microchip and integrated computer circuit that has ushered in the digital revolution, in which all information, whatever its form, can be reduced to a binary code and manipulated or interwoven. "Being digital," says Nicholas Negroponte, "creates the potential for new content to originate from a whole new combination of sources" (1995, 19). For some, the new information and communication technologies amount to a new "techno-economic paradigm" which moves us from energy-intensive to information-intensive production, from standardized to customized goods, from single to networked firms, and from centralized to distributed intelligence (Rosell et al. 1995, 26–29).

These technological changes have been the foundation of major economic transformations. As Courchene (1994) notes:

> It is the process of the increasing internationalization of manufacturing and, progressively, of services as well. Firms now compete with truly global strategies involving selling worldwide, sourcing components worldwide, and locating activities in various parts of the globe to seek out absolute advantage. Globalization in this sense decouples firms from the factor endowments of a region or country. (p. 233)

First, of course, has been the development of a complex international trading system. After World War II, a host of international institutions and conventions were established to create the beginnings of a true international economic system: the General Agreement on Trade and Tariffs (GATT—now superseded by the World Trade Organization or the WTO), the International Monetary Fund (IMF), the World Bank, and the Bretton Woods agreement on currency transactions. The logic behind these initiatives was twofold: first, to create a set of supranational decision-making bodies that would create stable and harmonized international regimes dealing with a host of issues from trade to communications; second, to knock down those major barriers between countries that impeded exchange or communication. The postwar efforts were successful on both counts. Both the movement of people and goods increased exponentially in the postwar years. Tourist travel grew tenfold between 1950 and 1990 (United Nations *Statistical Yearbook* 1952–1994), and tourism is now the globe's largest industry (Naisbitt 1994). Figure 2.1 shows the increase in global trade in goods and personal/business travel since World War II. As borders become more porous, people, goods, services, and information travel more freely across political lines. In a pre-globalized world,

Figure 2.1   **Global Trade**

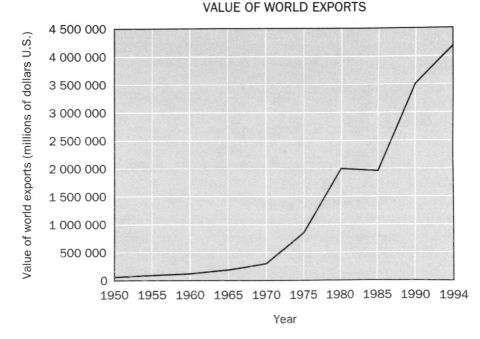

VALUE OF WORLD EXPORTS

Source: United Nations Conference on Trade and Development (1994).

those lines on maps mark territories where, through public policy as well as forces of history, society, economy, and governance, "national systems" coincide. At the most elementary economic level, for example, national boundaries mark economic systems. The whole idea of a national economy presumes that there is more internal than external trade. Globalization implies the opposite, and Canada, always a trading nation, crossed an important threshold recently. As Figure 2.2 shows, all provinces, with the exception of Prince Edward Island, now trade more with the rest of the world than they do with each other.

A second economic dimension of globalization is the well-known phenomenon of transnational corporations. Companies operating across the globe are not in themselves new; think of the Hudson's Bay Company (chartered in 1670) or the British East India Company (founded in 1600 to trade with Mogul kings in what is now India). But these companies were

Figure 2.2 **Interprovincial and International Trade**

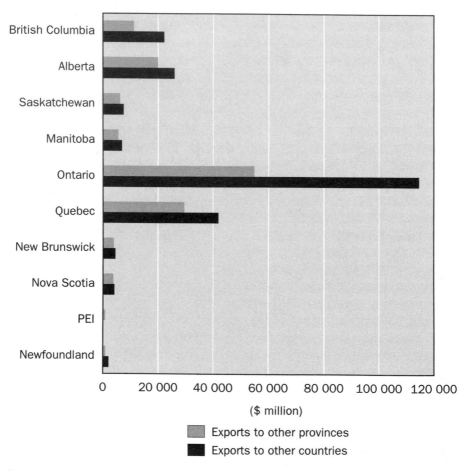

Source: Statistics Canada.

instruments of an imperial system of mercantilism, tools of imperial governments. What was different about postwar multinational commercial firms is that their commercial interests are primary, they operate across the globe, and their national home base is relatively unimportant. Table 2.1 lists the world's top fifty companies, their revenues, and country of origin, illustrating both their size and the continuing importance of U.S.-based companies.

Country of origin mattered at one time, but in the contemporary phase of economic globalization it is less and less important (Reich 1988). This is

Table 2.1   Leading Multinational Firms

Rank	Company	Country	Revenue (millions of U.S. dollars)	Number of Employees (thousands)
1	Royal Dutch/Shell Group	Netherlands	109 853	104.0
2	General Motors	United States	168 829	709.0
3	Exxon	United States	107 893	84.0
4	General Electric	United States	70 028	219.0
5	Bank of Tokyo-Mitsubishi	Japan	55 243	20.1
6	Toyota Motor	Japan	111 139	142.6
7	Philip Morris Cos.	United States	53 139	158.0
8	Ford Motor	United States	137 137	347.0
9	International Business Machines	United States	71 940	222.6
10	Nippon Telegraph and Telephone	Japan	82 002	231.4
11	Wal-Mart Stores	United States	93 627	648.5
12	HSBC Group	United Kingdom	26 682	101.1
13	Industrial Group of Japan	Japan	38 694	5.3
14	Citicorp	United States	31 690	84.0
15	Mobil	Unites States	64 767	54.5
16	Sanwa Bank	Japan	34 913	14.4
17	Fuji Bank	Japan	31 597	15.8
18	El du Pont de Nemours	United States	36 508	106

Table 2.1   Leading Multinational Firms (cont.)

Rank	Company	Country	Revenue (millions of U.S. dollars)	Number of Employees (thousands)
19	Nestlé	Switzerland	47 767	220.2
20	Procter and Gamble	United States	34 923	99.2
21	Chase Manhattan	United States	26 220	75.2
22	Sumitomo Bank	Japan	29 611	17.2
23	British Petroleum	United Kingdom	56 992	58.2
24	Dai-Ichi Kangyo Bank	Japan	30 312	18.1
25	Federal National Mortgage Assn.	United States	22 249	3.4
26	Hewlett-Packard	United States	33 503	102.0
27	Unilever	Netherlands	49 638	308.0
28	American International Group	United States	25 874	33.5
29	AT&T	United States	79 609	301.9
30	Deutsche Bank Group	Germany	38 418	74.1
31	ENI	Italy	34 924	86.4
32	BankAmerica	United States	20 386	81.0
33	Allianz Worldwide	Germany	43 486	67.8
34	Tokyo Electric Power	Japan	50 343	43.1
35	Chrysler	United States	53 195	112.5
36	Hitachi	Japan	84 233	331.9
	Sakura Bank	Japan	25 976	20.3
	ING Group	Netherlands	33 236	52.1

Table 2.1 Leading Multinational Firms (cont.)

Rank	Company	Country	Revenue (millions of U.S. dollars)	Number of Employees (thousands)
39	ABN-Amro Holding	Netherlands	26 533	63.3
40	PepsiCo	United States	30 412	475.5
41	Union Bank of Switzerland	Switzerland	18 496	29.1
42	Barclays	United Kingdom	23 202	92.4
43	NationsBank	United States	16 327	59.3
44	Matsushita Electric Industrial	Japan	70 454	265.4
45	National Westminster Bank Group	United Kingdom	23 533	81.8
46	Siemens Group	Germany	60 673	376.1
47	Lloyds TSB Group	United Kingdom	18 653	87.0
48	Motorola	United States	27 037	137.0
49	Amoco	United States	27 066	42.9
50	British Telecommunications	United Kingdom	22 618	135.2

Source: *Forbes,* July 15, 1996, p. 243.

because of a shift in the way in which these firms operate. The first phase of multinational development entailed exports to foreign markets of goods produced domestically (e.g., cars made in the U.S. or Japan exported elsewhere). The second phase was the establishment of production facilities in these foreign markets, facilities that would still be quite dependent on the parent corporation for services, inputs, and strategies. A third phase has seen multinational firms begin to operate as transnational firms, that is, to organize their production process globally. What this means is that an

American car will have parts produced in a variety of countries, with final assembly in a completely distinct location. This is a significant change in the nature of globalization, since it implies a much more tightly integrated international market. As Thurow (1996) notes, "For the first time in human history, anything can be made anywhere and sold everywhere" (p. 113). Global sourcing means that companies will shift production to the most attractive sites, either in terms of expertise or labour costs. It presumes an international or global production market, and by the same token an emerging global consumption market. In other words, if production is organized globally and consumption is increasingly similar in terms of the goods and services that people buy, then it makes less and less sense to talk about domestic and foreign markets since there is just one global market or economic space.

A final aspect of economic globalization is the increase in capital flows and mobility. Large financial institutions such as banks, insurance companies, and investment brokers have gradually developed systems to allow virtually instantaneous transfers of capital anywhere in the world. This is based in part on new technology and in part on the emergence of large international institutions and multinational corporations. The results are unprecedented. The global bond market, which only started in 1989, was trading US$78 billion in 1994 (Coleman & Porter 1996, 58). Enormous quantities of liquid capital are shifted from country to country, stock exchange to stock exchange, in response to business opportunities as well as perceived risk. These shifts in capital have consequences for domestic interest rates, stock prices, and exchange rates. From a policy perspective, clearly the most daunting implication has been for large government deficits. Deficits are covered by borrowing, and with a long enough string of deficits, governments have to go beyond domestic sources of capital to international ones. Reliance on international investors means keeping them happy, and in recent years these investors have not been very happy at all with deficits and high spending. In short, international capital fluidity has become a means of disciplining domestic governments in their budgetary policy. In most instances this has involved cuts in social spending, the size of government, and the scope of intervention in the market. This is particularly true for countries with a high reliance on exports, such as Canada, but most of Europe has been affected as well because of efforts to coordinate economic policy throughout the European Union: "European governments of all ideological stripes are held hostage even more tightly than Washington by bond and currency traders, who daily pass ruthless judgment about economic and political performance by sending interest rates and exchange rates up and down" (Stevenson 1995, 1).

What does all this mean? Details will be explored in subsequent chapters, but economic globalization has had several consequences that together change the terrain of modern policy-making and analysis. There are two major implications. First, the development of international trading regimes means that governments have had fewer policy instruments at their disposal to protect domestic markets, what Michael Porter calls the "home base" (Porter 1990). As Schultz notes with respect to regulatory instruments: "Regulation, as currently manifested in some sectors, may not be tenable where consumers can escape from the coercive power of the state" (1995, 273). Second, the traditional boundaries between policy fields begin to dissolve. In a technological society, natural resources matter less than human ones, and social policy (education, welfare, training) becomes an element of economic policy, and vice versa. Trade and industrial policy used to focus on the international and the domestic sides of the economy respectively, but globalization explodes that distinction as well, and the policy fields coalesce. These two broad implications suggest constraints, but demands on governments paradoxically increase in many respects because of the destabilization that comes with economic globalization. In Richard Simeon's words, "Globalization thus sets up paradoxical forces—it undermines and weakens the state's capacity and yet engenders political mobilization to use the state as a shield" (1995, 36).

As Prime Minister Chrétien noted in a speech in 1995, the "nation-state is not powerless" to influence the financial flows that buffet the world economy, but Canadians "cannot stop globalization, we need to adjust to it" (Howard 1995, A1). Part of that adjustment is thinking differently about public policy.

Cultural Globalization

Globalization is about more than economics, however. It relies, for instance, on technologies of communication that also have had a dramatic effect on culture. Once again, the central issue is the degree to which borders matter less as an element of cohesion in defining national cultures and societies. We have already noted how markets have become uncoupled from territorial boundaries, and the same is increasingly true of culture and communications. One line of argument about this phenomenon is that all around the world people are rapidly becoming homogenized. Globalization of culture means sameness. The massive penetration of

American culture through icons such as Coke, McDonald's, and Hollywood means that there is a pervasive sameness to capital cities no matter where one goes on the planet. Consumers "around the world are beginning to develop similar cultural expectations about what they ought to be able to buy as well as about what it is they want to buy" (Ohmae 1995, 28).

However, local cultures do have a resilience and carve out niches for themselves even in the shadows of what Barber (1995) calls "McWorld." Indeed, the counter argument to this view of global homogenization is that globalization really portends a growing awareness of differences (Kincaid 1994). In this scenario, which seems supported by the tenacity of ethnic differences and conflicts around the world, people retain their local cultural idioms, but globalization no longer makes it possible for them to conceive of their own culture as somehow natural, or the only possible world.

The telecommunications and information revolution has taken a giant leap forward with the popularity of the Internet. This integrated global network of computer networks cuts against the grain of traditional debates about the effects of telecommunications and broadcasting on community and culture. Accurate numbers are hard to come by, but recent estimates are that in "the population 16 years or older in the U.S. and Canada, 13 percent have used the WWW(World Wide Web) in the 6 months preceding March '96. Only 8 percent had used the WWW in the 3 months prior to August '95" (Nielsen Media Research Unit 1996). The highest density of use is in the industrialized countries, as one would expect, but the most rapid growth is being experienced in former communist countries and Africa (Neubarth 1995). The Internet is an astonishing development for several reasons. First, since it connects your computer directly to a myriad of other computers, creating a network, it is as though the information stored on all the computers on the Internet were available to you. This places virtually unlimited information at the disposal of ordinary citizens, as well as interest groups and other political actors. Second, the instantaneous nature of communications through the Internet means that both time and space are obliterated. No one controls the Internet, least of all governments, and so this capacity to instantly connect with anyone else on the planet and exchange unlimited amounts of information is perhaps an even more powerful assault on territory than the development of economic globalization. Third, whereas traditional broadcasting had a homogenizing effect in cultural globalization, since so much of it was produced for American sensibilities and sent around the world, the Internet has the potential to permit the development of differences and indeed of new communities of interest and of affinity (Rheingold 1993). At the stroke of a key, any individual can "broadcast" to thousands of others, and the most minute interests can develop followings. Cyberspace is so uncontrolled that it can be a hospitable environment for marginal political and social tendencies, both good and bad.

The Internet has been called a prototype of the information highway, a technological development that will possibly merge telephones, cable, TV, and computers, and deliver a cornucopia of services to individuals in their homes. The "infobahn" is a dream cherished and being pursued by major media conglomerates, and the struggle over whether the Internet model of maximum connectivity with minimum regulation and control will triumph is unclear. It seems hardly likely, however, that the Internet will disappear, and there are some interesting signs that corporate domination may not be successful. This, in addition to new technologies that promise even greater connectivity (e.g., satellite telephone systems that will provide each phone with a unique number, no matter where it is on the planet), mean that what *The Economist* (1995) called the "death of distance" is a fait accompli.

The overwhelming implication of these developments is to drive policy-making and analysis "beyond territory" (Elkins 1995). Governments have traditionally had a comparative advantage over their citizens in access to information. The Internet destroys that advantage, and gives global information-producing powers to nongovernmental organizations (NGOs). Cultural affinity has traditionally tended to coincide with territory, so that people define their relevant communities in terms of the territory defined by the state. Now communities can develop through connections that effortlessly transcend boundaries. At one time, governments had cultural policies. In the information age, where access to culture through communications cannot be easily controlled or regulated, a cultural policy looks increasingly like an oxymoron. Finally, if culture depends on communication, then the communications and information revolutions mean that communication is now global, suggesting the emergence of certain global understandings or standards. This is the third aspect of globalization, the development of international standards of conduct.

International Standards

The best example of these emerging standards is the human rights conventions that have evolved since 1945. The United Nations came into being on October 10, 1945, and its Economic and Social Council was instructed to establish a commission to draft an international bill of rights. The UN Charter itself referred to the "principle of equal rights" and the importance of universal respect for "human rights and fundamental freedoms for all." The Council established a Commission on Human Rights that produced the Universal Declaration of Human Rights which was passed in December 1948. The Universal Declaration was nothing more than a declaration without force of international law and without any enforcement mechanism. It recognized the "inherent dignity and the equal and inalienable rights of all members of the human family" and proceeded to list virtually every conceivable human right, from traditional civil and political ones to newer economic ones such as social security, work, rest, leisure, the right to an adequate standard of living, education, and free participation in the cultural life of the community. At the time these were lofty ideals indeed, and brought together in one document two sets of rights that coincided with the emerging global divisions around the Cold War: civil and political rights central to liberal democracies, and social and economic rights championed by socialist and communist states.

The history of human rights since 1948 has seen the progressive elaboration of both standards and institutions to monitor and enforce those standards. The Universal Declaration, for example, was followed by two International Covenants that did have the force of treaties rather than being mere declarations: the International Covenant on Civil and Political Rights and the International Covenant on Economic, Social and Cultural Rights. Both were passed by the UN in 1966 and came into effect in 1976. In addition to these covenants, the UN has passed Conventions for the Suppression of the Traffic in Persons and of the Exploitation of the Prostitution of Others (1951), the Status of Refugees (1954), the Elimination of All Forms of Racial Discrimination (1969), the Elimination of All Forms of Discrimination against Women (1981), against Torture and Other Cruel, Inhuman or Degrading Treatment or Punishment (1987), and on the Rights of the Child (1990). These UN initiatives have been complemented by similar regional conventions, for example, in Europe and the Organization of American States (OAS).

Critics often dismiss this dense system of overlapping covenants and declarations as largely meaningless posturing by governments, many of whom are energetic violators of the very agreements that they have signed. But events such as the 1993 Vienna World Conference on Human Rights and the 1995 Beijing World Conference on Women demonstrate that a global moral community has emerged from these efforts. Human rights violations will continue, but no longer invisibly and without impunity.

Human rights activists and NGOs around the globe, aided by the very technologies and institutions mentioned earlier in this section, ensure that violators are exposed. Even Canada is not immune to this process: UN human rights committees have sanctioned Canada, for example, in 1993 for Québec's Bill 178 restrictions on non-French commercial signs, and again in 1995 for federal cuts to social programs. In short, the most important development is less the absence of enforcement mechanisms than the emergence of standards that millions of people, regardless of place or culture, now accept as worthy of enforcement. In large measure, of course, these standards are Western in origin, and so the call for universalism is in part a call for the universal application of a certain view of individual rights and obligations.

As with the other elements of globalization, the implications of the emergence of international standards, many of them contained in conventions and treaties which Canada has willingly signed, are that the policy process and the principles by which it is made are no longer delimited by purely domestic considerations. Cuts to social programs are a good case in point: policy-makers may decide that cuts and reconfigurations of programs make fiscal and programmatic sense, but they will nonetheless have to be prepared to defend their actions against the charge that they are violating obligations to certain standard economic and social rights. Another example is Aboriginal issues: there is a worldwide Aboriginal movement, as well as a complicated UN process to deal with Aboriginal rights. Any policies Canada develops will be measured against what other governments have done. In addition to standards and international institutions to monitor them, of course, is the emergence of what some have called a "global civil society" of NGOs and other actors who can be mobilized quickly around domestic policy issues. Canada's environmental and Aboriginal policies, for instance, are closely watched by various groups around the world such as the Sierra Club and the World Congress of Indigenous Peoples.

In short, the traditional association between public policy-making and the territorial boundaries of the nation-state has been severely challenged in the last decade. Both the source of policy problems and their potential solutions now lie as much outside the boundaries of the state as they do within. This is not to say that states are irrelevant or that they cannot tackle major policy issues. The nation-state will remain a fundamental organizing unit for contemporary industrialized societies, but the sort of control and dominance that it once enjoyed, both over the policy process and the intellectual resources required to analyze it, is waning. The ways in which policy problems are defined will change, as will the range of instruments and strategies to deal with them.

THE POLITICAL CULTURE OF DIVERSITY

Globalization helps us grasp changes that have occurred at the international level, along with their effects on domestic politics and policy-making. It would be surprising, however, if these international changes were not accompanied by equally significant changes in the ways in which domestic political communities see themselves and their relations to government. For example, how could international human rights regimes strengthen over the past fifty years without human rights simultaneously becoming more important as standards of civil conduct on the domestic level?

Political culture across the industrialized democracies has indeed changed significantly, no less in Canada than elsewhere. Evidence of this abounds: the collapse of communism in Eastern Europe signalled the triumph of liberal individualist values that seem secure even in the face of the resurgence of communist parties in some countries like Poland and the Russian Federation; people everywhere seem more prepared to articulate their political concerns in terms of individual rights; even while Western societies have become more materialistic and consumer-oriented, social movements have arisen around the globe to press for concerns such as the environment, peace, gender relations, and sexual orientation. Along with an emphasis on the universal rights of individuals, there has come a greater sensitivity to the issues of identity and diversity. This section will briefly sketch three closely interwoven aspects of this shift in political culture: the rise of postmaterialism, the new salience of rights, and a new emphasis on difference. Together, these comprise the "postmodern challenge" of identity: "how to construct and sustain any sort of consensus in a postmodern society that is characterized by multiplying and fragmenting systems of belief" (Rosell 1995, 38).

Postmaterialism in the West consists of a shift away from deference, away from concern with material gain, and away from economic issues per se. These are displaced by lifestyle concerns, social and even spiritual issues, all pursued in a much more participatory mode than was characteristic of the 1960s. "In this process, an emphasis on economic security gradually fades, and universal but often latent needs for belonging, esteem, and the realization of individual intellectual potential become increasingly prominent. Although individuals still value economic and physical security, they increasingly emphasize the need for freedom, self-expression, and improving the quality of their lives" (Abramson & Inglehart 1995, 9). This is a long-term process which, according to Inglehart, will gradually take root in successive generations. The consequences of a shift to postmaterialist values are potentially profound: greater support for democratic institutions, and in particular, greater support for participatory democracy and a politics of identity and recognition.

Clearly, the growth of postmaterialism has links to the development of what Mary Ann Glendon has called the dominance of "rights talk" as a mode of political discourse. In the previous section we discussed the development of international human rights regimes. This has been mirrored at the domestic level in the elaboration of human rights documents, institutions, and political discourse. Glendon is careful to point out that the American version of rights talk is only a "dialect" of a form of discourse that has spread rapidly throughout the world since 1945. There is now a universal language of rights, though the American dialect has peculiarities which, she feels, contribute to and are a symptom of "disorder in the body politic." She argues that while rights talk is impervious to other more complex languages whereby we regulate our social and political lives, it "seeps into them, carrying the rights mentality into spheres of American society where a sense of personal responsibility and of civic obligation traditionally have been nourished" (Glendon 1991, x).

American commentators are concerned that this new rights talk de-emphasizes "attachment to duty and obligations" (Hughes 1993, 10), and undermines the possibility of political compromise (Elshtain 1993). Whereas American debate on these issues has traced the growth of rights talk to informal social and institutional developments in the 1960s, particularly the civil rights movement and the independent role of the courts (Melnick 1994), Canadian analysis has been driven by a constitutional version of the "big bang" in 1982, which patriated the constitution and added the far-reaching Charter of Rights and Freedoms.

Alan Cairns has been the preeminent thinker on the Canadian equivalent of rights talk (Cairns 1991, 1992, 1993; for a critique of the Cairns thesis, with rejoinder, see Brodie & Nevitte 1993). His argument consists of several key points. First, the Charter should not be seen in isolation; as Glendon notes, it reflects an international movement toward specifying and entrenching individual rights against governments. Second, while the Charter was a symptom of this development, it nevertheless has had several specific effects on Canadian political discourse. Traditionally, Canadian politics has been organized through and around federalism, and its constitution has been a "governments'" constitution in the sense that it was primarily about the division of powers, with little reference to citizens and their rights. The 1982 Charter, for the first time, brought citizens' rights into the constitution, but more importantly articulated many of those rights in terms of minority group identities (racial, ethnic, gender, Aboriginal, disabled, aged, etc.). Third, it is the combination of these constitutional rights and the demographic realities of ethnic, linguistic, and racial diversity in Canada that give the Charter its explosive power. Fourth, this power is being channelled in ways that undermine the old constitution of governments and underscores the importance of rights-based citizens' movements. Cairns and others have noted the process whereby the Meech Lake Accord (1987) and the Charlottetown Accord (1992) both collapsed in part before an onslaught of citizens' groups and rights claims (for similar versions of this argument focusing on the failure of recent constitutional adventures, see Pal & Seidle 1993; Lusztig 1994).

The third element of the changed political culture in industrialized democracies, especially Canada's, is a new tension between individual and group rights. The former consists of the traditional collection of civil and political rights that aim to treat individuals exactly the same, regardless of their social and economic differences. The objective was a political community that, for public policy purposes, ignored group differences and concentrated instead on equal rights of citizenship. This is a noble political ideal, and one that still commands substantial support. However, this type of liberal individualism was vulnerable to the argument that differences did matter, particularly economic differences, and they impeded the practical achievement of real political equality.

The contemporary version of the argument about difference shifts ground, however. The old argument with liberalism was that differences mattered, but that they should be overcome or ignored. The new argument challenges the core assumptions of liberal individualism by insisting that differences matter in a positive way, that equal treatment of individuals as abstract citizens ignores fundamental social and cultural characteristics that define identities. In the words of Iris Young (1990), "To promote social justice, I argue, social policy should sometimes accord special treatment to groups" (p. 158). Kymlicka (1992) describes this position as cultural pluralism, and it has fundamental implications for the way we conceive citizenship.

Liberal individualism insists that equality will be achieved by treating people as individuals under a system of universally applicable and consistent rules. Cultural pluralism insists that equality can be achieved only by treating people on the basis of their group affiliation and, in some cases, by treating them according to different rules. Of course, not every group characteristic is important—blue eyes or left-handedness is something shared by millions of people but it hardly matters as a basis of group affiliation. Young argues that only social groups, defined in terms of salient social, cultural, or racial differences, that have experienced oppression qualify for different treatment. Her list, for example, includes racial minorities (in the American context, blacks and Hispanics), women, gays and lesbians, the disabled, and Aboriginals. These differences are basic and powerful enough to define shared interests, worldviews, and even cultural norms among members of the group. Moreover, these groups exist in a society marked by radical inequality and oppression. If groups were different, but these differences were already accommodated and addressed through social and political institutions, there would be little to discuss in terms of public policy. But the "politics of difference" argues that, in fact, these differences are routinely and systematically oppressed. Indeed, it is the fact of oppression that gives these groups special claims within the political system.

This cluster of ideas leads to the conclusion that the application of universal rules will only serve to further disadvantage these groups and suppress their legitimate differences. It is evident in the politics of employment equity, with its differential treatment of women, the disabled, visible minorities, and Aboriginals. Multiculturalism policy, though it has had fewer teeth than the equity agenda, has from its beginnings been a program that recognizes and celebrates difference. The whole sorry history of Canadian constitutionalism (and now separatism) is rife with what Charles Taylor calls the politics of recognition. The demand that Québec be designated a distinct society is based on the firm view that people in that province are distinguished from other Canadians in terms of language, culture, and historical experiences, and that these differences matter enough that they should be the basis of real powers and special treatment. The Meech Lake and Charlottetown Accord fiascoes demonstrated the difficulties of trying to accommodate cultural pluralism within the framework of liberal precepts of the universal application of rules. Both these documents started off trying to accommodate the claims of distinctiveness for Québec, but quickly became embroiled in the crossfire between those (principally from the West) who resisted "special" treatment for any part of the country and those who resented the fact that their specific group differences (women, Aboriginals, ethnic groups) were not being addressed, too. The politics of difference has complicated Canadian constitutional life, and has been reflected in a wide variety of issues, from the wearing of the hajib by schoolgirls, to turbans and Aboriginal braids in the RCMP, to cultural policy and worries about the "appropriation of voice."

From a policy perspective, the impact of postmaterialism, rights talk, and cultural pluralism is complex and often contradictory. For one thing, it has contributed to the widely noted "decline of deference" among the Canadian population and democratic citizenry in other countries. Peter C. Newman (1995) devoted an entire book to the subject, convinced that Canada has undergone a revolution in its traditional political culture of deference and trust: "Experience has made it impossible to believe any longer in responsible politicians, pious priests, sensible Royals, trust-worthy lawyers, peace-loving peacekeepers, reliable bankers, principled businessmen or honest diplomats" (p. 395). Citizens trust their govern-ments and politicians far less than they used to. If they trust less, then they inevitably demand a different type of policy process. They want to be consulted, they want to participate, and they want their voices heard. A senior public servant notes that in the 1950s major policy decisions could be undertaken without public consultation: *"think of C.D. Howe and the Trans-Canada pipeline—there were no intervenors, no hearings, no envi-ronmental impact studies ... "*

A more recent example was the 1980 National Energy Program (NEP), hatched among a few ministers, and sprung on both the Cabinet and the public without prior notice. Governments simply cannot do that anymore; the public will not stand for it. As another interviewee phrased it:

> *Another thing, and I think that it goes along with the debt and deficit issue, is that citizens are a little bit cynical about governments and bureaucracy. I think that politicians and the bureaucracy get very low marks in terms of other professions. And this cynicism has to be dealt with. You can't have a country where the people who are supposed to provide leadership and vision and stuff are despised. So it has to be a much more open process, if you want to drive away the cynicism and you want to have people feel that what is being done reflects their views and values. And there are times when you'll do things that won't, but it should be pretty understandable if you have to go off on a longer-term perspective on a problem.*

On the other hand, a few officials interviewed for this book argued that, as one put it, *"the pendulum is swinging back on this—we peaked out on consultation in the Meech Lake process, now there is a trend back to 'this is our job and let's get these things out.'"* The same individual noted that *"people talk a lot about participation and certainly a lot of work goes into it, but it's considered more of a necessary hurdle that you have to go through, but does it make a difference at the end of the day?"* Most practising policy-makers know that the terrain has changed, and that there is a high level of distrust out there that requires them to consult. Some think that consultation will yield better policy; others worry that it will bog down decision-making hopelessly. But everyone recognizes that there is a rising demand for participation, not just in Canada, but across the world:

> The desire of people to be involved in the management of their affairs, the need to be active in areas where government is unable or unwilling to act, and the development of new communication technologies that convey information broadly and help people interact across national borders are encouraging what some have called a global associational revolution. This is fuelled by the realization that so many of the issues requiring attention are global in scope. The idea that people have common interests irrespective of their national or other identities and that they are coming together in an organized way across borders to address these is of increasing relevance to global governance. (Commission on Global Governance 1995, 253–254)

Another consequence has been a new emphasis on identity and the politics of recognition. Demographics play an important role in this, and Canadian society is increasingly diverse. But new sensibilities abound as well, some of them encouraged through government policies like multiculturalism, bilingualism, and equity. People increasingly identify themselves strongly with nonterritorially based groups—religious, ethnic, gender, linguistic, sexual, or some exotic combination. They identify themselves as members of these communities, and rely on the integrity and health of those communities for their personal well-being. From a policy perspective, this raises two challenges. One is the potential for social fragmentation. Pluralism and diversity are certainly to be valued in any society, but by the same token, any society worthy of the name shares things in common. Without that, a pleasing diversity can quickly become a scattered collection of mutually exclusive groups. The second challenge is the introduction of thorny issues of "ways of life" and collective rights. Both citizens and policy-makers are willing to compromise on material interests, but ways of life are intrinsically more precious and demand our respect. The result is new difficulties in dealing with some policy questions (e.g., reconciling fish management programs and Aboriginal rights; linguistic policies in Québec), and a certain prickliness on the part of significant segments of the public who feel that public policy should not merely confer benefits but also afford dignity, recognition, and support. As one policy analyst put it:

> there has been a fragmentation of position and process, the process highlighted in the Charlottetown Accord, which showed a reduced willingness of the public to have spokespersons. This is part of a reduced credibility of national institutions like political parties and the legislature. There is an increased tendency to identify with and speak through smaller and smaller groups. This makes strategies of coalition building infinitely more difficult.

A final, and somewhat contradictory consequence of this shift in public values is a growing scepticism of traditional representative institutions. The decline of deference certainly induces people to be sceptical of politicians, but added to the new emphasis on identity and rights, it makes them suspicious of institutions that represent majoritarian interests. Parliament, political parties, and the electoral system are skewed toward the majority, but the new political culture sees rights as against majority interests, and minority rights as against majority rule. Institutions like the courts, which formally have no representative function, and which appear to be dispassionately concerned only with truth and justice, come off much better in this view. It is no coincidence that courts have become much more important in contemporary Canadian public policy, just as our political culture has become more rights oriented.

GOVERNANCE AND PUBLIC MANAGEMENT

The third major change in the context of policy-making and analysis has been in our idea of the proper scope of governance by the state and the nature of public management. These are of course entangled with the changes described above in the domestic economy, globalization, and culture shifts, and are probably the results of these changes more than independent forces in their own right. Nonetheless, it is a crucial category for policy analysis since it cuts closest to what governments see themselves as doing, and the new politics of governance and public management have rapidly developed their own dynamics, however much they might be a consequence of deeper factors.

Ideas about governance operate at several distinct levels. The most general is the view of the appropriate scope and nature of government:

smaller. Policy-makers themselves have less confidence in the capacity of governments to do things. One policy advisor remembers federal planning exercises in the early 1970s about what the government should do, and *"everything was open, everything was assumed to be a potential area of government activity; it never entered people's minds that there wouldn't be the money, or the tools or the support to do something."* The central issue today is the relationship between governments, markets, and civil society. Should governments provide services themselves, or should they facilitate the delivery of these services through either for-profit or nonprofit agencies? Can and should government "correct market failures," or is the medicine worse than the malady? To what extent should government encourage the pursuit of what are basically private interests, such as child care or a university education, through direct services or financial support?

Another, more specific level concerns the tools that governments realistically have at their disposal for policy development and implementation. Can governments control unemployment and inflation through monetary policy? Can they create jobs? Can they eradicate poverty or racism? Can they provide adequate housing? The more limited one's views of government capacity, the less the question of policy instruments will arise. However, even in cases where one thinks that the role of government should be minimal, there can be disputes over appropriate policy design. The final aspect of governance concerns management practices. Given a certain vision of the role of government and the feasibility of tools at its disposal for dealing with public problems, what is the best way to organize the administrative machinery of government to achieve those ends?

It is clear that ideas about governance and public management have changed radically in the last two decades. Politically, the movement has coincided with the political ascendancy of the right in most liberal-democracies, starting with Margaret Thatcher in Britain (who became prime minister in 1979) and Ronald Reagan in the United States (elected president in 1980). In Canada, the Progressive Conservatives were elected for two terms in 1984 and 1988, before being almost wiped out in 1993. Interestingly, the Liberals accepted many key elements of the Tory agenda: deficit reduction and government restructuring being most prominent. This mimics a pattern in other countries such as New Zealand, where the change in public administration and management was led by left-wing parties. But the gospel of smaller government, balanced budgets, and new management practices seems to have gained converts from both left and right.

What are its main features? First, at the most general level, the size and role of government vis-à-vis the market and civil society should be much smaller. Government over the past forty years has grown too big, absorbs too many resources, and is a drag on both economic performance and civic independence. Second, the new vision of governance argues that many conventional policy tools no longer work (if they ever did), or that they sometimes cause more harm than good. In a global economy, for example, there is relatively little governments can do about unemployment and inflation directly, not much they can do to control interest rates, and so on. Third, there is a belief that what Barzelay (1992, 5) calls the "bureaucratic paradigm" of carefully defined roles, reliance on rules and procedure, line and staff distinctions, tight financial control, and central agency oversight, should be replaced with a more client-focused, service-oriented system. There has been a narrowing of what one interviewee called *"the realm of the possible."*

One of the most widely read examples of the new public management thinking was the 1992 book, *Reinventing Government*, by David Osborne and Ted Gaebler. The most important aspect of the book's argument was its rejection of the hierarchical structure of most government bureaucracies. Close accountability requires close scrutiny and a minimum of bureaucrat discretion. This organizational tradition is alleged to be responsible for the stereotypical sluggishness and waste in government bureaucracy. The result is often inflexible, costly, lumbering organizations driven by rules rather than by results. Creativity is stifled, problem solving is discouraged in favour of following routine, and significant resources are devoted simply to managing people within the system, rather than achieving policy goals. Osborne and Gaebler distilled ten principles of reinventing government from the cases they reviewed. These principles are grounded in the assumption that government is necessary, but it does not necessarily have to act like government.

> Most entrepreneurial governments promote *competition* between service providers. They *empower* citizens by pushing control out of the bureaucracy, into the community. They measure the performance of their agencies, focusing not on inputs but on *outcomes*. They are driven by their goals—their *missions*—not by their rules and regulations. They redefine their clients as *customers* and offer them choices—between schools, between training programs, between housing options. They *prevent* problems before they emerge, rather than simply offering services afterward. They put

their energies into *earning* money, not simply spending it. They *decentralize* authority, embracing participatory management. They prefer *market* mechanisms to bureaucratic mechanisms. And they focus not simply on providing public services, but on *catalyzing* all sectors— public, private, and voluntary—into action to solve their community's problems. (Osborne & Gaebler 1992, 19–20)

These may seem like abstract principles, but they summarize concrete initiatives that have been undertaken by governments all around the world, as well as in Canada. For example, when asked what was different about the policy environment today, one federal policy analyst answered:

I guess my first point is that there is a view now that the government can't solve everything. A recognition that it can't solve everything and it should limit itself to what it can do effectively and persuade others to take action where they are more appropriately placed to take action to solve, to analyze problems and then solve them. So the whole relationship with the private sector has changed from one of near rivalry twenty years ago, certainly in Canada, I think in the Trudeau era, the big expansion of the public service, to today where there is a sense of cooperation and partnership across just about every field you can imagine, whether it's in industrial policy, whether it's fisheries, or whether it's financial policy. So that is one big change. I guess the second change is that what government does do, it does in much closer contact with the client, or with the impact group. And thirdly, in order to do that, there is much more prior consultation before the government ever makes a move. So there is less surprise, there is more packaging, so that new policies and new directions pretty much have all the bases covered.

In the United States, the Clinton administration launched a National Performance Review on government, headed by Vice-President Al Gore, in March 1993. Its first report contained 384 recommendations for improving federal governmental performance, touching on virtually every agency and program in the American federal government (National Performance Review 1993). Despite criticisms that the process was stalled, within months of the release of the report, Kettl and DuIulio (1995) conclude that it led to real change in, for example, governmental culture, procurement practices, and cuts to some government agencies, though the long-term future of the reforms is more doubtful. Initially, this Democratic effort at reform was eclipsed with the Republican victory in midterm Congressional elections in 1994. A key ingredient to that victory was a platform of policy reforms entitled "The Contract with America." While short on details of how government management would be revised, it took a more extreme view of the need to reduce the size and scope of government in the United States. In the first 100 days, for example, the Contract promised, among other things, a balanced budget amendment (which was passed and led to a confrontation between President Clinton and Congress in January 1995 that shut down the American government for several days), a crime bill, welfare reform, tax cuts, and a stronger national defence. However, Republican popularity waned considerably in the run-up to the American Presidential election in November 1996.

The British and New Zealand examples are perhaps more relevant to Canada because they too are parliamentary democracies. In Britain today, two-thirds of "government employees" do not work for traditional departments, but instead for executive agencies that have been contracted to provide certain services. A wide range of reforms has been underway since Margaret Thatcher's prime ministership, but two initiatives, the Next Steps Program and the Citizen's Charter, illustrate the organizational revolution that has taken place (Jenkins and Gray 1993; Doern 1993).

Next Steps had its origins in the Financial Management Initiative of 1982, which tried to underscore the importance of management in government by introducing better practices and giving managers greater autonomy over budgets and operations as long as they met certain performance and output targets. By the late 1980s, the reform had bogged down, and so efforts were redoubled to take the "Next Steps" of the original Financial Management Initiative in decentralizing government services. The plan called for as many agencies as possible to be converted to "departmental executive agencies" that would act as businesses delivering public services. The chief executive officer of each Next Step agency was to negotiate a contract with the department specifying performance goals and targets, but would then have substantial freedom to operate the "business" as he or she saw fit.

In a little over a year, eight agencies were created. By April 1993, there were 89 such agencies employing almost two-thirds of the civil service. Among them were: the Central Statistical Office, the Employment Service, the Prison Service, the Royal Mint, and the Social Security Benefits Agency. These are not privatized agencies; they remain parts of government and their employees are still civil servants. The key change is the introduction of substantial managerial autonomy. Each agency has a framework document or agreement that is negotiated between the parent department and the Treasury, and is subject to some renegotiation later by the chief executive officer. The framework document differs for each agency, though all of them outline the agency's objectives and targets, resource management guidelines, and the pattern of agency-department relations. The result is the provision of government services in markedly new ways. The Next Steps agencies, for example, no longer need to follow general government guidelines on expenditures as long as they work within their framework agreement. Agencies can set salary levels and classify jobs as they see fit. Managers can take risks, be more entrepreneurial, and the agency as a whole can respond more effectively to its "customers."

The U.K. Citizen's Charter was introduced by John Major in 1991 after he had assumed the prime ministership from Margaret Thatcher. The Charter's principles, however, are entirely consistent with the Next Steps project of remaking the way that government works. Whereas Next Steps introduced fundamental organizational changes, the Charter is designed to alter bureaucratic practices in order to raise the quality of public services. The Charter was launched with a White Paper that laid out four key themes: (1) the improvement in the *quality* of public services, (2) the introduction, wherever possible, of greater *choice* through competing providers of public services and consultation with citizens about the type of services they wanted, (3) the clear statement of *standards* of services, to enhance accountability, and (4) the assurance that taxpayers would receive *value* for their money. In addition, the White Paper listed seven principles of public service: clear standards, openness, ease of access to information, choice, nondiscrimination on the basis of race or sex, accessibility to suit the needs of the public rather than civil servants, and responsiveness when things go wrong. The Citizen's Charter applies to all central government agencies and departments, nationalized industries, local governments, the health service, courts, police, and private and publicly regulated utilities.

The New Zealand experience saw equally radical changes in the nature of governance and public management (Boston 1991). Starting in 1984 under a Labour government, New Zealand moved rapidly to privatize a host of state agencies, drastically reduce expenditures, and restructure the public sector so that government agencies were more clearly devoted to policy-making rather than delivery functions.

By contrast with the United States, Britain, and New Zealand, Canadian management innovations to date have been relatively tame. At the provincial level, the governments of Alberta and Ontario have attracted the most recent attention, though some important administrative changes to the health and education sectors have also been made in most of the other provinces. The Alberta government passed a Deficit Elimination Act that committed it to that goal for 1996 to 1997, but actually achieved a balanced budget a year earlier through deep spending cuts (and unexpectedly high resource revenues). It restructured its welfare services, closed hospitals, consolidated school boards, and privatized its liquor stores (Mihlar 1995). A Conservative government was elected in Ontario in 1995 on the platform of its "Common Sense Revolution," which promised virtually the same policy configuration as Alberta's. In the words of Premier Mike Harris, "I am not talking about tinkering, about incremental changes, or about short term solutions. After all, the changes we have all experienced in our personal lives have been much more fundamental than that. It's time for us to take a fresh look at government. To reinvent the way it works, to make it work for people" (Conservative Party of Ontario 1995, 1). This high rhetoric, however, actually reflects massive changes underway in all the provinces. After a survey of their administrative reform projects, Lindquist and Murray (1994) conclude:

> All governments have enacted forms of wage restraint and have been involved in combinations of downsizing, delayering, and consolidation of departments and agencies, or perhaps their elimination. Service quality precepts are ubiquitous; many governments are moving toward "single window" offices, and some are experimenting with different organizational forms such as special operating agencies to provide more focused service. The rhetoric in official documents and interviews often calls for greater delegation of authority from central agencies or senior management to frontline staff, more emphasis on results or performance to ensure accountability, and more open budgetary processes. (p. 488)

At the federal level, the vehicle for a new public management has been the Program Review, launched in 1994. The scope and impact of the review only hit home with Canadians in the February 1995 federal budget statement. The language of that budget was as uncompromising as that in the *Common Sense Revolution*: "The Program Review will lead to long-standing structural change in *what* government does" (Department of Finance 1995, 32). Program review was guided by six tests or questions: "serving the public interest; necessity of government involvement; appropriate federal role; scope for public sector/private sector partnerships; scope for increased efficiency; and affordability" (Department of Finance 1995, 34). According to Paquet and Shepherd (1996), these tests imply a principle of subsidiarity: "The principle is built on two assumptions: that individuals are competent and capable of taking primary responsibility for their own welfare, and that help to individuals can be provided more effectively, efficiently, and caringly by organizations in close proximity to them than by governments, which can and must play only a subsidiary or supportive role in providing such help" (pp. 40–41). They believe that this fundamental review of governance was eventually eclipsed by expenditure reduction priorities, which were relatively successful. Federal program spending will be 21.5 percent lower in 1997–98 than in 1994–95, the lowest level in almost half a century (Minister of Finance 1996, 12). Whatever the degree of success of the Program Review and expenditure exercises, however, it is clear that Canadian governance is fundamentally different from the assumptions that guided most of the postwar period, what Eden and Molot (1993) call the second national policy of "compensatory liberalism" with its emphasis on "macroeconomic management, the creation and maintenance of a welfare state, and Canadian participation in the construction of a liberal postwar international economic order" (p. 237).

These examples show that ideas about governance and public management vary by political jurisdiction, but that there are still clear patterns. As Pollitt puts it: "One senses an 'official line' advanced, with local inflexions, by most national government leaders" (1995, 204). This official line has coalesced around a strong political emphasis on certain techniques: decentralization of budgeting, performance indicators, performance-related pay, an emphasis on quality and standards, the contractualization of relationships, and evaluation coupled with a concern about value for money. The picture gets even more confusing when it is realized that academic versions of the new public management, as well as some practical real-world examples, suggest a variety of sometimes inconsistent models (Peters 1995).

The emphasis on empowerment and the distrust of bureaucracy, for example, is just as likely to lead to a greater emphasis on broad political participation in policy-making as it is to market-based prescriptions (Denhardt 1993). And the enthusiasm with which new visions of governance have been seized by politicians has not been mirrored by analysts. For many students of public administration, wide-sweeping changes were often implemented without public consultation or popular mandates (e.g., New Zealand), and for others the new public management is yet another postwar fad that kowtows to the market as the only credible model for human organization (Savoie 1995). What this model forgets is that traditional public administration was couched in an understanding that politics is different from economics: in politics, it is citizens and not merely customers or clients that interact; they interact with an eye to the common public interest and not to personal interests. In democratic politics there has to be a heavy premium on accountability and public debate. For others, the new public management does provide some important improvements to the conventional bureaucratic model (Borins 1995).

CONCLUSION

Are the forces described in this chapter permanent? Yes and no. Globalization, increasing cultural diversity, the decline of deference, and the information revolution are virtually impossible to reverse. Governance, or our systems of public policy and administration, are reactions to these forces, and can be expected to change and vary over time. For example, the budget cutting and downsizing that has characterized Canadian governments for the past few years were indeed compelled by globalization, but different governments handled that process in different ways. Saskatchewan and British Columbia, under New Democrats, cut spending but also raised taxes. Alberta simply cut expenditures. Ontario cut spending and taxes, and launched a revolution in the organization of government. New Brunswick opted for an aggressive strategy that combined training, information technology, and trade. Moreover, once the books are balanced, basic choices are open once again about what to spend tax dollars on. And of course, the same forces that constrain governments generate demands for policy to protect or help the victims of those forces. As one official put it, the paradox is that *"people's confidence in government is less, but they still want governance."*

So it would be a mistake to think that these forces somehow mark the end of policy-making. They do, however, impose constraints and offer new opportunities, and they have forced us to change our notion of the role of government. The initial response to these forces came from the political right, and so for some people these changes simply reflect a right-wing, neoconservative agenda. As noted in the previous paragraph, choices can be made, ones that differ substantially from those taken by conservatives. However, the consensus on the fundamentals is impossible to deny. This book will focus on those fundamentals, and think through what they mean for the art and craft of policy analysis.

SUMMARY

Globalization

- globalization in its modern form is qualitatively different from the internationalism that marks most of human history; it is driven by new technologies, and is both deeper and wider in scope

- economic globalization is driven by the new technologies, particularly the merging technologies of communications and computers

- economic globalization is marked by (1) complex trading systems, (2) transnational corporations and global sourcing, (3) fluid capital flows

- cultural globalization is marked by (1) growing similarity of consumer tastes and expectations, (2) a heightened sensibility about cultural, national, and ethnic differences, and (3) the emergence of common, global standards of conduct

Diversity

- postmaterialism is a deep cultural shift that appears to be affecting most industrialized countries, and consists of a higher priority for lifestyle concerns, participation, and identity over purely material interests

- "rights talk" is a specific type of political discourse that views issues through the dual prism of individual and collective rights (as opposed, for example, to feasibility or cost)

- "politics of difference" is a new sensibility about cultural, racial, gender, or other "differences" which reflects both the oppression by majority society and the tenacity of "ways of life," and calls for both the recognition of these differences and accommodations in public policy to demands grounded in those differences

Governance

- new public management is a loose framework that draws its inspiration from the private sector, and urges public sector institutions to be more businesslike through contracting out, alternative service delivery, and client/customer responsiveness

- National Performance Review: redesign of American federal government institutions, launched by the Clinton administration and under the leadership of Vice-President Al Gore

- Next Steps: redesign of British government institutions launched by Prime Minister John Major

REFERENCES

Abramson, P. R., & Inglehart, R. (1995). *Value change in global perspective.* Ann Arbor, MI: University of Michigan Press.

Barber, B. R. (1995). *Jihad vs. McWorld.* New York: Times Books.

Barzelay, M. (1992). *Breaking through bureaucracy: A new vision for managing in government.* Berkeley, CA: University of California Press.

Borins, S. (1995). The public management is here to stay. *Canadian Public Administration, 38*(Spring), 122–132.

Boston, J. (Ed.). (1991). *Reshaping the state: New Zealand's bureaucratic revolution.* Melbourne, Australia: Oxford University Press.

Brodie, I., & Nevitte, N. (1993). Evaluating the citizens' constitution theory. *Canadian Journal of Political Science, 26*(June), 235–259.

Cairns, A. C. (1991). *Disruptions: Constitutional struggles, from the Charter to Meech Lake* (D. E. Williams, Ed.). Toronto: McClelland and Stewart.

Cairns, A. C. (1992). *Charter versus federalism.* Montreal: McGill-Queen's University Press.

Cairns, A. C. (1993). The fragmentation of Canadian citizenship. In W. Kaplan, (Ed.), *Belonging: The meaning and future of Canadian citizenship* (pp. 181–220).Montreal: McGill-Queen's University Press.

Coleman, W. D., & Porter, T. (1996). The internationalization of Canadian banking and securities policy. In G. B. Doern, L. A. Pal, & B. Tomlin (Eds.), *Border crossings: Internationalization and Canadian public policy* (pp. 55–81). Toronto: Oxford University Press.

Commission on Global Governance. (1995). *Our global neighbourhood: The report of the Commission on Global Governance.* Oxford, England: Oxford University Press.

Courchene, T. J. (1994). *Social Canada in the millennium: Reform imperatives and restructuring principles.* Toronto: C. D. Howe Institute.

The death of distance: A survey of telecommunications. (1995, September 30). *The Economist,* pp. 5–27.

de la Mothe, J., & Paquet, G. (1996). Competition and governance: The new challenges. In J. de la Mothe & G. Paquet (Eds.)., *Corporate governance and the new competition* (pp. 3–22). Ottawa: PRIME at the Faculty of Administration, University of Ottawa.

Denhardt, R. B. (1993). *The pursuit of significance: Strategies for managerial success in public organizations.* Belmont, CA: Wadsworth Publishing Co.

Department of Finance (Canada). (1995). *The federal budget.* Ottawa: Ministry of Finance.

Doern, G. B. (1993). The UK citizen's charter: Origins and implementation in three agencies. *Policy and Politics, 21,* 17–29.

Eden, L., & Molot, M. A. (1993). Canada's national policies: Reflections on 125 years. *Canadian Public Policy, 19*(September), 232–252.

Elkins, D. (1995). *Beyond sovereignty: Territory and political economy in the twenty-first century.* Toronto: University of Toronto Press.

Elshtain, J. B. (1993). *Democracy on trial.* Toronto: Anansi.

Glendon, M. A. (1991). *Rights talk: The impoverishment of political discourse.* New York: The Free Press.

Hood, C. (1995). *Explaining policy reversals.* Buckingham, England: Open University Press.

Howard, R. (1995, May 20). Canada must adjust, PM says. *Globe and Mail,* A1–2.

Hughes, R. (1993). *Culture of complaint: The fraying of America.* New York: Oxford University Press.

Jenkins, B., & Gray, A. (1993). Reshaping the management of government: The Next Steps initiative in the United Kingdom. In F. L. Seidle (Ed.), *Rethinking government: Reform or reinvention?* (pp. 73–109). Montreal: Institute for Research on Public Policy.

Kettl, D. F., & DuIulio, Jr., J. J. (Eds.). (1995). *Inside the reinvention machine: Appraising governmental reform.* Washington, DC: The Brookings Institution.

Kincaid, J. (1994). Peoples, persons, and places in flux. In G. Laforest & D. Brown (Eds.), *Integration and fragmentation: The paradox of the late twentieth century* (pp. 53–84). Kingston, ON: Institute of Intergovernmental Relations.

Kymlicka, W. (1989). *Liberalism, community and culture.* Oxford, England: Oxford University Press.

Kymlicka, W. (1992). *Recent work in citizenship theory.* Ottawa: Multiculturalism and Citizenship Canada.

Lindquist, E. A., & Murray, K. B. (1994). Appendix: A reconnaissance of Canadian public administrative reform during the early 1990s. *Canadian Public Administration, 37*(Fall), 468–489.

Lusztig, M. (1994). Constitutional paralysis: Why Canadian constitutional initiatives are doomed to fail. *Canadian Journal of Political Science, 27*(December), 747–771.

Melnick, R. S. (1994). *Between the lines: Interpreting welfare rights.* Washington, DC: The Brookings Institution.

Mihlar, F. (1995). *Alberta mid-term report: The Klein government.* Vancouver: Fraser Institute.

Minister of Finance (Canada). (1996). *The budget plan.* Ottawa: Canada Communication Group.

Monahan, P. J. (1991). *Meech Lake: The inside story.* Toronto: University of Toronto Press.

Naisbitt, J. (1994). *Global paradox: The bigger the world economy, the more powerful its smallest players.* New York: Morrow.

National Performance Review. (1993, September 27). *From red tape to results: Creating a government that works better and costs less* [On-line]. Available: http://sunsite.unc.edu/npr/np-realtoc.html

Negroponte, N. (1995). *Being digital.* New York: Alfred A. Knopf.

Neubarth, M. (1995). The Internet: A global look. *Internet World, 6*(November), 94–101.

Newman, P. C. (1995). *The Canadian revolution, 1985–1995: From deference to defiance.* Toronto: Viking.

Nielsen Media Research Unit. (1996, September 27) [On-line]. Available: http://www.commerce.net/work/pilot/nielsen_96/exec.html

Ohmae, K. (1995). *The end of the nation state: The rise of regional economies.* New York: The Free Press.

Osborne, D., & Gaebler, T. (1993). *Reinventing government: How the entrepreneurial spirit is transforming the public sector.* New York: Penguin.

Pal, L. A., & Seidle, F. L. (1993). Constitutional politics 1990–92: The paradox of participation. In S. Phillips (Ed.), *How Ottawa spends, 1993–94: A more democratic Canada?* (pp. 143–202). Ottawa: Carleton University Press.

Paquet, G., & Shepherd, R. (1996). The program review process: A deconstruction. In G. Swimmer (Ed.), *How Ottawa spends, 1996–97: Life under the knife* (pp. 39–72). Ottawa: Carleton University Press.

Peters, B. G. (1995). The public service, the changing state, and governance. In B. G. Peters & D. J. Savoie (Eds.), *Governance in a changing environment* (pp. 288–320). Montreal: Canadian Centre for Management Development and McGill-Queen's University Press.

Pollitt, C. (1995). Management Techniques for the Public Sector: Pulpit and Practice. In B. G. Peters & D. J. Savoie (Eds.), *Governance in a changing environment* (pp. 203–238). Montreal: Canadian Centre for Management Development and McGill-Queen's University Press.

Porter, M. E. (1990). *The competitive advantage of nations.* New York: Free Press.

Progressive Conservative Party of Ontario. (1994). *The common sense revolution.* Toronto: Progressive Conservative Party of Ontario.

Reich, R. (Ed.). (1988). *The power of public ideas.* Cambridge, CT: Harvard University Press.

Rheingold, H. (1993). *The virtual community: Homesteading on the electronic frontier.* Reading, MA: Addison-Wesley.

Rosell, S. A. (1995). *Changing maps: Governing in a world of rapid change.* Ottawa: Carleton University Press.

Savoie, D. J. (1995). What is wrong with the new public management? *Canadian Public Administration, 38*(Spring), 112–121.

Schultz, R. (1995). Paradigm lost: Explaining the Canadian politics of deregulation. In C. E. S. Franks et al. (Eds.), *Canada's century: Governance in a maturing society* (pp. 259–277). Montreal: McGill-Queen's University Press.

Simeon, R. (1994). *In search of a social contract: Can we make decisions as if democracy matters?* Toronto: C. D. Howe Institute.

Simeon, R. (1995). Globalization, domestic societies, and governance. In C. E. S. Franks et al. (Eds.), *Canada's century: Governance in a maturing society* (pp. 25–42). Montreal: McGill-Queen's University Press.

Stevenson, R. W. (1995, November 12). Deficit-cutting's international. *New York Times,* section 4, p. 1–4.

Thurow, L. C. (1996). *The future of capitalism: How today's economic forces shape tomorrow's world.* New York: William Morrow and Co.

United Nations. (1952–1994). *Statistical yearbook.* New York: United Nations.

United Nations Conference on Trade and Development. (1994). *Handbook of international trade and development statistics*. New York: United Nations.

Young, I. M. (1990). *Justice and the politics of difference*. Princeton, NJ: Princeton University Press.

Chapter 3   Problem Definition

Policy-making is in large measure about trying to solve problems, and so the nature of those problems—how they are defined—is central to the entire process. But defining problems is not merely a technical exercise, it entails political and strategic manoeuvres, insofar as problem definition sets the tone for successive stages in the process. Framing problems draws on a wide variety of ingredients, from scientific expertise to conventional wisdom and rhetoric. In a democracy, it always means shaping arguments in ways that capture public attention. This process is connected to interests and institutions, of course, but the study of problem definition and framing clearly underscores the importance of ideas in policy-making. The second part of the chapter explores ways in which both the substance and the process of problem definition are changing in the face of the forces described in Chapter 2.

The core of any public policy is the triad of problem definition, goals, and instruments. Know them, and you know the policy. But if we view policy more dynamically, which of these elements comes first, or what is the prime mover in the policy response? There is universal agreement that the key factor is the problem, or at least the definition of a situation considered problematic (the two are not the same). Policies are responses to problems, and so the character and shape of the problem will deeply affect the nature of the response. At the most extreme, if a problem is not widely recognized at all, there will be little or no policy response. The existence of widespread and systematic poverty in the United States in the late 1950s was largely ignored, for example, until the publication of Michael Harrington's *The Other America: Poverty in the United States* (1962). The same could be said of modern environmentalism: until Rachel Carson's *Silent Spring* (1962), the notion that what we were doing to the environment was a problem simply did not occur to many people. A striking Canadian example comes from research conducted by the Canadian

Advisory Council on the Status of Women in 1987 on domestic abuse: the study entitled *Battered but Not Beaten* by Linda MacLeod took something from the shadows of private family life and exposed it as a major social problem. As with the Harrington and Carson books, something that had been invisible as a policy problem was suddenly and powerfully illuminated.

It would seem that there should be another end of the continuum to complement problem invisibility, a point where problems are so well defined and understood that the policy response seems obvious and uncontroversial. In fact, there are very few of these, at least with respect to proposed solutions. On some issues, such as child pornography, consensus is overwhelming about both the character of the problem (universally despised) and the solution (a strong prohibition). However, in other areas of even strong consensus about the need to tackle a problem, like the deficit, for instance, there will be differences over solutions. So it is clear that problems are not simply either recognized or not, they have to be discerned, shaped, and articulated. There are so many different elements that can conceivably go into a problem definition, that people may see the same situation quite differently, even if they agree on its general aspects, and so will offer very different solutions.

The idea that people disagree in their perceptions of problems and solutions is hardly news, so it may come as a surprise to learn that until the last decade, policy analysis held out the hope of trying to "get it right," in other words, to achieve the correct definition of the problem. As Rochefort and Cobb (1994) describe it:

> Through the accumulation of information, a troubling social condition comes to light and is documented. Next it is the job of public officials to assess that problem and its causes and to respond as efficiently as possible through such means as new legislative enactments. Attention continues until the distressing concern is alleviated. (p. 56)

As Stone (1988, 106) puts it: "In conventional policy analysis textbooks, as well as in the larger rationality project, a problem definition is a statement of a goal and the discrepancy between it and the status quo. In this conception, problem definition is a matter of observation and arithmetic— measuring the difference between two states of affairs." A dozen years ago, a leading text could refer to the possibility of making "mistakes" in the problem definition or initiation phase of policy design (Brewer & deLeon 1983, 35). The idea of "making mistakes" would strike Stone as very odd, since to her, "there is no objective description of a situation; there can only be portrayals of people's experiences and interpretations" (1988, 106). When everything is open to interpretation, there is no clearly superior way of discerning a situation, and so all interpretations are equally valid. This explains the problem-saturated policy environment within which we live. The media, interest groups, experts, analysts, think tanks, and political parties subject us to a constant barrage of crises and problems. Not only is the number of problems apparently large, but the range of solutions seems bewilderingly wide.

Governments do not have infinite resources or time, however, and every government faces the ultimate test of having to choose among definitions and solutions and doing what it was elected to do—govern. It is this combination of epistemological variety and political reality that shapes the agenda of questions that occupy the literature on problem definition: (1) by what process are problems defined, (2) what are the generic elements of a problem definition, (3) how are some problems chosen to be on the political/policy agenda while others languish in obscurity, and (4) what impact does problem definition have on subsequent stages of the policy process? The good news is that most of the answers to these questions are interesting and insightful. The bad news is that they are not systematic, nor could they really be expected to be. Problem definition has a strong sociopsychological dimension; it is one component in the imaginative construction of reality, with heavy doses of creativity, intuition, and serendipity. Moreover, problem definition is embedded in fluid political and policy processes, where accident and luck play a great role. It is not surprising, therefore, that the literature is dominated by case studies which, while interesting themselves, often conclude that "it all depends."

However, the questions, and some of the general answers to them, are worth exploring, if only because they do provide an organized way of thinking about problem definition and formulation. Contemporary policy analysis needs to go beyond this to recognize that some key elements of both the substance and process of problem definition have changed dramatically in the last decade in response to the forces described in Chapter 2. In terms of the substance of public policy problems, globalization, diversity, and the role of government in actually causing problems rather than solving them, are new parameters within which any policy analysis will have to take place. The generic nature of problems is being reconceptualized as well: policy itself is increasingly viewed suspiciously as a cause of problems. The tools needed to deal with policy problems in this new environment are different from what they were in the past, and this chapter closes with a consideration of the demands this places on analysts.

PROBLEM DEFINITION: KEY ISSUES

What constitutes a problem? The most common definition in the field is that a problem is a "substantial discrepancy between what is and what should be" (Dery 1984, 17). There are three components to this definition: reality (what is), a desired state of affairs (what should be), and the gap between them (the discrepancy). But why should the simple fact of a discrepancy or gap between reality and the ideal constitute a problem? Clearly it does not, and note that the definition addresses what should be, and not what could be. There have to be realistic opportunities for improvement. So this is a first clue on the nature of problem definition—it is incomprehensible without some understanding of the goals being pursued, or the standards being used to judge "what should be."

If standards are always involved in defining the desired state of affairs, the other key ingredient is discerning the gap or discrepancy. Indeed, this is the first phase in the process of problem definition. Before problems can be defined they have to be recognized. This is a prior stage in the sense that it usually involves just a first tremor that something is wrong, that there is a difference between reality and our preferred standard. Strict constructionists (in the sense that all problems are socially constructed) like Deborah Stone (1988) and Joel Best (1989) see this as a highly unpredictable and strategic process: it depends on both the values and interests of the observer.

While this has a measure of truth to it, it also tends to underestimate the degree to which some standards are in fact widely shared and hard-wired into the political process itself. Problem recognition, according to Kingdon (1995), is often stimulated by indicators and routine monitoring that turns up discrepancies or patterns that hint that something is amiss.

> Fairly often, problems come to the attention of government decision makers not through some sort of political pressure or perceptual sleight of hand but because some more or less systematic indicator simply shows that there is a problem out there. Such indicators abound in the political world because both governmental and nongovernmental agencies routinely monitor various activities and events: highway deaths, disease rates, immunization rates, consumer prices, commuter and intercity ridership, costs of entitlement programs, infant mortality rates, and many others. (p. 90)

Kingdon goes on to say that while pressure campaigns and dramatic events are certainly important in attracting notice to a problem, in fact people pay attention "rather straightforwardly because there actually is a demonstrable problem that needs their attention" (p. 93). This occurs in those instances where there is a reasonable degree of consensus about the indicators and what they mean. Canadian debates about poverty, for example, are universally based on the low income cutoffs developed by Statistics Canada. However, these cutoffs were never intended to be a measure of poverty, but rather an indicator of when the consumption of an "average" package of goods would become difficult (Sarlo 1992). Nonetheless, when the numbers of Canadians who fall below that threshold increases, there are immediate concerns about rising poverty in the country. Changes in other indicators such as the gross national product (GNP), the exchange rate, crime statistics, and average life span, also convey messages, not about what the problem is, but that there may be a problem that needs attention.

As Kingdon and others have pointed out, however, indicators have to be interpreted. In more cases than is usually acknowledged, the range of interpretation is fairly narrow. Today, for example, it is virtually beyond discussion, from either the right or the left, that the country faces a deficit problem. And while there is much debate about the causes of that problem and the appropriate solutions, there is broad agreement that the problem has to be addressed primarily through reduced expenditures rather than increased revenues. Governments across the country, as noted in Chapter 8, have launched different versions of the same bundle of strategies to cut their deficits through expenditure reductions.

Indicators can be contrived through research or can consist of routine feedback mechanisms attached to programs themselves. These types of indicators are different from what Kingdon calls "focusing events" which can be sudden catastrophes or crises that grab attention. Sometimes an event may not be significant in itself, but may convince people that there is a deeper malaise. By themselves, focusing events are not usually enough to generate concern, and usually have to be supplemented by other factors such as a receptive public mood, energetic politicians willing to push the issue, or some sense that trends are developing beyond acceptable thresholds. But whatever is at work, the most that happens at this stage is the development of a sense that there may be a problem that needs attention. Beyond problem recognition there has to be a phase of problem definition.

Problem definition is the more arduous process of taking some indicator that a problem exists and answering three fundamental questions. The first question is about the indicator itself. An airline crash and high dropout rates from high school both indicate a problem, but in each instance the first step is an investigation of the event or the numbers. In the case of an air crash, how many casualties, where, and when? In the case of dropout rates, one might ask questions about precise levels, trends, and breakdowns among different groups or regions in the country. The second question is also about the indicator, but now shifts to causality. Why did this happen and how? What matrix of cause and effect is at work? In wildlife management, if there is a sudden decline in the population of a certain species, that is an indicator that something might be wrong. After checking the numbers carefully (the indicator), the key question would be why the drop occurred. It might be due to hunting, natural rhythms in the population, decline in food stocks, migration, disease, and so on. Each one of these hypotheses would have to be considered and tested in some fashion. And this is a relatively easy case: imagine trying to determine the causes of economic decline or of Québec separatism! The third question is about what action to take in the event that there is a "real" problem at stake. Is this a problem that can be solved, and who should solve it? Most importantly, is this a problem that government should solve? Is it in the public sphere, or is it a matter either for private initiative or nongovernmental collective action?

It is rare for these questions to be answered in detail except by specialists. Scratch the surface of any policy debate, go deeply into it, and you will find mountains of argument and discussion around these three categories of questions. Few of us, however, have the time to be that well acquainted with a policy definition. Most of us, even in cases where we are quite interested in a given policy issue, will tend to summarize it in what Baumgartner and Jones (1993) call "policy images." Policy images are a "mixture of empirical information and emotive appeals" that explain the issue and justify the public policy response (p. 26). Moreover, since these images are shorthand, they convey more than information; they give a sense of the tone of the issue, in positive or negative terms. Baumgartner and Jones cite the changing tone in the policy image surrounding civilian nuclear power from a largely positive association with economic progress to a negative connotation linked to environmental damage. As discussed above, a policy issue may be framed in various images, depending on the interests and actors in the field. Stable policy fields tend to coalesce around one dominant policy image, and policy challenge and change is largely about mobilization through the "redefinition of the prevailing policy image" (p. 239).

As noted earlier, recognizing some event or condition as a problem depends on one's goals and values. But given that, simple assertions are not enough. The process of problem definition is one of shaping a persuasive argument about the nature of the problem and, of course, the solution. Of what does that argument and persuasion consist? Rochefort and Cobb offer a scheme that captures the key elements, summarized in Box 3.1.

Not every problem definition will contain all these characteristics, but most will be present. The definer has to deal with the question of causation. Without an idea of why the problem exists there is no way to figure

---

Box 3.1   SUMMARY OF ASPECTS OF PROBLEM DEFINITION

causality	• individual causation versus systemic (the former stresses choices and culpability; the latter stresses impersonal and unavoidable forces)
	• intentional versus accidental causes
	• causes due to character of values
	• complex causal systems versus simple causal agents
severity	• this distinguishes between the acknowledged existence of a problem (e.g., recession) and how serious it is
	• severity is usually measured against some backdrop or context, such as trend lines ("this will soon go away" or "this is getting worse"), specific populations ("this is a big problem only for group X") or what is considered normal or deviant
incidence	• who is affected generally?
	• what subgroups are affected and how?
	• what patterns of incidence are most important?
novelty	• is the issue or problem new?
	• is it unexpected?

proximity	• this refers to how close a problem "hits home"
	• depends on how "home" is defined (i.e., children are valued for any social group's survival, so by definition anything that affects children negatively is bad)
crisis	• largely a rhetorical device to signal urgency
problem populations	• problem definitions can also define the people who are potential targets of policy interventions
	• deserving vs. undeserving of assistance
	• sympathetic vs. deviant definitions of groups
	• definitions that emphasize capacities vs. those that emphasize dependency
instrumental vs. expressive orientations	• difference between focusing on ends (the instrumental intent to solve the problem) and the means (the degree to which what you do expresses an important symbol or value—e.g., refusing to negotiate with terrorists even if it harms hostages)
solutions	• solutions sometimes actually precede the problem and help shape it (e.g., a commitment to vouchers as a policy instrument to deal with a host of problems)
	• are solutions available—can something actually be done to solve a problem, or merely take action for its own sake?

Source: Adapted and amended from Rochefort & Cobb (1994).

out what to do about it. The "causal pictures" we use can differ in their emphasis on individual responsibility or systemic sources. Is poverty a result of individual decisions and choices, or of large economic forces? Definitions can also differ in the degree of complexity of their causal portraits. Inevitably, however, policy action can only be taken across a narrow range of factors, so that the causal assumptions in most policy-relevant problem definitions are usually limited. The severity of the problem is another important characteristic. A problem may be acknowledged, but it might be innocuous enough not to matter in policy terms (e.g., physical fitness of the general population). This often gets connected to the incidence of the problem in the sense of how different groups in the population are affected. Concerns about violence against women or date rape focus on the incidence and severity of these phenomena on women. Novelty, proximity, and crisis are all elements that help heighten the urgency of a problem. The way in which a problem definition portrays potential target populations of policy interventions has received more attention in recent years (Schneider & Ingram 1993; Lieberman 1995; Ingram & Schneider 1995), on the sound assumption that policies are more than just instruments for solving problems. They also convey signals about how policy-makers picture recipients of government programs. Welfare programs are typically paternalistic, conveying the image that welfare recipients cannot plan their own lives and must be watched carefully for fraud. This is another aspect of the symbolic or expressive dimension of policy. Often what matters most about a problem is not whether it can be solved, but how it will be solved. This is because of the simple fact that what we do (in this case, collectively as a political community) says much about who we are.

There is no science of problem definition, and providing the sort of checklist found in Box 3.1 is at best an approximation of the elements that go into the process of persuading others that a problem exists and that it should be addressed. What is clear, however, is that much of the time the process of problem recognition and definition is one of making arguments and persuading others (Majone 1989). Postpositivist policy analysis is correct to emphasize that there can be no absolutely conclusive proof of anything outside of a shared paradigm of understandings. Within those worlds, of course, according to their own canons, it is possible to make a case that will be widely judged as "more true" than the next. Across those worlds, different values and standards of evidence and persuasion will make it difficult to come to firm and widely accepted conclusions. However, there is neither an infinite variety of conceptual paradigms nor of standards of what constitutes good argument. While rhetoric and presentation are always important, there are both inherent constraints within issues themselves, as well as broadly shared understandings at any given point in time that form a common backdrop for the debate about public policy issues.

For example, in their study of five cases of agenda setting (supply-side economics, the greenhouse effect, child abuse, drunk driving, and comparable worth) Milward and Laird (1996) identified the way in which an issue is framed as "critically important to the success of the issue on the public agenda" (p. 63). They argue that some of these issues, such as child abuse and drunk driving, were clearly framed, and that this clarity contributed to their success on the public policy agenda. "A clearly framed issue is one that succinctly states what the problem is in plausible terms and embodies an easily understood solution" (p. 64). Moreover, issues are not infinitely malleable, but have characteristics that make them more or less amenable to clear framing. Supply-side economics, for example, is difficult to personalize, but child abuse and drunk driving both leave victims that can put a human face directly onto a policy problem. Issues that are driven by powerful underlying demographics, such as pensions today because of the greying of the boomers, develop an urgency that can move them up the agenda quite rapidly. The same is true of issues that have no credible opposition. As Milward and Laird argue, there are no "spokespersons for 'killer drunks' or child abusers" (p. 70).

Issue framing or problem definition consequently has two dimensions. The first is analytical, and emphasizes the logical elements that make up an argument or claim. William Dunn (1993), for example, offers a schema to decipher the different statements that comprise a policy argument around the impact of strict traffic enforcement on highway fatalities. Data are offered on the positive correlation between the speeding crackdown and fewer deaths; warrants back up the causal claim that it was the speeding crackdown that led to the result; claims are made that the crackdown was worthwhile; and rebuttals are offered (by sceptics) as to other reasons for the reduction in fatalities. The point of an exercise like this is to outline the types of analytical statements that are made in a typical argument, and sketch their logical relationships to each other.

Policy arguments can also be viewed from the perspective of rhetoric. In this view, the analytical statements are less important than structural elements of language that stimulate almost unconscious reactions to the argument. For example, there is growing interest in the way in which policy arguments are actually framed as narratives, or as stories. We are all familiar with certain archetypical "story lines," and a policy argument that can tap into one of these draws on the power of the narrative structure itself. Arguments about social policy and the deficit can be seen as "redemption stories." In the past, good will and good intentions built a welfare state to meet important needs, but then temptation led us astray and we indulged in excesses and financial debauchery. Our problems got worse, but we ignored them and continued our profligate ways. Now the only option is a complete renunciation of our past sins, and with much pain and suffering we will be redeemed. No wonder finance ministers sound like preachers these days. Their "narrative line" is about nothing less than weakness, temptation, and eventual, if painful, redemption.

Consider the way in which certain words are used to tilt meaning and stimulate reactions. Labels are summary words that convey subtle but powerful meanings: "gay" versus "homosexual," "vagrant" versus "homeless," "tax" versus "user fee," "prostitute" versus "sex-worker," "pro-choice" versus "pro-life." Intense policy battles are often fought over labels, because labels are often the first way in which the public is acquainted with a policy issue. Metaphors are another weapon in the linguistic arsenal. Consider some of the most famous: Cold War, Iron Curtain, Third World, porkbarrel, social safety net, spaceship Earth, global village, and of course, war metaphors such as the War on Poverty, line in the sand, and so on—and this does not even include the ubiquitous sports metaphors!

As Kingdon (1995) points out, getting people to see new problems or see old ones in new ways, "is a major conceptual and political accomplishment" (p. 115). At any given time, there is a host of problems competing for public attention. Some are old and familiar, some are new twists on old issues, and a very few are completely new. The first hurdle is the one mentioned earlier, of providing persuasive indicators that something of importance is actually going on. The next step is a fuller description or definition that will likely take into account some or all of the elements outlined in Box 3.1. A critical aspect of this process is one that was briefly alluded to earlier: defining the problem as one that falls in the public sphere, and indeed as a problem to which the government can offer a credible and feasible response. Even if successful in all this, however, the problem still has to be positioned high enough on the public agenda to receive attention. This is the process of agenda-setting. Why do some problems or issues get onto the agenda when others do not, and what explains the relative positions of issues on that agenda?

We already have referred to the importance of issue framing, and to the vague but important principle of some broad public consensus that determines which ideas (and issues) are plausible and important. At any given time, the number of such "ideas in good currency" as Donald Schon

(1971) termed them, is quite limited. They change slowly, and lag behind present circumstances, but provide a point of reference for policy debates. According to Schon, beneath every policy debate "there is a barely visible process through which issues come to awareness and ideas about them become powerful" (p. 123). Some examples of ideas in good currency from the 1950s included competition with the Russians, the space race, and basic research. Certainly the 1990s list would include competition, sustainable development, and fiscal prudence. Kingdon (1995) captures much the same idea with the notion of the "national mood."

> People in and around government sense a national mood. They are comfortable discussing its content, and believe that they know when the mood shifts. The idea goes by different names—the national mood, the climate of the country, changes in public opinion, or broad social movements. But common to all of these labels is the notion that a rather large number of people out in the country are thinking along certain common lines, that this national mood changes from one time to another in discernible ways, and that these changes in mood or climate have important impacts on policy agendas and policy outcomes. (p. 146)

Baumgartner and Jones (1993), while emphasizing the turbulence and change in American politics, also note that periods of policy stability are marked by substantial consensus over policy images: "One of the clearest findings from our research is the extent to which a prevailing conception of a policy issue dominates both press coverage and official behavior during periods when policy subsystems are especially strong" (p. 238).

Ideas in good currency and the policy images that dominate a given policy field at any given time, help clarify the boundaries and constraints in agenda-setting. The political system as a whole can only handle a limited number of ideas at one time. It is rare for new ideas to come out of nowhere. Fresh policy proposals typically are framed in ways that resonate with existing ideas in good currency, but if they fail, they drop off the agenda into a sort of twilight zone for policy innovations that might be mobilized again later, when the opportunity affords itself. This process of ideas struggling for attention and then fading away has supported the image of an agenda-setting cycle where issues arise, enjoy some intensive debate and perhaps success, and then gradually fall off. An early and influential example of this image was Anthony Downs's "issue attention cycle" (1972), but a cyclical image underpins most discussions of agenda-setting.

Baumgartner and Jones (1993) have borrowed the idea of "punctuated equilibrium" to convey a process that simultaneously combines a greater degree of stability with a higher level of challenge and turbulence.

A great deal of the agenda-setting process is contingent on unpredictable factors and personalities, or as Kingdon puts it, the "opening of policy windows." Windows sometimes open regularly (e.g., cabinet shuffles and budget speeches), but who jumps through successfully or not is still a matter of chance and skill. It is clear that some issues are driven onto the agenda by fundamental characteristics of a political community and economy itself: in Canada, for example, the perennial question of Québec and our relationship to the United States. Modern welfare states have a wide range of important redistributive social programs that are of vital importance to recipient groups (e.g., pensions and the elderly), and so issues of this type are usually high on the public agenda. Massive changes in economic circumstances, or powerful shifts in technology also have a way of rippling through the political system and generating issues for public discussion. But these structural explanations can only illuminate the broad shape of the public agenda. Too much depends on political jockeying, policy entrepreneurs, and combinations of complex and unpredictable forces. The best that one can hope for in this field is a grasp of the institutions, the actors, and the opportunities, as well as the importance of shaping a coherent problem definition. As we will argue shortly, however, the dynamics and circumstances of problem definition have changed significantly in the last decade, and some of the old assumptions no longer apply.

What is the relation of problem definition to policy solutions? The conventional argument in the literature is that the way in which a problem is defined has a dramatic impact on the proposed solutions. At one level this makes sense: if you have to hit a nail, use a hammer, or something that hammers, which could just as easily be a shoe or a brick. Problem definition shapes solutions primarily because of the causal explanations that are its heart. Unemployment, for example, is a problem, but to deal with unemployment we need to know what causes it. If it is due to an international recession, there is not much the government can do to insulate the economy. If it is due primarily to poor training, then the obvious answer is training programs. According to Statistics Canada (1996) 16 percent of Canadian adults are functionally illiterate (defined as being unable to read a product label), but how to deal with this? Better early education? Better diagnosis of persons with reading disabilities? Adult literacy programs? It would depend on the fundamental causes at work.

There are, nonetheless, important variances between problem definition and solutions. First, problems are not always so easily defined. Many social problems are "squishy" in that they don't lend themselves to mathematical formulation and are politically controversial (Strauch 1976, 134), or "messy" in that they are deeply entangled with other problems (Ackoff 1976, 21). The less clear the causal underpinnings of a problem, or the more irreducibly complex a problem appears, the less likely unique solutions can be derived from the definition. Second, even if the causal connections are clear, it is not always feasible to deal with "root" causes. Sometimes, Band-Aid solutions are all that we have. Third, most problem definitions deal with clusters of issues, and raise questions about what governments should do across a range of options. This poses the question of what combination of solutions to apply and what emphasis government should place on any single solution. Just as there is no science of problem definition, there is no clear science of solutions.

PROBLEM DEFINITION: BEYOND OLD CATEGORIES

The preceding section sketched out the conventional theories of problem definition and agenda-setting. But as Chapter 2 argued, the context within which policy analysis is practised today has changed substantially, and some of the key assumptions about the reality to which these theories apply—the substance as well as process of problem definition and agenda-setting—need to be reexamined. This section comes at problem definition and agenda-setting from this angle: what are the implications of globalization, culture shift, and governance for the ways in which we define public policy problems? Problem definition cannot be easily disentangled from the other phases of the policy process, but this chapter will concentrate on sources of policy problems, ideas in good currency, and the role of policy actors in problem definition. More detailed aspects of policy design, implementation, policy communities, and evaluation will be taken up in subsequent chapters.

Sources of Public Policy Problems

Problem sources refers both to the origins of policy problems and the default causal matrixes that people assume underpin those problem situations. One of the most important changes in the sources of policy problems is that many of them are now generated beyond our borders, due to the phenomenon of globalization. As was argued in Chapter 2, the dynamics of globalization and internationalization mean that borders are much more permeable. But that permeability is coupled with a new level of integration in the international political economy. It is important not to exaggerate this phenomenon. There have been many areas of public policy in the past—finance, communications, foreign policy, agriculture, trade, to name a few—that have traditionally been highly exposed to international forces and tightly integrated into international systems. By the same token, there remain many policy areas today that will continue to be insulated from the direct influence of these international forces or systems, for example, health care, social security, or overland transportation. Rather, what has happened is that the intensity of international exposure has increased in many policy fields traditionally marked by global influences, and a host of other areas have been indirectly affected by these wider forces. Policy-making systems in the 1990s have essentially shifted away from a preponderant concern about problems generated domestically within national borders, to problems generated internationally. The policy challenge is how to respond to these new types of problems.

As argued in Chapter 2, the primary drivers in this new internationalization are economics and technology. As we shall see in a moment, a major shift has occurred in the salience of the budget and fiscal balance as a broad idea in good currency, but this shift is itself directly connected to the tighter integration of financial markets. In 1993, Canadian business and governments borrowed $29 billion abroad. As Paul Martin, the federal minister of finance proclaimed in his March 1996 budget: "That was reduced to $13 billion in 1995 and will be reduced again next year and the year after that. In short, Canadian economic sovereignty is being restored" (Department of Finance 1996a). The connection that governments now make between fiscal balance, low interest rates, and job growth through exports is clear, and that link is directly based on the new global economic realities of fluid financial and trade transactions.

> Our overriding policy objective since the very beginning of our mandate in 1993 has been to create more and better jobs for Canadians. However, we realized that simply throwing money at the economy is no durable solution to the problem of unemployment. So, in Canada we have acted to create the necessary conditions for strong economic growth and job creation. This has meant reducing our budget deficits while keeping inflation low, which, in turn, helps get interest rates down and keep them down … The strong growth

in employment that has occurred since October, particularly in the private sector, is a sign that our policies are paying off, one which will provide a further boost to domestic demand by raising household incomes and consumer confidence. Export growth, which has been our principal source of growth over the past several years, should also be strong in 1996, since growth in the U.S. economy is picking up once again. (Department of Finance 1996b)

The governor of the Bank of Canada made the connections even more explicit in a March 1996 speech to the Fraser Institute in Vancouver, B.C. With falling trade barriers and increasing capital movements, international trade is increasingly the path to job creation. Successful economic performance depends on a combination of private sector investment, stable prices, and balanced budgets. In the Canadian context, and indeed for many other countries both developed and developing, this mix is more than a matter of adjustment—it is a wrenching virtual-reality ride of deep public program cuts, rising unemployment, and significant changes to the very nature of government.

However, these ongoing globalization trends and adjustments to new technology do imply changes in the structure of national economies ... Why is it that in Canada we seem to have had a more difficult time of it? There are a number of reasons for this ... The depreciation of the Canadian dollar in the mid-1980s, by easing the pressure from foreign competition, blunted the urgency to adopt more efficient production processes. And through much of the second half of the 1980s, because many Canadians were still acting on expectations of accelerating inflation, we were devoting a good part of our energies and resources to speculative activities, rather than investing in improvements in productivity and competitiveness. Rising government deficits, which were absorbing increasing amounts of domestic savings, were not helping either. Thus, with poor productivity growth, rapidly rising wages and generally weak cost control, Canadian businesses and exporters found it increasingly difficult to compete, especially at the end of the 1980s, when the Canadian dollar had reversed its earlier depreciation ... Thus, we have had two major structural adjustments vital to our economy taking place back to back. Indeed, over the past year, these adjustments have been overlapping, and that may continue for some time. And while a good deal of the restructuring in the private sector has already occurred, the adjustment in the public sector still has some way to go. (Bank of Canada 1996)

In economic policy, which of course drives a good deal of everything else, both the source of our problems, and our eventual salvation, lie beyond our borders. This is not as dramatic a shift for Canada as it has been for some other countries, since we have always been a trading nation. But as noted in Chapter 2, the proportion of our economic wealth now accounted for by trade is rising steadily (exports drove the expansion in 1996), and most regions in this country now trade more with the outside world than with each other. Whereas at one time economic policy tried to push and pull domestic levers in order to stimulate demand, the focus now is global. This does not mean, of course, that there is no role for government to play in the domestic economy. As we will note in Chapter 4, there are a host of things to do about infrastructure, training, and promotion, but the key point is that the drivers of our economic problems are international. Our response is primarily domestic, though as the major drivers shift to the international level, we can see governments more actively trying to establish stable international regimes to manage those sources of instability and turbulence. A dramatic example of the integration of world financial markets was the Mexican peso crisis of December 1994. Political uncertainty in Mexico made international investors skittish about a government devaluation, which developed into a run on the peso that saw its value drop by 40 percent in mere days. An international financial rescue mission—with over $20 billion from the United States, American banks, and other countries, as well as almost $30 billion in credits and loan guarantees from the International Monetary Fund and central banks— had to be mounted to protect against further deterioration in Mexico that might drag the rest of the world economy down with it.

Another example of how our frames of reference have shifted to the international level comes from environmental policy. Canada has now officially adopted the principle of sustainable development to guide its environmental policy, and while once again there is a great deal to do domestically, international forces and actors are an increasingly important part of the equation. The concept of sustainable development was invented by the UN World Commission on Environment and Development (the Brundtland Commission) in 1987 in its report *Our Common Future*. In turn, it became the foundation concept for "Agenda 21," the action plan adopted at the United Nations Conference on Environment and Development held in Rio de Janeiro in June 1992.

Canada's third report to the Commission on Sustainable Development was tabled in 1996, and leaves no doubt of the scope of the domestic-international linkage:

> In accordance with the Commission's multi-year work plan, issues covered include strengthening the role of major groups; environmentally sound technology; combating poverty; changing consumption patterns; promoting education, public awareness, and training; integrating environment and development in international legal instruments and mechanisms; protection of the atmosphere; and protection of the oceans and other seas. (Department of Environment 1996)

It is a point too obvious to belabour that the environment does not respect boundaries, and so that from its inception, this policy field has had an international character. But as noted in the first part of this chapter, issues have to be framed, and there have been previous images of our environmental policy problems that have placed less emphasis on the global connection. As Doern and Conway (1994, 212) note, the policy paradigm in the early 1970s stressed industrial pollution rather than ecological dangers like global warming and the ozone layer, not to mention toxic wastes. Even though Doern and Conway argue that sustainable development is at best a "latent policy paradigm" because it has not yet been clearly defined or incorporated into Canadian public policy processes, it still clearly embraces both a wider domestic scope, as well as a stronger domestic-international linkage. While the definition of sustainable development included in the amendments to the Auditor General Act that established a new Commissioner of Environment and Sustainable Development is indeed anaemic ("development that meets the needs of the present without compromising the ability of future generations to meet their own needs"—this is taken directly from the UN's *Our Common Future*), the more detailed versions that the Department of Environment has circulated incorporate just about every conceivable aspect of quality of life: income, health, education, cultural diversity, and community.

The ecological disaster of the cod fishery on the East coast had its international connection in the 1995 fish war with Spain, and the emerging crisis of West coast salmon stocks is entangled with claims of overfishing by Alaska and Washington state residents. Our forestry policy has been targeted by international environmental groups, not to mention softwood lumber producers in the United States, and a great deal of Canadian government effort in 1996–97 will be going into building the groundwork for a Forestry Convention at the 1997 meeting of the Commission on Sustainable Development in Geneva. Canada wants to develop a stable international regime around sustainable forest practices that will then help it combat attacks from international environmental nongovernmental organizations. In short, most of our major environmental issues have a clear international connection.

A final example of the new importance of the global arena as a source of problems comes from Canadian foreign policy. Foreign policy, of course, is about the pursuit of domestic interest on the international plane. That is precisely why the new policy framework announced in *Canada in the World* is so interesting: it shows that the international context can be framed in a new way, one which stresses the connectedness of a wide variety of global forces to our domestic well-being in a way that goes well beyond the conventional foreign policy categories of military security and economic trade. Noting that there is no distinction anymore between domestic and foreign policy, the document argues that the traditional focus on military security that characterized the Cold War world is no longer adequate to a period without the Soviet Union as a nuclear enemy. Whereas previous foreign policy documents from the 1980s had featured a combination of expanding trade and defence from communist machinations around the globe, *Canada in the World* sees the threats differently.

The heightened integration in a global economy means that we face new threats: "in particular, threats that transcend political borders and affect whole regions or even the globe. International crime and disease, global warming and mass involuntary migration are examples of the more negative aspects of greater global integration" (Government of Canada 1995, 3). Our security is now dependent on the security of others, but in a much wider sense, including economic, social, environmental, and even cultural security. "All this demands a broadening of the focus of security policy from its narrow orientation of managing state-to-state relationships, to one that recognizes the importance of the individual and society for our shared security" (Government of Canada 1995, 25).

Ideas in Good Currency

We noted in the first section of this chapter that problem definition is a crucial phase in the policy process, but that it is not unconstrained. Better or worse arguments can be made, and not all issues can be addressed simultaneously. Moreover, there is a rhythm to the agenda-setting process wherein issues rise and fall (and maybe rise again!) and jostle for position.

A good deal of the success of policy entrepreneurs and policy communities in getting their issues on the agenda depends on good luck and political skill, but luck and skill have to be placed against the backdrop of what Schon calls "ideas in good currency" or others term the public mood. The two are not quite the same, since ideas in good currency may not necessarily reflect (at least in the first instance) a groundswell of public opinion. Indeed, the public mood might be influenced by a sense of changes in important structuring ideas, ideas that many people might at first find unfamiliar or even disagreeable, but which over time they will come to accept as a standard of importance and plausibility.

Any list of such foundational ideas will have a strong dose of subjectivity to it, but at the same time, if the concept of ideas in good currency has any validity at all, a well-constructed list should "sound right" to most people who hear it. First, consider what might plausibly have been a list from the 1970s and early 1980s, before the influence of the Reagan revolution in the United States and its echo in the Mulroney regime, and just around the time of the passage of the Canadian Charter of Rights and Freedoms. Its central tone or themes were equity, cooperation, a strong national government, "made in Canada" solutions, social justice, and social needs. While being careful not to exaggerate—after all, despite their conservative sabre-rattling, the Mulroney Conservatives passed employment equity legislation and more than doubled the federal debt—it is clear that the mid-1980s was a transition period to something with a different emphasis. Certainly, from the vantage point of the mid-1990s, the flavour and tone of what counts as "common sense" in public policy has changed dramatically. Note, however, that it is a matter of tone and emphasis, and not of a complete sea change in public discourse. As most analysts cited in the first section of this chapter argue, new ideas do not completely displace old ones in public discourse, and indeed some of the older ones float in a purgatory of lost causes, to ascend again to political heaven when the time is propitious.

Interviewees for this book were apparently sensitive to this subtlety. One noted that it was impossible to cite any single cause or event for the changed context of policy-making, but that it was more like *"cascading interactions that only make sense in retrospect."* Another nicely expressed the odd mixing of old and new, of fundamental agenda items that characterize the country along with change:

> There's as much continuity in social policy as change … The changes
> have been fundamental, though not well understood generally. That

being the case, what's interesting is that, yes we have globalization, we have changes in the labour market, we have changes in the economy. But a lot of the dynamics of social policy reform are real old: Quebec and the rest of Canada, interprovincial squabbling, feds versus provinces, class-based interests in terms of pension reform. I don't think that those categories have become any less relevant in talking about the politics of social policy reform. But there have been major, major changes.

While these major changes have affected almost everything that governments do (and we will be looking at these in later chapters), at the level of ideas in good currency, the single most important change has been in the perceptions surrounding the fiscal capacities of government. In policy-making, of course, as in most things, bucks always matter. But what has changed dramatically is the sense of how many bucks governments have, and what they should do with them. It has been a change, however, not simply in rhetoric, but in reality as well. Canadian governments since the mid-1960s, when they launched major, expensive social programs such as Medicare, the Canada Pension Plan, and certainly since the oil crisis and inflation of the mid-1970s, have constantly wrung their hands and worried publicly about rising deficits and overspending. While they took periodic and often quixotic action on the budgetary front—with perhaps first prize for budgetary bluster going to the Mulroney Conservatives in their almost decade-long, and ultimately futile fight against the deficit—deficits continued to rise. The last time the total government sector in Canada (on a national accounts basis) was in surplus was in 1974 (Doern, Maslove, & Prince 1988, 17). By 1992, Canada had the second highest level of total government debt as a percent of gross domestic product (GDP) after Italy (Purchase & Hirshhorn 1994, 29). Through the 1980s, Canadian governments continued to borrow to cover their deficits, piling up the public debt (even as they raised taxes) as interest rates began to climb and economic performance slowed down. In this sense, the deficit was "structural" rather than "cyclical" in that the debt itself was so large that not even an economic upturn would do much to reduce interest payments.

That, at least, is the narrative that now suffuses public opinion on government spending and certainly has been the leading motif in budget-cutting exercises at the provincial and federal levels since the early 1990s. While in the 1980s there used to be debate about whether the deficit was a "real problem" or whether it was merely an artifact of high interest rates, a sluggish economy, and tax privileges for the wealthy, by the 1990s all political tendencies, both left and right, agreed that deficits were bad. The debate then shifted to ways of dealing with it, either on the expenditure side (which most governments have done), the revenue side (some arguing for higher taxes on corporations and the middle class, while most governments have opted for revenue generation through various fees and charges), or lower interest rates. The shift in what Kingdon calls the national mood, along with government determination to reflect that mood (or lead it), has been remarkable. In mid-1996, seven of ten provinces had balanced budgets. Saskatchewan and Alberta had led the way, and the first Ontario budget in 1996 echoed the importance of deficit elimination (the Harris government cut the provincial deficit by $3 billion or 27 percent in its first year in office). Paul Martin proudly pointed out in his March 6, 1996, budget that "Measured relative to the size of the economy, the decline is even more dramatic. By 1998–99, program spending will have been reduced to 12 per cent of GDP, down from close to 20 per cent just over a decade ago. In fact, it will be at its lowest level in 50 years" (Department of Finance 1996a).

The effects of this new emphasis on the fisc, or the national treasury, in problem definition have been profound (we will revisit the effects on other stages in the policy process in later chapters). First, if the deficit is the problem, then it implies the government itself is a problem, since the deficit is a reflection of government activity and management. No ministerial musings on the deficit, from Canada to the United Kingdom to New Zealand, have been complete without an explicit attack on the style of government that produced it. As one interviewee noted, this connects with *"a reduction in the scope of what we consider to be a public responsibility—now we think that individuals, corporations, the third sector, whatever—should take on problems."* The ferocity with which government itself is attacked as a source of problems varies from conservatives to liberals, but the general view is that at a minimum, government should "get itself right," and in doing so will provide the best "solution" to its negative impact on the economy and society.

A second, mirror-like effect of this new emphasis on deficit elimination is that spending itself is now considered to be a generator of possible policy problems. The argument is that our current policy frameworks need to be reworked, but that usually requires fundamental changes in structure or delivery. Our past spending habits and the reliance on money as the policy cure-all made it easy to avoid hard choices. As one interviewee put it:

*It's taken the policy community a long time to switch gears from solv-
ing problems by throwing more money at them, versus solving problems by doing structural reform in the system itself, which is quite a
different problem. [It is] much more controversial, because you have
to piss off the existing community before you can deal with your
problem, instead of building on the status quo.*

This is linked with a third fascinating phenomenon: the sense that a key
policy problem today is the undue influence of those wedded to past solutions. Insofar as those solutions often called for spending, and certainly for
a fairly large role for government, the network of advocacy or public interest organizations that has grown up in this country is now perceived by
some as part of the problem. Cardozo (1996) notes, for example, that
recently,

> just as our national political institutions have come under criticism,
> so has the legitimacy of national groups been publicly challenged ...
> The effect of these new dynamics on public policy development is
> noticeable ... For those elements in society who want to see rapid
> change, this interference with the work of these groups is welcome.
> After all, according to the conventional neo-conservative wisdom,
> these groups are only "defending their turf" and the policies that
> they are interested in, without caring about the larger picture of
> fiscal policy and the new evolving role of government in Canada. (pp.
> 303–304)

An interviewee put the same point this way: *To be blunt about it, most of
the social policy community are stuck thirty years ago, they're still there.
They are therefore irrelevant to the policy process, they just aren't part of
it any more, they've marginalized themselves. Old language, old ideas.*

In combination, this new emphasis on the global sources of our policy
problems, the interconnectedness of our domestic situation and international developments, and the emphasis on the deficit and spending have
changed the "climate of ideas" quite significantly and created new
constraints on problem definitions in some major policy areas. When the
federal Social Security Review was launched in 1994, for example, a background paper entitled *The Context of Reform* argued that "Market globalization and technological change have a heavy impact on the Canadian
economy and labour market: we are in a period where the very nature of
what happens in the economy and in employment is changing rapidly"
(Minister of Human Resources Development 1994, 9). To be sure, the

social security picture consists of domestic factors such as demographics, family structures, and cultural patterns, but the backdrop is now global. What people count as a "sensible" solution has changed: not piecemeal tinkering, not a significantly greater role for government (especially the federal government), and certainly not more spending.

Entrepreneurs and Policy Actors

The literature on problem definition and agenda-setting generally agrees that ideas matter, but it also urges the importance of entrepreneurs and broader policy communities in the framing of issues. We will take this up in greater detail in Chapter 6, and have already referred above to how some policy constituencies have in fact been defined as part of the problem, given their close association with previous modes of policy-making. But there is another dynamic that springs from the new combined context of globalization and fiscal prudence, one that affects the process of problem definition within government. Interviewees for this book highlighted two aspects that, in their view, are changing the way in which policy development occurs in government.

The first and most visible is that, in the words of one analyst, *"the fiscal context has changed the environment in terms of the weight that the different players bring to bear—the Department of Finance has a stranglehold on the policy process."* Another interviewee put it this way:

> *I'm not sure that the public is where the problem definition tends to come from. In fact, the most significant place that it comes from these days is the Department of Finance, basically setting the agenda. Budget cutting tends not to be "take 10 percent off your budget and do what you will." The Department of Finance tends to say "you will take so much off such-and-such a program in such-and-such a way, in such-and-such a time frame, and once they've said all of those things, you really have a fairly small box to start playing in, in terms of figuring out how to do it, and it may or may not have much social policy content, as much as it has fiscal policy content. There's no doubt that budgets play a big role, and it permeates everything. The Speech from the Throne might be a Speech from the Throne, but I can tell you that there is an awful lot of Finance finger in the pie behind the Speech from the Throne, like the budget plays a large role in that as well. There's nothing in there that they haven't figured out how to finance.*

Major announcements of government policy are now routinely made in the budget, not separately by ministers responsible for their own portfolios. As managing the fisc has become the key to government credibility, and as the cuts have been deep and wide, the position of Finance has grown commensurably. This is true of provincial as well as the federal governments. There are nuances here, of course. For example, in its Program Review exercise, firm reduction targets have been given to departments, who have then decided internally on how to meet them. There are also broader government agendas that drive the policy process along with the financial one, and might even contradict it (e.g., at the federal level, the perennial national unity file). However, insofar as policy development has been driven by fiscal concerns, those with fiscal expertise hold the whiphand.

The other change that has reinforced this Finance dominance has been the expenditure management process, coupled with the effects of cuts on the internal policy capacity of departments. A senior official put it this way:

> *In the past what you'd do is analyze your problem, come up with your options, and they all had costs associated with them, and you'd go to Cabinet. There would be a policy envelope that you could access. If your issue was compelling enough, if your problem was significant enough, you more or less went into the auction, effectively, and at the end of the year or two or three times a year, they'd kind of line up all the contenders. If you were good enough, you'd get financed, if you weren't, you'd lose out. But now, if a department identifies a problem, it has to also identify a source of funds for the solution. It's a closed loop, by and large. And that changes the name of the game, very, very quickly. It's almost at your peril that you think of a problem, unless you have a corporate consensus around the need to resolve this problem and a view of what the reasonable trade-offs within the department are. It changes the dynamics a lot.*

Another analyst noted that while the same pressures exist to produce instant policy advice on very complex issues, governments usually have limited analytical resources. Some of that may be due to cuts, and there was no consensus among interviewees that overall capacity was declining because of cuts. However, there was a sense that the combined effects of cuts and an increasingly complex policy agenda were straining what capacity there was left.

There is a tendency to think that infinite intellectual capacity exists in government to look at old programs, review current ones, and plan for future initiatives. In fact it's a desperate situation. Take the West coast salmon: it's an ecological issue, it's a federal-provincial issue, it's a white versus native issue, it's a fisheries issue, it's a trade issue, and so on. It's incredibly complex. And how many people do you think we have to deal with it? Ten? Maybe fifteen? Governments don't have the policy capacity that they did twenty years ago, partly because of the demographic change. The people who are pulling the cart are tired. Twenty years ago these guys were thirty and had lots of horsepower; now they're fifty.

CONCLUSION

No one should read this chapter as claiming that everything about our processes of problem definition and framing has suddenly shifted to the United Nations and consists of nothing more than carping about money. There are still plenty of problems bubbling at the local level and which are primarily domestic in origins and solutions: drugs, petty crime, literacy, pollution, housing, waste disposal, prostitution—in short, things that matter to people on a daily basis. The simple point of this chapter is that the context and processes of problem definition are never set in stone, and that they have changed in important ways in the last decade. Put it this way: urge a large, new spending program like national child-care, and see what the reaction is. At the very least, it's more of an uphill climb than it would have been even ten years ago.

One of the most important, if subtle, effects of this new environment is what it implies for policy development. As fiscal considerations and resource constraints become uppermost in the minds of policy-makers, they are forced into a different mode of thinking. One senior policy manager put it this way:

The fiscal overlay on everything is, I think, the single biggest change in policy development terms. Policy development used to be identifying a problem and then programming against its solution with a policy framework. That is no longer the case at all. Now, you are looking at problems in an entirely different context. Policy development is intermingled with fiscal issues, with management issues, with implementation issues, with "who is going to do this" issues. And so you have what used to be a cascading system where policy was approved, and then you'd go into program design, and then you'd find the money, and then you go find your delivery agent and then you'd go implement. That hierarchy or cascading is absurd now. Not only are you asking different questions to start with, you are now looking at those things in their totality. You now look at policy in horizontal terms, not vertical terms.

There are some important caveats to this, however. First, our fiscal woes will not last forever, given the rate of deficit reduction. While the federal government has taken a slower approach (its 1997–98 target is a deficit at 2 percent of GDP, or $17 billion), most of the provinces have balanced their budgets and Alberta is now launched on a debt reduction course. New Zealand, which set the global pace of deficit elimination in the mid-1980s (Boston 1991; Douglas 1993), announced a $4 billion surplus in its 1996 budget (New Zealand Minister of Finance 1996). Both Alberta and New Zealand have devoted a substantial portion of their surpluses to debt elimination, but some of that money is going back into programs, principally health, education, and income security. Policy debates and discussions will once again turn on substantive issues, rather than purely fiscal ones, though how soon this will happen depends on levels of debt (even draconian repayment schemes will not substantially reduce public debt at the national or provincial levels for many years). With respect to Finance's dominant role, a senior official noted:

It's half true. Finance's primary responsibility is getting the deficit under control. Their instinct is to also set policy while they do it. And depending on the moment and the department, they do more or less of it. They don't care enough about [my department's policy] to set it. We tend to push them more in a policy direction than they push us ... It also depends very much on who the deputy is, how strong the minister is in Cabinet, whether Finance can push them around. It's not only a policy question, it's the psychosocial political dynamics of the moment. But Finance's power is probably going to diminish as time goes on, because it's going to be a reallocation game and Finance ain't going to be able to play. As soon as we get close to the zero deficit, Finance won't be distributing money or taking it away. He who can reallocate intelligently is the one who will win the day ... Reallocations between portfolios are going to happen, but I don't think they're going to happen by Finance, I think that's going to be a question of whether or not the Cabinet process can work.

However, fiscal prudence will continue to be the backdrop to these debates, even when there is some cash in the coffers.

Another caveat is that the global economic forces that are driving our perceptions of policy problems are also at the root of new, more intense demands for local and community action. If anything, Canadians' sense of security (the key theme in the federal February 27, 1996, Speech from the Throne) is being eroded by this relentless pressure to compete globally. Exposure to world markets sends tornadoes of social and economic change throughout society, as people shift jobs, homes, and communities in the "adjustment process." These are clearly policy problems, rooted in international developments, but policy problems nonetheless that emphasize a more defensive role for governments. Neoconservatives have been slower to pick up on this, and have stressed the relentless reduction of government as a buffer between citizens and the world. But whatever sympathy Canadians have for this agenda (and recent elections and polls show that it is fairly high and solid) will be tempered by the realization that there are huge risks to our social and community fabric in an untempered embrace of the "new realities."

SUMMARY

Problem Definition: Key Issues

- a problem is a substantial discrepancy between what is and what should be

- constructivism: the view that "reality" is socially and politically constructed, that we can never know "truth" in some absolute sense, and that social structures and dynamics determine in large part what we believe to be true

- indicators: signals from the environment that can trigger a sense that there is a problem that needs addressing

- focusing event: some crisis or unusual occurrence that concentrates attention on an issue

- problem recognition: the first perception, without much elaboration, that "something is wrong"

- problem definition: the fuller, analytically based attempt to work out the details of the problem, both in terms of key features and causal patterns; it involves questions about indicators, causality, and what action to take

- policy image: the usual way most of us make sense of a policy issue—a mix of facts and emotive appeals, both positive and negative

- labels and metaphors: key elements in the rhetoric of problem definition; the use of language to frame issues either positively or negatively (label), and the use of analogies (metaphor)

- agenda-setting: the process whereby issues are not only defined but are ordered on an agenda for action

- policy windows: opportunities to carry a policy issue forward

Problem Definition: Beyond Old Categories

- globalization means that many of our policy problems are now seen to have both sources in the international arena, as well as solutions at that level

- the climate of ideas has changed to emphasize the deficit and the negative consequences of high spending policies

- finance ministries have become much more powerful in the agenda-setting and problem formulation stages

REFERENCES

Ackoff, R. L. (1976). *Redesigning the future: A systems approach to societal problems*. New York: John Wiley & Sons.

Bank of Canada. (1996, September 27). *The Dr. Harold Walter Siebens lecture by Gordon G. Thiessen, Governor of the Bank of Canada to The Fraser Institute, Vancouver, B.C., 6 March 1996* [On-line]. Available: http://www.bank-banque-canada.ca/english/spmr6.htm

Baumgartner, F. R., & Jones, B. D. (1993). *Agendas and instability in American politics*. Chicago: University of Chicago Press.

Best, J. (1989). *Images of issues*. New York: deGruyter.

Boston, J. (Ed.). (1991). *Reshaping the state: New Zealand's bureaucratic revolution*. Melbourne, Australia: Oxford University Press.

Brewer, G. D., & deLeon, P. (1983). *The foundations of policy analysis*. Homewood, IL: The Dorsey Press.

Cardozo, A. (1996). Lion taming: Downsizing the opponents of downsizing. In Gene Swimmer (Ed.), *How Ottawa spends, 1996–97: Life under the knife*. (pp. 303–336). Ottawa: Carleton University Press.

Carson, R. (1962). *Silent spring*. Boston: Houghton Mifflin.

Department of Environment. (1996, September 27). *1996 Report of Canada to the United Nations Commission on Sustainable Development* [On-line]. Available: http://www.doe.ca/agenda21/96/hompgeng.html

Department of Finance. (1996a, September 27). *Budget speech, March 6, 1996* [On-line]. Available: http://www.fin.gc.ca/budget96/speeche/speeche.html

Department of Finance. (1996b, September 27). *Notes for an address by the Minister of Finance of Canada, Paul Martin, to the IMF Interim Committee Washington, DC, April 22, 1996* [On-line]. Available: http://www.fin.gc.ca/newse96/96-032e.html

Dery, D. (1984). *Problem definition in policy analysis*. Lawrence, KS: University Press of Kansas.

Doern, G. B., & Conway, T. (1994). *The greening of Canada: Federal institutions and decisions*. Toronto: University of Toronto Press.

Doern, G. B., Maslove, A. M., & Prince, M. J. (1988). *Public budgeting in Canada: Politics, economics, and management*. Ottawa: Carleton University Press.

Douglas, R. (1993). *Unfinished business*. Aukland, New Zealand: Random House.

Downs, A. (1972). Up and down with ecology: The issue attention cycle. *Public Interest, 28*, 38–50.

Dunn, W. N. (1993). Policy reforms as arguments. In F. Fischer and J. Forester (Eds.), *The argumentative turn in policy analysis and planning* (pp. 254–290). Durham, NC: Duke University Press.

Government of Canada. (1995). *Canada in the world*. Ottawa: Department of Foreign Affairs and International Trade.

Harrington, M. (1962). *The other America: Poverty in the United States*. New York: Macmillan.

Ingram, H., & Schneider, A. L. (1995). Response. *American Political Science Review, 89*(June), 441–446.

Kingdon, J. W. (1995). *Agendas, alternatives, and public policies* (2nd ed.). New York: HarperCollins.

Lieberman, R. C. (1995). Social construction continued. *American Political Science Review, 89*(June), 437–441.

MacLeod, L. (1987). *Battered but not beaten: Preventing wife battering in Canada.* Ottawa: Canadian Advisory Council on the Status of Women.

Majone, G. (1989). *Evidence, argument, and persuasion in the policy process.* New Haven, CT: Yale University Press.

Milward, H. B., & Laird, W. (1996). Where does policy come from? In B. G. Peters & B. A. Rockman (Eds.), *Agenda for excellence 2: Administering the state* (pp. 38–75). Chatham, NJ: Chatham House Publishers.

Minister of Human Resources Development. (1994). *Improving social security in Canada: The context of reform. A supplementary paper.* Ottawa. Minister of Supply and Services Canada.

New Zealand Minister of Finance. (1996, September 27). *Budget and fiscal strategy report 1996* [On-line]. Available: http://www.treasury.govt.nz/pubs/bmb/budgets/1996/toc_bud.htm

Purchase, B., & Hirshhorn, R. (1994). *Searching for good governance.* Kingston, ON: Queen's School of Policy Studies.

Rochefort, D. A., & Cobb, R. W. Problem definition: An emerging perspective. In D.A. Rochefort & R.W. Cobb (Eds.). (1994). *The politics of problem definition: Shaping the policy agenda* (pp. 1–31). Lawrence, KS: University of Kansas Press.

Sarlo, C. A. (1992). *Poverty in Canada.* Vancouver, BC: The Fraser Institute

Schneider, A., & Ingram, H. (1993). Social construction of target populations: Implications for politics and policy. *American Political Science Review, 87*(June), 334–347.

Schon, D. A. (1971). *Beyond the stable state.* New York: W. W. Norton & Company.

Statistics Canada. (1996, September 27) *International adult literacy survey* [On-line]. Available: http://www.statcan.ca/Documents/English/MediaRel/IALS/home.html

Stone, D. (1988). *Policy paradox and political reason.* New York: HarperCollins.

Strauch, R. E. (1976). A critical look at quantitative methodology. *Policy Analysis, 2*(Winter), 121–144.

Chapter 4 Policy Design

Policy design is a mix of inspiration and technique. The inspiration comes in framing the policy issue (discussed Chapter 3) in ways that make sense of the problem and provide a broad sketch of how to tackle it. The technique (though not without its creative side either) comes in the detailing of what tools to use, in what combination, to achieve a given end. The tools will vary with the task at hand, sometimes involving expenditures, sometimes regulation, partnerships, or the exchange of information. It usually will draw on all of these and more, and be bundled into programs. The conventional discussion of policy instruments usually proceeds by laying out the basic categories and outlining some of the objective characteristics of each of the instruments; when and why, for example, regulation makes more sense than direct program provision by government. This chapter will honour that format in briefly describing the main categories, but it will also show how the menu of choices has changed in recent years. While the reality of instrument choice has always been more constrained than theory might suggest, the old, full menu of the past has been replaced with something closer to a table d'hôte with a more limited range of items. But just to show that even a limited menu can be quite filling, the chapter closes with a snapshot of government policy instruments in a new policy field—building the (as politicians love to call it) "information superhighway."

Policies are sometimes best thought of as creative solutions to challenging puzzles rather than just dry legislation and programs. The creative dimension breaks through conventional definitions of the issue and comes up with something people had not thought of before. This does not mean, of course, that those creative solutions are the correct ones, only that they offer an unanticipated or surprising approach. Shortly after the 1995 Québec Referendum, for example, Prime Minister Chrétien attempted to honour his promise of immediate and substantial constitutional change by introducing legislation that "lent" the federal government's constitutional veto to provinces and regions according to certain rules. This was a novel, though highly dubious, way of amending the constitution without actually amending it. During the fish war with Spain in 1995, Fisheries Minister Brian Tobin went to New York and had a huge net put on display that he claimed proved that Spanish trawlers were using illegal gear to overfish turbot stocks off Newfoundland. He used the visual impact of the media as an instrument to his policy ends. While no policy instrument or technique is ever completely new, they can be combined in fresh ways to achieve policy goals.

Policy design is about choosing the most appropriate instrument to deal with the policy problem as it has been defined in order to achieve a given policy goal. This implies that a key criterion in instrument choice and policy design is effectiveness—getting the job done. Efficiency—getting the job done with the least resources—is typically considered as another key criterion. The reality of politics means that popularity and re-election cannot be left out of the mix of motives, indeed, they may be overpowering at times. But if one puts together the inevitably creative aspect of policy design, with the range of criteria by which that design might be judged, it is clear that coming up with a list of tools is no easy task. In fact, while lists abound, and while there is some agreement on at least the major policy instruments and their characteristics, there is little agreement (or knowledge) of how and when particular mixes of instruments should be used in policy design. Like a list of the letters in the alphabet, the keys on a piano, or all the possible ingredients in five-star French cooking, the best that an inventory could provide is a sense of the possibilities of language, music, or cuisine. Choice and design are marked more by art and circumstance.

Nonetheless, thinking through at least the major categories of ingredients is a useful exercise. The first section of this chapter will do this with brutal economy, splitting only enough hairs to make sense of major alternatives and some of the broad dynamics of choice. Policy instruments will be distinguished here from implementation, which we take up in Chapter 5. There is an overlap between the two, of course, but policy instruments usually refer to the technical means of achieving a goal, such as a tax or a regulation, while implementation refers to the organizational structure and processes to execute that instrument. Policy instruments and implementation overlap most obviously in cases where a particular organizational format is the technical means of achieving the policy goal, such as a partnership between a nongovernmental agency and a government department. But we will leave this for Chapter 5.

The theme of this book is that the world of policy-making is changing, and so the bulk of the chapter will take up these new dynamics, and also link the question of instrument design to a question that increasingly troubles policy-makers: how to fashion democratic and cooperative social institutions as a bedrock for most of the other things a people might wish to accomplish collectively.

INVENTORY AND THE DYNAMICS OF INSTRUMENT CHOICE

The technical means whereby we pursue goals are a reflection of the ways in which we perceive problems and the goals that we are pursuing. For example, income security programs only made their appearance as full-blown policy instruments when Western governments (grudgingly) came around to the view, during the Depression, that income inequality was a problem, and that it was a legitimate goal of government to try to redistribute incomes. Any inventory of policy instruments will therefore be more like a snapshot of what is considered legitimate and efficacious at any given time. There is a sense of appropriateness or legitimacy to the use of policy instruments that varies in much the same way as Chapter 3 argued that "ideas in good currency" will change from time to time. This sense of what is legitimate rests on several ethical foundations, and in a country like Canada, principally on a cluster of ideas such as equality, equity, liberty, and rights. There is no point in trying to define these ideas, since they are constantly contested, but it is fair to say that at this point in Canadian history, most of us look to the Charter of Rights and Freedoms and the courts for inspiration as to the proper scope and limits of government action in our lives. Policy analysts have to know which way the wind is blowing in these areas, or instruments that they may recommend for good policy reasons may turn out to have little or no legitimacy among the wider public. As we shall see in the next section, the wind has been blowing quite hard and long.

The history of attempts to classify governing policy instruments begins with Kirschen (1964). His system presented sixty-two different types of economic policy instruments, and the various contributors to the field since have tried various ways of combining aggregate categories with the more finely grained instruments within them. Doern and Phidd (1992, 97), for example, argue that there are really only five broad categories: (1) self-regulation, (2) exhortation, (3) expenditure, (4) regulation (including taxation), and (5) public ownership. Based on earlier work by Doern and Wilson (1974), this typology assumed that as one moves from the first category to the last, one moves roughly along a continuum of legitimate coercion. The argument was that all government in a liberal democracy involves some degree of imposition or coercion, and that politicians generally prefer to use the least coercive instrument possible. Within these broad categories, Doern and Phidd (1992) identify as many as twenty-six finer "graduations of choice" such as grants and subsidies, guidelines, and speeches (p. 112).

Another well-known typology by Hood (1984) developed what he called the NATO scheme, standing for the different resources that governments have at their disposal to effect policy change. N stands for nodality or information resources, A for authority, T for treasure or money, and O for organization or personnel. These struck Linder and Peters (1989) as too broad, and in their valuable article on the question, they developed their own schema that tries to draw on several existing schemes, including Hood's. Four basic classes appeared over and over again in the literature they reviewed, but not always the same four, and so they combined them into a group of seven major categories of policy instruments: "1) direct provision 2) subsidy 3) tax 4) contract 5) authority 6) regulation (the only consensus class), and 7) exhortation" (p. 44). They too provide a finer gradation of choice, based on their view that what really matters is the way in which policy-makers themselves subjectively perceive the choices that they have before them. As is evident from the list reproduced in Box 4.1, this finer gradation does not have a clear pattern. Nor do several other attempts at classification (e.g., McDonnell & Elmore 1987; Schneider & Ingram 1990; Howlett & Ramesh 1995), all of which adopt a different classificatory principle (e.g., government resource versus impact or ends).

How then to proceed? It is important to understand that in the run of normal or routine politics, the range of instrument choice is generally limited by the existing array that is already embedded in the policy field. Policy-makers think through their options on the basis of what is currently in the field or underpinning policy efforts. If evaluation shows that some instruments are not working, they can be amended, but as long as normal politics is incremental politics, the temptation is to build upon already existing and fairly finely graduated policy instruments. A good example is unemployment insurance, the previous legislative basis for which was first passed in 1971, and not completely overhauled until 1996. The act and the program were, however, changed almost constantly over that twenty-five-year period (Pal 1988), but only rarely were entirely new instruments introduced. In periods of greater policy turbulence, policy-makers will

---

Box 4.1   **A SAMPLE OF POLICY INSTRUMENTS**

- cash grant

- loan guarantee

- certification/screening

- administered contract

- quality standard

- information/ demonstration

- loan

- public investment

- government- sponsored enterprise

- tax break

- government provision

- quota

- jawboning

- procedural guideline

- licence/permit

- franchise

- in-kind

- transfer

- fee/charge

- fine

- prohibition

- public promotion

- insurance

- price control

---

actually begin to think in broader instrument categories, because in turbulent times policies are often fundamentally restructured, forcing a consideration of instrument types.

From the policy-maker's point of view, virtually every policy instrument involves expenditure—even giving a speech will entail the cost of speech-writers and distribution of materials. So, money is a ubiquitous and universal resource that governments use to effect policy, and rarely, if ever, can expenditure as an instrument be avoided. The point about expenditure-based policy instruments, however, is that it is money itself that is the instrument—implying that the problem is a lack of funds or resources. The specific ways in which money is transferred can vary, as can the conditions attached to the transfer. Straight grants, for example, often have fairly light conditions attached to them. Subsidies are usually seen as more specifically geared to some outcome (e.g., wage subsidies for the employment of a given number of workers). Income transfers under programs like employment insurance or pensions also have varying conditions attached. The key point is that in using expenditure-based policy instruments, the policy-maker has to answer at least the ten questions listed in Box 4.2. Clearly, the answer to the first question has to be yes in several senses. First, it is the lack of funds that is the principal problem. In income security programs, for example, we transfer money under employment insurance or pensions because during unemployment and retirement, people typically receive little employment income. The unemployed and the retired may have a range of other needs, from training to health care, but a big part of what defines their status (and their capacities) is low income. This would be as true of grants or contributions to organizations like an Aboriginal band, a research institute, or a university or hospital. The organizations have certain needs that only money can buy, and so providing money is a means of supporting them. But the government could always provide those needs directly (e.g., research data or health services). The problem therefore is not entirely a lack of funds, but is entangled with at least three other assumptions: (1) the recipient has the capacity to spend those funds wisely, (2) the recipient can spend those funds more effectively than a third party, and (3) it is important to respect the recipient's autonomy (i.e., avoid paternalism). Obviously, if the answers to questions 2 and 3 in Box 4.2 are no, one need proceed no further. If the policy agency has the legal capacity and the resources, then the design questions are encapsulated in questions 4 to 10. Note, however, that while this list provides a technical guide to sketching out the shape of an expenditure-based instrument, how one answers the core questions (e.g., on conditions or enforcement) depends on circumstance, program history, and the analyst's creativity.

Expenditure-based instruments always involve the transfer of funds in some fashion to help meet the needs of the recipient. But needs might be met directly through the provision of services. A good example is education. Parents need to have their children educated, but governments can elect to provide that education directly themselves, or they might provide parents with the funds (usually through some form of voucher) that they could then redeem for services as they saw fit, from either government providers, the private sector, or some mix. Any service directly provided by government, from garbage collection to education, will involve the expenditure of often very substantial amounts of money. Provincial and territorial governments spent $111 billion on health, education, and social services in 1994–95, out of total expenditures of $175 billion (Statistics Canada 1996). So "direct provision" is less an alternative to spending money than it is a means of spending money that reflects a different policy logic. It is a logic reflected in the questions listed in Box 4.3. Take municipal garbage collection as an example. The need in this case is the removal

Box 4.2   ## QUESTIONS TO ASK ABOUT EXPENDITURE-BASED INSTRUMENTS

1. Is the lack of money the main problem in this circumstance?
2. Do I have the legal capacity to spend money in this area?
3. Do I have the requisite resources to spend?
4. Are there no alternative sources of funds?
5. Do I have to provide all the funding, or is it possible to provide a portion?
6. Should the money be a loan (repayable in whole or part), a grant (the amount determined by criteria other than the strict needs of the recipient), a subsidy (the amount determined closely by the recipient's needs), or some contractually based exchange (a purchase of goods or services)?
7. Who is the legal recipient?
8. What conditions should be attached to the transfer?
9. How should the conditions be enforced and monitored?
10. What reporting requirements should be attached to the money?

of refuse, and municipal governments have traditionally provided this service directly by raising general tax revenues to cover the cost. Traditionally no fees have been attached. Municipal governments have had both the authority and the fiscal capacity to deliver the service. The nub of the issue is in questions 4 and 5. Are there alternative service providers? Absolutely. The garbage business in North America is huge. Laidlaw Environmental Services, Inc. alone has revenues of $800 million per year (Laidlaw Environmental Services 1996). What is the compelling policy reason to directly collect garbage with city workers rather than through a contract for service with a private company? Typically, the argument from public sector unions has been that the level of service (and the wages and working conditions of sanitary workers) will decline if private companies get into the act. Apart from that, most people only care that the can at the curbside is emptied weekly. This is essentially a question of

---

Box 4.3   **QUESTIONS TO ASK ABOUT DIRECT PROVISION OF SERVICE INSTRUMENTS**

1. What is the need or the problem, and what service or bundle of services will meet that need?
2. Do I have the legal capacity to provide the service?
3. Do I have the resources to provide the service?
4. Are there alternative service providers?
5. Is there a compelling policy reason to provide the service directly (e.g., safety, uniformity of standards, recipients cannot choose appropriate service levels)?
6. If the service is provided publicly, should there be fees attached?
7. If the service is provide privately, will recipients be able to pay for it, or should there be some subsidy? (See questions 4–10 in Box 4.2.)
8. If there is a subsidy, should it be paid to providers or recipients?
9. If the service is provided privately, by what sort of entity (e.g., for-profit, nonprofit).
10. If the service is provided privately, what oversight/regulation should government provide?

---

efficiency. If public sector workers can collect the garbage as efficiently as a private sector company can, there usually is little reason to change. Question 6, however, has risen with a vengeance in recent years. As the costs of garbage collection have increased dramatically across North America, and as pressure to hold the line on taxes has mounted, more and more municipal governments have decided to charge some sort of fee for collection. This can get quite creative, from charges per can or bag, to limits on the number of bags one can put out. The logic in both cases is the same: what was once a "free" service now has a direct cost attached to it. The other questions deal with the ways in which government can either support or regulate the private provision of services. As we shall see in Chapter 5, "alternative service provision" has become a central issue in the implementation of public policy. More and more jurisdictions are answering question 4 in the affirmative, but question 5 in the negative, and then the game turns into one of deciding how to structure a private sector/public sector partnership. Another implementation issue is, if the service is to be provided through a public agency, how should that agency be designed? Should it be a direct-line department, or an arm's length entity like a public or Crown corporation?

As the list of questions on service delivery suggests, governments can either provide the funds, regulate the provision of those services by third parties, or they can do a mix of both. Policy instruments are not mutually exclusive, but are usually combined in packages to deal with the different dimensions of the problem. Regulation draws on the most fundamental resource a government has, its capacity to command and prohibit. That capacity depends on a blend of legitimacy and effective sanctions for disobedience, with the greatest weight on legitimacy. If governments merely have power without authority, they will have little capacity to command. It is the legitimacy of their commands as perceived by the majority of citizens that permits them to efficiently use sanctions against the minority that disobey. A great deal of public policy is about achieving outcomes through ensuring certain actions or behaviours. Regulatory instruments define the bona fide actors in a policy field, and then circumscribe their behaviours. The ways of doing this are almost infinite, but the general logic of regulation underpins them all.

Defining the bona fide actors in a policy field can take several different forms. The most benign is simply to recognize certain individuals or organizations for some policy-relevant quality that they have or have achieved. Under the Indian Act, for example, the federal Department of Indian Affairs and Northern Development keeps a registry of all Indians so defined for purposes of the legislation (essentially those individuals descended from Indian bands with whom the federal government struck treaties in the 19th and 20th centuries). Appropriately enough, they are known as status Indians, and other Indians are described as non-status or non-treaty Indians. For the purposes of the Indian Act and what it permits, prohibits, and provides, it matters a great deal if one is status or non-status. Another example is the Green logo designed by Environment Canada. Products that meet certain standards can display the logo, and thereby send a signal to consumers. All that government is doing here is lending its authority to designate some actors as complying with the larger policy purpose. That designation carries a certain advantage to its recipients, but not much else.

When most people think about regulation, they think less about these forms of recognition or designation, than outright prohibitions unless one meets certain standards. This is indeed the classic formula of the regulator: first, generally prohibit some action (e.g., broadcasting TV signals, driving a vehicle, fishing for salmon, doing brain surgery); second, specifically permit that action for individuals or organizations who will respect some pre-defined criteria or conditions. The designation in this case is usually called a licence, and the conditions can be as detailed or as scant as the regulator likes. Of course, a third ingredient is defining sanctions for the unlawful (i.e., unlicensed) practice of the regulated act. Use of "regs," as seasoned policy analysts like to call them, is a marvelously flexible instrument in that it can define prohibited acts quite precisely, and can attach equally precise conditions to the licensee. The most extreme form of regulation is outright, blanket prohibition that follows the form of "Thou shalt not ..." The Criminal Code is the prime example of this sanctions aspect of the general power to regulate behaviour.

Regulations can broadly be classed as economic, social, or environmental, though each of these will have subsets based on the object (e.g., prices, safety) or targets (e.g., specific industries). Economic regulation typically addresses such factors as pricing, advertising and labelling, competition, some aspects of production, profits, and disclosure of financial information. The classic rationale for economic regulation is that markets are not working efficiently. This may be because of monopolies (the historical case for public utility regulation), oligopolies (hence competition regulation), or the simple occurrence of various forms of behaviour designed to maximize profits at the expense of workers and consumers (e.g., collusion, false advertising, union busting). Social regulation is designed to protect us less as consumers than as persons or citizens. This somewhat vague formulation is fairly clear when it comes to health and safety standards such as fire regulations. Though these frequently apply to products and services, they also affect our use of spaces and buildings as citizens. It is a lot less clear what criteria regulators have in mind as they move into the cultural realm with broadcasting regulations (e.g., Canadian content, nonstereotyping), and social justice regulations such as employment equity or speech codes. Environmental regulation struggles with the standards issue as well, since the science is often not precise enough to determine what the allowable limits of many toxic substances might be. Nor can we easily know the effects of the interaction of hundreds and thousands of substances in the air, land, and water.

Regulation can be seen as a response to issues of trust, failure, and common standards. One rationale asks whether individual organizations can be trusted to achieve outcomes desired by policy. For example, if our policy is competitive markets that respond to consumers' needs, rather than economic cabals that bilk buyers, can we trust companies to achieve the desired end? If the issue is one of trusting economic actors to do things that are not in their short-term interest, most of us would hesitate. This is a trust issue. The rationale of failure has less to do with motivations than with resources, and principally information resources. Many bad things happen because of imperfect information, or because information is too costly to obtain. Finally, governments have an interest in ensuring common standards for public goods, and often the easiest way to achieve that is to regulate those standards. Regulation of utilities, meat inspection, safety regulations, and antidiscrimination laws are all forms of regulation, yet they actually mix the various rationales. Airline safety regulations, for example, are based on all three: airlines cannot be completely trusted to enforce the highest safety standards because these are costly and can negatively affect the bottom line; consumers by the same token cannot be expected to compare airline safety records each time they fly; and there is a desirability in having the highest standards for something as risky as air travel.

A species of regulation is self-regulation, where the three rationales are turned on their heads, and it is assumed that only the suppliers in question can best regulate themselves. The professions (medicine, law, engineering) are the main examples, though there are some instances from other fields as well. In these cases, regulatory bodies are established by the groups themselves to enforce standards and monitor compliance. The assumption policy-makers have made is that these professions can be trusted not to take the short-term view or operate primarily for economic gain. Some authors include what is effectively "no-regulation" under the self-regulation category, on the assumption that if government leaves well enough alone it is apparently trying to achieve some policy goal through the voluntary action of individuals, families, and communities. As we shall see in Chapter 5, however, this fails to capture the real character the interlacing of public and private efforts for policy ends.

If governments cannot spend, deliver services, or regulate, what is left? Most typologies give them two more categories of weapons for their policy arsenals. The first is taxation. Governments tax, of course, to get revenue. They can have policies about taxation, in terms of the fairness and incidence of the tax regime. They can also use taxes as deliberate policy instruments. First, they can decide that services may either be free of charge to end-users or have some fee attached. At one level this is a decision with regard to service policy, but money matters so much that it deserves its own treatment. How much to levy, when, how, and on which users are complex questions of public finance. Second, tax instruments can be used to dissuade or encourage certain activities by raising or lowering the costs of doing them. Fiscal measures that lower taxes on some types of investment compared with others will, all other things being equal, make those investments more attractive. The sin taxes on alcohol and cigarettes are a means of discouraging their use.

The final category is information. In areas that depend on individuals or organizations acting for themselves, or more fundamentally, coming to conscious conclusions that will guide their actions, government can provide information of various sorts and varying degrees of intensity to shape hearts and minds. The Canada Food Guide helps us know how many legumes and lentils to consume per week; the chilling TV ads about the health effects of cigarettes will (the sponsors hope) give us pause the next time we light up.

The preceding has covered most of the major categories of instruments. What can we conclude from the discussion? First, no list is ever complete, and there are some instruments that some authors would include as separate categories (e.g., Crown corporations) and others would place under a broad category such as direct provision. Second, the sliding scale of authority idea is only moderately helpful in distinguishing these instruments. A high government charge on a service I need to use regularly will seem a lot more coercive to me than even the most detailed regulations covering a service I rarely access. Equally, a persistent series of hectoring ads about what the government believes to be naughty behaviour may seem more paternalistic than the income tax I am forced to pay once a year. This point takes on even greater force when we consider a third conclusion: no instrument is an island. Since they tackle clusters of problems, government policies use clusters of programs. These program clusters in turn bundle together groups of instruments. Education, for example, mixes big spending, direct service delivery, taxation (special education taxes), and lots of regulations.

This crude inventory has shown us what instruments we can choose, and some of the rationales behind their choice. But what actually explains instrument choice? Theoretically, some instruments are substitutable, meaning that from the point of view of cost and at least the major outcome desired by policy, it makes little difference which instrument you use.

Postsecondary education is currently funded in part by federal government transfers to the provinces. For years, federal ministers have mused about converting that transfer to vouchers that would go directly to students. The money would be exactly the same, and it could only flow into postsecondary institutions. The big difference would be the change from a cash transfer to governments to a voucher for students. The other aspect of this issue is comparing the pattern of instrument choice across governments. Expenditures across the OECD countries on health, education, and income security are much closer than the means used to provide these services.

Linder and Peters (1989) provide a comprehensive model for understanding the links between the broad policy system variables and decisions that policy-makers themselves undertake in given situations. They emphasize the importance of systemic variables, organizational characteristics, problem features, and the profile of individual decision-makers. Systemic variables include such broad factors as national policy style, political culture, and prevailing social cleavages. Organizational variables include the way that the sponsoring department is structured, its history, and its connections with its relevant policy communities. The problem context embraces questions such as how crowded the policy domain is, the political constraints of using a specific instrument, and the requirements of political support. Finally, individual level variables comprise perceptions, values, and experience of the policy-maker. This schema operates almost like a funnel, channelling these larger forces down from the systemic level to the individual decision-makers. Of course, national policy style and political culture are not actors on the policy stage; they only have influence through the decision-maker's implicit or conscious application. The current debate in some provincial jurisdictions over the use of private management companies to run public hospitals is an interesting illustration. This is contracting out to a third party in a policy area that jealously protects its public character. The decision to use this instrument will certainly depend on cost considerations and effectiveness (the problem context), but also on what is feasible or acceptable in that political regime (style and political culture).

NEW DYNAMICS

As we have argued throughout this book, the nature of governance is changing because of globalization, technology, culture, and governance systems. While the impacts on problem definitions are powerful, as we saw in Chapter 3, they are still somewhat difficult to conceptualize because problem definition and agenda-setting are such complex processes in their own right. In this chapter and in Chapter 5, we see clear evidence for new ways of making policy.

Fiscal Restraint

This factor was discussed in detail in the previous chapters, and the simple point is that for the first time in a quarter century, governments are single-mindedly attacking their deficits through expenditure reduction. At the federal level, that has been accompanied with a Program Review that has forced policy-makers to ask six fundamental questions (see Chapter 2) about each program they administer and reconsider modes of delivery (i.e., their instruments). The interviewees for this book were unanimous in saying that their policy context was completely different as a result of expenditure reductions. The consensus was simply that *"There is no money; we can't buy solutions."* But from a policy design point of view, what difference has that made? A surprising number of interviewees argued that now that the money is gone, much more imagination has to go into policy design. One respondent put it in uncompromising terms:

> *I think the days of spending sucked. I think it was stupid public administration. It was unimaginative. It was usually ineffective. And I love having no money. Because what we did is we always bought useless solutions because they were politically attractive, they didn't require any policy imagination, they didn't require going after the root causes of anything, they didn't require any political vision or leadership. Spending a few million dollars gives you a press release, an announcement, a speech. It rarely fixes anything. Lack of money does more than make you think harder, it forces you to do something useful. There are some problems you can solve with money. I mean, I know exactly what I'd do if I had a billion dollars—there's a lot of stuff I'd do. But overall, I think it [less money] will lead to more effective governance.*

Why? For one thing, the magnitude and unavoidability of the cuts faced by most spending departments in most jurisdictions across Canada have demanded a fundamental reevaluation of lines of business. When funding drops by 20 percent or 30 percent in two years, something has to change, and that change cannot be incremental. The federal Program Review, whatever its limitations, illustrates the connection between deep funding cuts and a reassessment of policy. Moreover, that reassessment evolves into a permanent monitoring function. As one administrator said, *"We tend to think about the basics on a weekly basis. You have to."* When the money dries up, another respondent said, you only go for it as a last resort. Instead, you seek *"policy power rather than spending power."*

Another consequence of fiscal restraint has been greater interlinkage in designing policy. In part, this stems as well from the growing appreciation of the interconnectedness of policy fields. Sustainable development, for example, can be defined to include health and social stability, in which case almost anything becomes relevant as "environmental policy." As fiscal concerns have driven policy-making in recent years, almost everything has come under the purview of departments of finance. As economic theory has highlighted the importance of human capital for competitiveness in high technology, information-based industries, social policy has merged to a large extent with economic policy. Nonetheless, reduced spending capacity has helped this new appreciation of linkages and leverage to emerge as well.

> *There are more linkages being made, and the notion of trade-offs. It is happening. It took us a long time to shift gears from a solution that was based on spending money, to the harder question of how do we fix the problem. And maybe it's still a funding solution, it's just that you work at a zero-sum game within your own program area, for example. I imagine that regulatory options are a lot more on the table than they used to be. But now the name of the game is to be less government, government is a facilitator rather than government as doer, "find yourself a partner," show leadership.*

It is important to remember that despite the recent cuts, governments in Canada still spend large amounts of money. As the fiscal situation improves, pressures to increase spending will rise. Is there anything different about the ways in which governments spend in this new environment, as opposed to the design implications of less spending on the ways in which policy is thought about? One tendency may be to target moneys much more specifically than was the case before. When less emphasis was placed on careful financial management, it was easier to turn money over to social partners such as school boards, universities, and hospitals. A trend among governments that cut is to attach many more strings to what is left in their spending envelopes. A good example is Alberta. Faced with a decision on how to spend its 1996–97 budget surplus, the government decided to "reinvest" in education. "In Alberta, as in other provinces, governments no longer hand universities a blank cheque. Even as it cut spending to universities by 21 per cent over three years, the Alberta government became more directive in how its remaining support would be spent on campus" (Lewington 1996, A3).

Another implication of reduced funds is to try to leverage what is left. To some degree this represents a countertrend to the one mentioned in the previous paragraph. Rather than try to attach more strings to remaining dollars, governments offer to fund some portion of an activity or outcome as long as the rest comes from nongovernmental sources. This usually means reduced government control over the project, but there are several benefits. First, the government agency does not have to fund the entire endeavour. Second, the willingness of businesses or individuals to contribute to the project is evidence of its viability. In some senses, of course, this strategy is as old as government itself, as funding arrangements in health and education attest. But recently there has been greater emphasis on leveraged funding as a means of effecting policy outcomes.

Everyone knows that governments are spending less on programs. What is not as evident, however, is that in spending less they are also being forced to design policies more comprehensively, and think about linkages across policy fields. As well, they spend what they have left differently than before, trying to both target and leverage their funds more strategically.

Regulation

Just as the character of expenditures as a policy instrument has changed, so have regulation and taxation. The pressures on regulatory instruments have been somewhat contradictory. On the one hand, all other things being equal, governments that have less money to spend will shift to less expensive regulatory instruments to achieve the same ends. But as we argued in Chapter 2, the very nature of governance has changed, and spending cuts are usually accompanied by a sense that government as a whole should pull back. That makes regulatory instruments less feasible, since they rely on the direct use of authority, which has less legitimacy among modern publics. On the other hand, both international agreements and economic and technological forces constrain the use of regulatory instruments in many traditional areas such as telecommunications and broadcasting, foreign investment, and marketing boards. We will try to make sense of these contradictory pressures by addressing constraints on regulation, demands for regulation, and shifts in regulatory venues.

The constraints on the use of regulatory instruments come principally from four sources: international trade agreements, technology, economics, and cost. A large subset of economic regulatory instruments have been devoted in one fashion or another to the protection of domestic industries from excessive internal or foreign competition. Classic examples included regulations that prevented foreign banks from operating in Canada, regulations that gave domestic Canadian oil companies advantages over foreign-owned competitors, foreign investment guidelines, broadcasting rules that protected Canadian advertisers and cable companies, and agricultural marketing boards for everything from milk to potatoes. The 1989 Free Trade Agreement, and its successor, the North American Free Trade Agreement (NAFTA), with Canada, the United States, and Mexico, expressly forbids some forms of regulation that would advantage domestic industries over competitors from the partner countries. Agricultural marketing boards, for example, are facing intense pressures under the NAFTA provisions on agriculture and food products. While environmental, health, and cultural regulations are in principle shielded from NAFTA, the larger free-trade logic of the agreement increasingly puts these provisions under some pressure. The new World Trade Organization (WTO), the successor to the GATT, was explicitly designed to establish clearer and more efficient institutional mechanisms to deal with a wider variety of trade issues (e.g., services, farming, as well as manufactured goods). On standards, for example, the Uruguay Round Agreement on Technical Barriers to Trade

> seeks to ensure that technical regulations and standards, as well as testing and certification procedures, do not create unnecessary obstacles to trade. The agreement recognizes the rights of countries to adopt such measures, to the extent they consider appropriate—for example, for human, animal or plant life or health, for the protection of the environment or to meet other consumer interests. Moreover, members are not prevented from taking measures necessary to ensure their standards of protection are met. The agreement encourages countries to use international standards where these are appropriate, but it does not require them to change their levels of protection as a result of standardization. The agreement sets out a code of good practice for the preparation, adoption and application of standards by central government bodies as well as provisions under which local government and nongovernmental bodies should

frame and use technical regulations. It requires that procedures for determining the conformity of products with national standards be fair and equitable, particularly between domestically produced goods and the equivalent imported goods. In addition, it encourages the mutual recognition of conformity assessments—in other words if the authorities of the exporting country determine a product to be in conformity with a technical standard, the authorities of the importing country should normally accept that determination. (World Trade Organization 1996)

As we note below, however, internationalization has also provided a fresh context for "re-regulation" that brings domestic policy targets into a wider, international regime. This can actually strengthen domestic regulation, not constrain it. An excellent example is the Canadian Endangered Species Act, introduced in November 1996. This act flowed directly from new commitments formed at the biodiversity convention, which the 1992 United Nations Conference on Environment and Development (best known as the Rio conference) brought about (Toner and Conway 1996).

These organizational constraints on regulatory instruments mirror the constraints that some of these instruments face as a result of technological and economic changes. The key to regulatory instruments is the government's ability to first forbid some activity or outcome, and then permit it under certain conditions. This assumes that the activity or outcome in question can indeed be controlled and monitored. When regulatory authorities can be bypassed, then the regime collapses or becomes irrelevant. Substantial changes in technology and competitive markets were the foundation for the massive deregulation movement in trucking, airlines, and energy in the 1980s (Schultz 1994). Technology and markets, of course, have no independent effect of their own. They work through their impacts on existing political and economic coalitions. As Hood (1995) notes, social changes "such as the growth of business travel and of telecommunication-linked services may have played a part in producing more concentrated consumer muscle in areas of traditional pro-producer regulation ... [I]t seems hard to ignore the effect of long-term changes in technology and related social behaviour in accounting for policy change" (p. 148). Before the advent of satellite dishes, for example, what Canadians watched on TV could be controlled by the regulator. It is less clear what the Canadian Radio-television and Telecommunications Commission (CRTC) can do about what Canadians watch in a 500-channel universe where most of those channels are being broadcast by entities beyond the CRTC's control.

The bypass problem is related to the cost of regulation. While most discussions of instrument choice and policy design refer to the low cost of regulatory instruments in comparison with direct spending, some species of regulation can be quite costly indeed. To take the case of the CRTC again, if the regulatory target is Canadian broadcasters, cable companies, and telephone companies, then it is relatively easy to monitor and enforce regulations. The Canadian Environmental Assessment Act, on the other hand, potentially requires the federal government to do environmental impact assessments of hundreds of projects across the country. There are thousands of toxic substances for which standards have to be established and enforced. Every aspect of the environment and economy is potentially implicated in these regulations, and so the scope of investigation and enforcement is very wide and quite costly. This does not mean the regulation will be abandoned, but in tight fiscal circumstances it directs pressures in two ways: (1) reduction of government overhead by shifting some of the costs onto third parties (e.g., polluters themselves or those proposing projects), and (2) reducing the economic impacts of regulation by streamlining decision processes.

These forces help us understand the constraints and limits on regulatory instruments. However, there are countervailing pressures that make regulatory instruments attractive. Ironically, the argument that government should be reduced and restructured can work to the advantage of regulatory instruments. The downsizing comes principally in expenditures and direct service provision, leaving a stronger role for governments in the establishment of framework legislation or regulation. Governments, so the argument runs, should steer not row, and this draws them toward regulatory instruments. As well, some areas of regulation remain quite popular with the public, whatever the apparent rising antipathy to government as a whole. In mid-1996, for example, the Harris government in Ontario was working hard to reduce environmental regulation in the province. Public opinion polling, however, showed that most voters, even those who want smaller government, support strong environmental regulations (Mittelstaedt 1996, A4). Indeed, even as major areas of economic regulation were being cut back in the 1980s, social regulations were, in some cases, actually increasing. Human rights legislation, regulations against discrimination, and efforts to control violence and pornography have enjoyed continuing support. Moreover, the forms of regulation may adapt. As Schultz (1994) notes, "I think it more accurate and appropriate to describe Canadian deregulation as constituting a reformulation and recasting of aims and instruments of government intervention in regulated sectors" (p. 142).

One of the most important changes to regulation as a governing instrument and as part of policy design has been the internationalization of regulatory regimes. If we think of regulation in its broadest sense—rules and standards about conduct, backed by sanctions of some sort—then many of our domestic regulatory regimes are becoming linked with international ones. This reflects one side of the process of globalization discussed in Chapter 2. As the forces and factors important to policy shift to the international level, governments will increasingly have to cooperate at that level in order to continue to have some influence on their domestic practices. Simply put, interdependence compels reflection on inconsistencies, and builds pressures for harmonization. In his review of Canadian competition policy, for example, Doern (1995) notes:

> Canadian competition policy authorities have always had to deal with some international issues and pressures. But … economic globalization in the 1980s and early 1990s, coupled with the establishment or strengthening of trading blocs such as the European Union and the North American Free Trade Agreement (NAFTA), have greatly internationalized the nature of competition policy decisions and brought the presence of comparative institutional models more forcefully to the attention of Canadian authorities. (p. 165)

As the quote suggests, harmonization or linkage means several things. At the very least, it means a greater awareness of the comparative context and what it is that other governments are doing about similar problems. One interviewee noted: *"The influence of globalization has been one of providing models and information, and the development of international policy communities that can help you come to grips with some of the bigger issues."* At another level, it involves actually meshing and coordinating regulatory regimes at the international and domestic levels. The WTO was mentioned earlier as a prime example of the development of a global trading system, but the same is true of human rights. Canada's Charter of Rights and Freedoms directly incorporates language from the International Convenants on Civil and Political Rights and on Economic, Social and Cultural Rights. Indeed, Canada's commitments under these covenants and other international human rights instruments mean that our domestic laws must be consistent with these international regimes (Cooper & Pal 1996).

The story for regulatory-based instruments is less clear than it is for spending-based ones. Whereas spending, for the time being, is out, regulation is both out and in. There seems to be a general prejudice against regulations that impede market efficiency (red tape) or individual choice (the nanny state). However, regulatory instruments directed to facilitating market efficiency and competition, or reducing trade barriers between Canadian provinces, continue to enjoy support. As well, the environmental field, health and safety, and community standards on at least some key moral issues are not witnessing dramatic declines in regulation and, in some instances, have actually seen government regulatory activity increase. Finally, the international linkages and harmonization of regulatory regimes continues apace, so that the would-be policy designer has to be cognizant of these international regimes as well as what other countries are doing about broadly similar problems.

Taxation

The final report of the 1996 Ontario Fair Tax Commission took up more than 1000 pages. This review of tax instruments will have to be much shorter. The main story line in the taxation field since the 1980s is that the tax burden has increased substantially in an effort to come to grips with rising deficits. As Purchase & Hirshhorn (1994) show, total tax revenues in Canada "increased from 31.3 percent in 1983 to 37 percent in 1992" (p. 36). Moreover, while corporate taxes actually declined in this period, "taxes on individuals have increased sharply" (p. 37). As we noted above, the deficit elimination strategies of Canadian governments in the 1990s have deliberately eschewed increased taxation in favour of cuts in expenditures. In part, this was because of a growing view that spending would never come under control if there was always an option of increasing revenues. As well, the globalization argument was that since the overall Canadian tax burden was already high compared to trading partners and the G-7, any further increases would reduce competitiveness. Ralph Klein took this notion to its extreme in promoting what he called the "Alberta advantage" of low taxes compared to other Canadian provinces. From the policy designer's point of view, then, new tax schemes would not appear to be an available instrument.

Or are they? It depends largely on how one defines taxation. If it is defined as a general levy on all citizens, such as an income tax or a sales tax, then increases of this type have indeed fallen off the policy table. However, various charges and fees for special benefits or services are, if anything, growing in use. The deepest reasons for this are also the murkiest, and perhaps the most controversial: as citizens become more resistant to redistributive government, they become more resistant to redistributive (i.e., general) taxation. Fees and charges seem to link services more directly to beneficiaries. Special benefits enjoyed by only a minority of citizens are thereby paid for in whole or in part by that minority. One study estimated that user fees accounted for 17 percent of total government revenues in 1990, and that reliance on them, by at least Ontario municipal governments, was increasing (Sproule-Jones 1994, 7). In a related development, governments also seem more willing to "earmark" certain tax revenues to cover specific expenses (Thirsk & Bird 1994, 130).

The experience of cost-cutting governments across the country in the past few years has seen user charges and fees of various sorts increase. On July 16, 1996, for example, the Ontario government instituted a co-payment scheme for the fee for drugs dispensed to seniors and welfare recipients. The last province to do so, Ontario's plan called for a minimum dispensing fee of $2 for each prescription, and for higher income groups, the complete payment of the first $100 in drugs, and "then a dispensing fee of up to $6.11 for each prescription" ("Ontario Drug Fees," 1996, A4A). Alberta's budget cuts in 1992 began with a reduction of early childhood education subsidies, forcing many parents to make up the difference. Major highway construction in Ontario will rely on tolls for funding (a routine measure used in the U.S.). There are several equity arguments against user fees, such as that their incidence is greater on lower income groups, as well as technical considerations, since only goods and services that are easily packaged for individual consumers are amenable to the technique. Nonetheless, there is huge scope to recover at least part of the costs of many government services through charges and fees, and this instrument is likely to remain important even when most governments have gotten their deficits under control.

New Emphases

The mark of the inventive policy designer is the ability to come up with new ways of doing things, and there have been some fresh techniques or devices both discussed and implemented in some countries in recent years (e.g., tradable pollution permits). This section will focus, however, on three categories of policy instruments and how emphasis has shifted to make them comparatively more important than ever before. They will be discussed in greater detail in Chapters 5 and 6.

Exhortation, or the use of information and entreaties by government, is typically listed in instrument inventories as a sort of sad, weak cousin to the more robust regulatory and spending instruments. We have already seen that spending, regulatory, and taxation instruments have been constrained in the new governance environment. Information-based instruments, by the same token, have increased in importance. As Ryan (1995) notes:

> The federal government, including its crown corporations, became the country's largest advertiser in the mid-1970s and has led the country in advertising almost every year since. The government has used advertisements to inform us about "children's needs," remind us that we can talk to other family members during breakfast, convince us that fish are "modern and exciting," persuade us that the Goods and Services Tax (GST) is "fair, visible and modern" and assure us that "Yes We Can" compete in the global marketplace. (p. 264)

He argues that "advertising to promote federal institutions, shape Canadian identity, modify individual behaviour and promote government policies has increased dramatically" (p. 266). The reasons for this are both peculiar to Canada and a reflection of larger forces. The specifically Canadian reasons (reasons that make Canadian governments comparatively larger advertisers than most other G-7 countries) have to do with the fragile legitimacy of our governments and major policy shifts at the federal level in the early part of the decade. Ottawa used advertising to win hearts and minds around the unity issue, and will do so again through a recently launched Canadian Information Office. It was announced by Deputy Prime Minister Sheila Copps on July 9, 1996, although she was "unable to say what kind of information the office will provide, how it will distribute it or where its budget is coming from" (Winsor 1996, A5A). Government spending on "information" around issues like the constitution and free trade were massive.

The larger forces have had to do with the importance of new policy targets. As governments in the 1970s and 1980s began more vigorously to pursue equity-related policies such as antidiscrimination and women's equality, they inevitably got into the persuasion game, since the policy problems here are primarily attitudinal. Policy concerns about health and lifestyle in this period also contributed to the importance of changing hearts and minds on key issues such as exercise and eating habits. Contemporary concerns about violence, stereotyping, and abuse ensure that policy instruments that both convey information and try to exhort certain behaviours will remain important. In addition, however, governments increasingly find themselves with less money, and greater reliance on partners for the delivery of programs, as explained in Chapters 5 and 6. This interdependency depends on the exchange of information and the building up of relationships. Lindquist (1992) has even urged policy-makers to conceptualize their role as "stewards" of policy communities. Stewardship depends on information exchange. The more that government finds itself operating in networks, relying on partners, and enhancing and facilitating the capacities of societal actors to do things, the more its primary role is to provide critical information, help circulate it, and encourage policy learning. This can go beyond simple distribution of information to calling attention to new policy problems—providing leadership, in short. An official in the environmental policy field notes the difference:

> *We did a thing trying to find a federal role, and one of the key roles we came up with was leadership. And we defined it as identifying issues of national significance. And that's not just a facilitator. Ozone is going to give us cancer. Climate change matters. We are losing habitat at such and such a rate. So it's very science based, and it's using the power that government has in the sense of being able to know ... so to identify issues is one part of leadership. The next part was mobilizing the actors ... And then the last part was doing the federal bits of it ... And it's really those three elements of leadership, which is very different from command and control.*

A new emphasis on partnerships is another development in policy targets and hence policy instruments. Partnerships will be discussed in greater detail in Chapter 5, but the basic logic is that government can either get out of some of the things that it has traditionally done and leave them to the private or nonprofit sectors, or it can continue to do those things in direct partnerships with those sectors. The first mode suggests an oversight capacity for government once the service has been devolved. The second implies a direct partnership with a community association, industry group, or NGO. If partnerships are conceived of as a policy instrument, then they will not simply appear, they have to be created. This requires some skill, as well as a grasp of the different types of partnering that can be undertaken (e.g., one of consultation versus a roundtable format or working together to implement programs).

The third new emphasis in policy is the international system itself. The traditional organization of the foreign policy dossier called for a single foreign affairs department that would channel issues from domestic departments into the international system. With the internationalization of so many policy fields, and with the substantive policy expertise in fact lodged in "domestic" departments, more and more of these departments are engaged in international negotiations. The Department of Foreign Affairs and International Trade tries to coordinate this at the national level, but the sheer scope of international representations by every government body, from local municipalities to federal departments, makes it a difficult task. Yet, international agreements and international negotiations are becoming a routine instrument in the pursuit of domestic policy. Moreover, it is not simply a matter of single policy fields being projected upward to the international level, but linkages across policy fields being developed by international agencies. A good example is environmental issues being entwined with economic and development questions, not to mention technology transfer and agriculture. *"There are more and more forums that are specifically addressing the linkages ... [The venues at the international level for linkage across issues are] limitless. Environment Canada has someone in Paris, someone in Geneva, someone in Manila, every day. You cannot go into Mirabel without bumping into someone from Environment Canada."* Box 4.4 makes the same point with regard to the international calendar (as of July 1996) of coming events involving Human Resources Development Canada (HRDC) on social policy issues.

A final effect—one that is not linked to a single instrument, but rather to combinations of instruments in the policy development process—is the degree to which governments have had to think more holistically about policy problems (in part related to the fiscal drivers mentioned in Chapter 3), and consequently have tried to respond with large policy initiatives. One of the paradoxes of the modern policy environment is that while governments complain about restricted resources and limited capacities, most of them are busy with massive redesigns of huge programs in virtually every field. Often these entail cuts and reductions, but also substantial reconfiguration of policy instruments. As one interviewee put it:

> *One of the problems we're living with is the accumulated inventory of piecemeal solutions. Frankly, if you really unwrap the onion on any vertical ministry right now, you'll see the craziness and absurdity of decisions in the '60s, laid on by the '70s, the '80s, and the '90s. Everything then becomes a monster to manage.*

Another senior analyst reflected on how things have changed in the last twenty years:

Box 4.4   **HUMAN RESOURCE DEVELOPMENT INTERNATIONAL CALENDAR**

1. UN International Year for the Eradication of Poverty (1996)

2. UN Economic and Social Council (ECSOC) meeting (New York, June 1996)

3. OECD Meeting of the Working Party on Social Policy (Paris, July 1996)

4. International Council on Social Welfare: Committee of Representatives and Executive Committee (Hong Kong, July 1996)

5. Meeting of the OECD Economic and Development Review Committee (September 1996)

6. UN General Assembly (New York, September–December 1996)

7. OECD Meeting of the Group of the Council on Rural Development (Paris, September 1996)

8. Six Countries Social Security Meeting (Ottawa, September/October 1996)

9. Bilateral China-Canada (China's Ministry of Labour will host six-member delegation of experts from HRDC for a seminar likely focused on employment programs and vocational training) (Beijing, Fall 1996)

10. Bilateral China-Canada (China's Ministry of Personnel will host senior HRDC delegation for Sino-Canadian seminar on human resource development) (Beijing, Fall 1996)

11. Belmont Conference (New Zealand, October 1996)

12. Meeting of the OECD Employment, Labour and Social Affairs Committee (Paris, October 1996)

13. European Centre for Social Welfare Policy Research, National Liaison Officials Meeting (Vienna, October 1996)

14. Council of Europe, European Social Security Committee Meeting (Strasbourg, November 1996)

15. 27th Session of the International Labour Organization (ILO) Governing Body (Geneva, November 1996)

16. International Labour Office, Forum on Enterprises (Geneva, November 1996)

17. OECD High Level Conference on "Welfare on the Eve of the Third Millennium" (Paris, November 1996)

18. OECD Meeting of the Directing Committees of the Co-operative Action Program on Local Economic and Employment Development (November 1996)

19. Asia-Pacific Economic Co-operation (APEC) Meeting of the Human Resources Development (HRD) Working Group (Australia, January 1997)

20. World Initiative on Lifelong Learning, Second Global Conference on Lifelong Learning (Ottawa, March 1997)

21. Canada host to the APEC 16th Meeting of the Working Group on HRD (Vancouver, May/June 1997)

22. Meeting of the OECD Employment, Labour and Social Affairs Committee at Ministerial Level (Paris, Autumn 1997)

23. UN Regional Conference of Ministers Responsible for Social Affairs (Vienna, Fall 1997)

Source: IIRD International Calendar, July 9, 1996.

The context for policy-making had more to do with an incremental buildup of what the government wanted to do. There was a consensus in the public, acknowledged by government, that we were there to help and assist to do good things. By the late '70s a lot of the fundamental pieces of the social policy fabric were there, and you were simply filling in those pieces. What I'm seeing now, and the policy context within which I work, is infinitely more complex. There is a greater attention to the impact of the finances, much greater attention to accountability issues, a lot more attention to and a lot more rigour in the policy analysis, in terms of looking at ... everything. Right from legal issues to individual rights and appeal mechanisms through to doability, how the policy will actually work and roll out on the ground, labour relations issues, issues of social justice. In this policy context, you really have to look at it all. It was much more segmented. Now there is much more requirement to work between ministries and across governments. I think it's better policy, because ministers see the entire picture. As you bring forward options, you're expanding the horizons of your options. Your options are not narrow little tinkering things. They tend to be of wider scope.

CONCLUSION

We should address two questions in closing this chapter. First, is there a uniform tilt to the new toolbox of policy instruments? Second, has the toolbox become so small and empty that governments are virtually powerless to do anything worthwhile?

Readers will have noticed that there does appear to be a tilt to the way in which instruments and policy design have been going. Deficits and globalization, combined with citizen disaffection, generally propel governments not simply to do more with less, but to do less with less. If possible, policy should depend on market mechanisms and individual choice, and minimize spending and regulation. In practice, of course, this is precisely the prescription adopted by Canadian governments in the last few years, whatever their political stripe. Conservative governments have had more blood lust on this question, slashing with greater determination and less regret than NDP or Liberal governments, but the latter have adopted much of the same rhetoric and policy approaches. Small government and unobtrusive instruments seem to be the order of the day.

The picture is more complicated than this, however. First, as we noted in Chapter 2, postmaterialist values are not uniformly promarket, for example, when it comes to the environment. Second, there is substantial angst about some major social policy questions such as youth crime, violent pornography, decaying family structures, racism, school behaviour, and educational performance. It is far from clear that governments or citizens in these areas are prepared to accept nostrums of minimal government and market mechanisms. Third, the same market forces that drive globalization and competitiveness generate anxieties about jobs, communities, and lifestyle. Some more extreme scenarios draw a grim portrait of highly polarized societies, with a small elite of global citizens jetting off to their next conference or business meeting while the majority drifts in a world of intermittent employment, corroded infrastructure, and the commercialization of virtually every aspect of life.

The policy literature is coming to recognize this, principally by urging the importance of values in public policy. Though this is a larger issue than instrument choice, the discussion in this chapter has shown that the tilt of the toolbox is to maximize individual choice and minimize government intervention. But public policy is not purely instrumental, it sends signals to citizens about who they are and how they should behave. For better or worse, it gives them a picture of appropriate social and political relations. Policy implementation that depends increasingly on market mechanisms and individual choice will encourage citizens to see their relations to government and to each other as primarily ones of exchange—a set of quasi-economic transactions for individual benefit. As Aaron, Mann, and Taylor (1994) point out: "In the jargon of the social scientists, analysts have begun to recognize that values and norms are not 'exogenous,' or independent of public policy. And the idea that values can change, combined with the recognition that responses to policies depend on people's preferences—that is, their values—leads to thinking about how public policy might change values directly or indirectly and thereby change the responses of public policies themselves" (p. 3). Their point is twofold: (1) effective public policies depend on a certain temperament of cooperation and support from citizens, and to neglect the nurturing of that temperament would be a huge mistake, and (2) governments have a legitimate, though carefully balanced, role in supporting and developing some key social values, such as trust, community, and empathy.

These are ultimately questions of policy design for democracy, an issue that the literature on policy instruments studiously avoids and that practising policy-makers usually sidestep. But it is worth asking these questions. What effect will downsized government have on citizenship? How far should we go in encouraging individual self-reliance before ensuring common bonds and a public space? Marc Landy (1993), for example, defines citizenship as "a station that lies between self-absorption and absorption with abstractions … It involves an ongoing effort to synthesize questions of 'what is best for the world' with 'what is best for me'" (p. 20). This is a vision that stresses duty, responsibility, and democratic deliberation. March and Olsen (1995) define the civic temperament this way: "democratic civility achieves its primary claims by stimulating empathetic feelings in citizens, attitudes that allow for sympathetic consideration of the plights and possibilities of others, capacities for feeling sorrow and joy in concert with others. Civility in conflict is encouraged by encounters of understanding, generosity, and restraint" (p. 61).

These phrases sound soft when compared to the tough talk usually associated with developing economic competitiveness. That tough talk has served to justify smaller government. Some recent economic thinking about what truly makes economies competitive, however, suggests that these softer policy targets may be vitally important. Recent work on social capital, for example, seeks to explain both efficient government and competitive economies in terms of social bonds of association and trust. The phenomenal success of Robert Putnam's *Making Democracy Work* (1993) suggests that concerns about social capital cut across ideological lines. Francis Fukuyama (1995) has argued that economic performance depends on social capital and is a function of trust, which he defines as the "expectation that arises within a community of regular, honest, and cooperative behaviour, based on commonly shared norms, on the part of other members of that community" (p. 26). Both economic and political "performance" can be seen as forms of "collective action" problems, where what is rational from a collective point of view (say, a clean environment) runs up against incentives for individuals to free-ride and maximize their self-interest (say, the profits that can be made when all your competitors install antipollution equipment but you do not). If people cooperate, they are all better off. As Putnam (1993) puts it:

> Success in overcoming dilemmas of collective action and the self-defeating opportunism that they spawn depends on the broader social context with which any particular game is played. Voluntary cooperation is easier in a community that has inherited a substantial stock of social capital, in the form of norms of reciprocity and networks of civic engagement. (p. 167)

Governments are clearly aware of the importance of trust, community, and social cooperation as the foundation for almost any public policy, though firmly conservative governments like Ontario's seem obsessed with an agenda of smaller government and greater reliance on the market, with only passing reference to (or robust faith in) the voluntary sector and our social capacities. Excerpts from the February 27, 1996, federal Speech from the Throne show that the quality of the social fabric is a policy issue that weaves itself through the unity question, as well as social and economic policy.

Canadians are concerned about economic uncertainty, the sustainability of social programs and the unity of the country. The scope and enormity of the challenges are such that no individual, municipality, province or region acting in isolation can expect or hope to address them successfully. It will take the will to reason together and to pull together. Each of us must join with those with whom we have the most in common, with whom we share the most at the most basic level—at the level of values …

The federal government has an important contribution to make in preserving and modernizing Canada's social union so that the caring society remains Canada-wide in scope. In particular: The Government will work with the provinces and Canadians to develop agreed-upon values and principles to underlie the social union and to explore new approaches to decision making in social policy. (Governor General of Canada 1996)

The above should help provide the answer to our second question of whether the tool kit has shrunk or been emptied. As has been mentioned many times in this book, modern governments have had their hands tied by fiscal pressures, internationalization, and shifts in ideology that demand less intervention. Governments today have less to spend than they did before, as well as less room to tax. Internationalization means that the domestic economy is much more exposed to global competition, and investors sit ready to judge government policy by pulling out of currency and bond markets if they see something they dislike.

This is not the whole story, however. As we noted earlier in this chapter, the same forces of globalization that constrain governments create powerful pressures for them to act on behalf of their domestic constituencies. Governments remain massively involved in health, education, and social security. New problems such as youth unemployment, Aboriginal self-government, information technologies, and building social capital also demand attention. What is different is that policy-makers have to be a bit more clever than they once were. As our interviewees said, without the easy option of throwing money at a problem, policy suddenly demands more imaginative use of other instruments. If internationalization threatens an important domestic industry, the trick is to find a way, within the rules, to help. For example, we mentioned earlier that agricultural marketing boards were under pressure through international trade agreements like the NAFTA and the WTO. In fact, in joining the WTO, Canada had to change its protective instrument from import quotas to tariffs, some-times as high as 351 percent. The Americans then said that these tariffs were in violation of the NAFTA, which calls for the eventual removal of all tariff barriers between the two countries. On July 16, 1996, it was reported that a NAFTA trade tribunal had ruled in Canada's favour, allowing it to maintain its WTO-sanctioned tariff barrier. The moral of the story is that there is more than one route to a policy objective, and good policy design depends on understanding the substantial room that is left to manoeuvre, the substitutability of instruments, and the multiple levels (local, national, international) at which instruments can be invoked.

Rather than end on an abstract note, let us look at a concrete example of the range of policy instruments at the disposal of government as it tries to tackle a modern policy issue. In 1994 the federal government appointed an Information Highway Advisory Council to investigate issues surround-ing the information highway in Canada. The council submitted its report in September 1995, with over three hundred recommendations. In May 1996, the Minister of Industry responded with an action program entitled *Building the Information Society: Moving Canada into the 21st Century*. Box 4.5 summarizes the initiatives. A glance at the list shows that govern-ment, even in an area as dramatically affected by the forces described in Chapter 2, can still do an awful lot. Note, however, that most of the initia-tives call for (1) small expenditures that are usually leveraged through the private sector, (2) the development of regulatory or legal frameworks to enable the private sector to operate in a consistent context of rules that encourage competition, (3) partnerships and collaboration among govern-ments and industry, (4) the use of the government's capacity to circulate information and research, (5) the use of the government's capacity *as government* to set standards through its own behaviour, (6) the reliance on small pilot projects to both explore whether something might work, and demonstrate how things can work, and (7) the interlinkage across policy fields, departments, and jurisdictions.

This is not policy anemia. There is still a formidable toolbox. But as this chapter has argued, the scope of instruments has changed, and they involve the deft use of fresh strategies to cope with a changed policy-making environment.

Box 4.5	**POLICY INSTRUMENTS FROM BUILDING THE INFORMATION SOCIETY**

Action	**Description**

Building Canada's Information Highway

Creating a Competitive Environment

Convergence policy	• framework for competition between cable TV and telephone companies
Harmonization of ownership rules	• harmonization of rules between cable and telephones to allow cable companies easier access to foreign capital
Overseas telecommunications policy	• participation in G-7 and OECD to develop rules favouring the rapid evolution of global networks and services

Encouraging New Services

Advanced satellite services for multimedia	• partnership with private sector (government $141 million; private sector $600 million) for a commercial multimedia satellite system
Global mobile satellite policy	• new framework to encourage telecommunications companies to invest in global and regional mobile satellite services
New wireless broadband services	• call for licences in February 1996 to provide full range of wireless broadband services (such as TV, high speed data, and telephone services)
Personal communications services	• licensing of four companies to develop PCS devices (wireless) with private investment of $3 billion

Digital television and radio	• task force and CRTC developing policy framework for transition to digital TV and radio

Stimulating Information Highway R&D

Science and Technology Strategy	• encouragement of information highway related research in universities, private sector, and government through government R&D spending ($3.2 billion plus $1 billion in tax credits); coordination between Industry Canada's Communications Research Centre and the private sector
Phase 2 of The Canadian Network for the Advancement of Research, Industry and Education (CANARIE)	• consortium of government and over 200 companies to test commercial applications of advanced networking technologies and applications; funding of $78.5 million over four years

Making Networks Talk to Each Other

Further measures on standards	• joint government-industry effort to develop open standards
Standards setting with industry	• use of government purchases to encourage open standards, combined with government–industry cooperation in the Telecommunications Standards Advisory Council of Canada and the Government Enterprise Network

Growing Canadian Content

A Strategy for Canadian Cultural Content

A comprehensive strategy	• development of a common policy framework with provinces and territories

Content and Information Industry Development

Access to capital for multimedia producers	• working with Minister of Canadian Heritage to improve access to capital
Export development strategy	• working with Department of Foreign Affairs to enhance exports
Canadian content in Canadian classrooms	• emphasis on French and Aboriginal content through SchoolNet

Digitization of Canadian Content

Government Task Force on Digitization	• coordination among agencies and departments (e.g., National Library, National Museum of Science and Technology, and National Film Board) to digitize their collections
Canadian Heritage Information Network	• established 23 years ago to offer on-line access to 25 million objects in the national inventories of Canadian museum collections
Access AMICUS	• bilingual fee-based information system of the National Library of Canada
Imaging Centre	• partnership between Kodak and the Canadian Museum of Civilization to create photos of objects
Digital Collections Program	• aimed at youth projects to digitize Canadian materials

Copyright Protection

Determine need for
further revision of Act

- resolution of outstanding copyright issues with stakeholders; emphasizing more efficient enforcement and administration

**Creators and the New
Technologies**

Development of pilot
projects for training and
R&D

- combined initiative of ministers of Canadian Heritage and Human Resources Development to encourage collaboration among creators

Realizing the Economic Benefits for All Canadians

**Realizing the Economic
Benefits**

Creating the basis for
electronic commerce

- government (through Treasury Board) continuing to convert to electronic commerce as preferred means for conducting business

Preparing Canadian
companies for the information age

- encouragement of use of knowledge-based technologies

Making federal R&D
more available

- transfer research

Technology Partnerships
Canada

- $250 million in investment support for the near-market end of R&D cycle

More financing for
knowledge industries

- Business Development Bank will receive additional $50 million for new technology investments

Strategies	• Canada's largest business Web site (and one of the largest in the world) with over 60 000 reports and 500 000 pages of searchable text on markets, export information, economic analyses; managed by Industry Canada
Support for strategic intelligence and alliances	• encouragement of industry-government alliances
Canadian Technology Network	• 300 member organizations
Trans-Forum	• helping Canadian universities market technology and expertise to private sector
The Student Connection Program	• subsidization of university students' wages hired to introduce and train managers in 50 000 small and medium enterprises in Information Highway business applications
Spirit of Aboriginal Enterprise	• Web sites for Aboriginal entrepreneurs
Canadian Spatial Data Infrastructure	• minister of natural resources in cooperation with provinces and industry will create digital maps accessed through a single electronic window
Agricultural and rural development information	• Agriculture and Agri-Food Canada information access system
Marine Data Environmental Service	• Fisheries and Oceans information access system
The Green Lane	• Environment Canada information access system

Labour adjustment strategies	• convening of a national forum with labour leaders to assess impacts of new technologies on work
Labour standards	• monitoring application of Canada Labour Code
CanWorkNet	• Human Resources Development initiative to develop electronic directory of Internet sites related to work, training, community development, and other topics

Realizing the Social Benefits

Building a lifelong learning culture	• fostering closer collaboration among "governments, learning institutions, sectoral councils, the private sector, business associations, labour organizations, associations for learning, technology professionals, women's groups, community groups and other non-governmental organizations"
Office of Learning Technologies	• Human Resources Development agency
SchoolNet	• two-year government-industry program to put all Canadian schools on-line by June 1997
First Nations SchoolNet	• 447 Aboriginal schools to be linked by Fall 1997 through SchoolNet
Integrated health information network	• development of national strategy to establish an integrated health information network

Conditions for Success

National access strategy	• development by 1997 of a national access strategy using policy and regulatory measures to ensure affordable access to all Canadians

Community Access Program	• prototype of an access framework, providing up to $30 000 to remote communities for equipment, connectivity, support, and training
Disability Access Program	• determination of special needs
Security and public key infrastructure	• public key infrastructure (a means ensuring secure electronic communications) in place in government by 1997 and with external partners by 1998
Framework legislation to protect privacy	• development of legislative framework for protection of privacy
Law enforcement and offensive conduct	• review by Department of Justice on enforcement mechanisms

Getting Government Right

Quick and Easy Access

Seamless electronic government access	• ensuring compatibility
Availability of government information at public access	• ensuring access to government information at all community centres, libraries, and schools
Canada Site on Internet	• continuing work on Government of Canada Web site (http://canada.gc.cd)
Open Bidding Service	• French and English concordance of technological terminology

Electronic Commerce by Government

| Electronic commerce strategy for government | • Treasury Board to convert to electronic transactions |

Electronic commerce in private sector	• government acts as "model user" of technologies
Public key infrastructure	• as above
Business Number	• unique identifier for dealings with Revenue Canada
Intelligent transportation border crossing system	• speeding up customs, immigration, and toll collection
Customs Automated Data Exchange	• automatic transfer of data and tolls
Optical card for Canada–U.S. travellers	• optical card for frequent travellers between Canada and the United States
Direct deposit and standard payment systems	• streamlining government financial operations

Improved Efficiency in Government

E-mail across government	• government-wide E-mail system, now accessible by public
Locally Shared Support Service	• 250 pilot projects underway

A Common Electronic Information Infrastructure

Integrated approach to privacy, security, and access to information	• Public Works Canada manages internal network
Technology Standards Program	• promotion of open standards

Source: Government of Canada (1996). The original distinguishes between actions taken and actions planned.

SUMMARY

Inventory and the Dynamics of Instrument Choice

- policy instruments are the means whereby policy objectives are accomplished through spending, regulation, exhortation, or taxation (to mention just a few)

- instruments are different from implementation, which consists of the organizational means of putting an instrument into effect

- almost everything government does involves spending, but expenditure-based instruments have as their primary rationale the idea that lack of financial resources is the key policy problem in some field

- direct provision of services involves government as the main deliverer of those services, in contrast to their parties or partnerships

- regulation relies on the government's capacity to issue authoritative commands to prohibit or permit certain actions; it typically involves permitting those actions only under certain conditions (i.e., licence requirements)

- there are several types of regulation—economic (prices, working conditions, safety, product standards), social (rights, standards of conduct, safety), and environmental (toxic substances, production processes)

- self-regulation is a policy instrument that delegates the state's regulatory powers to a specific group—examples include the professions and some economic sectors (e.g., agriculture)

- instruments typically come in bundles, which in turn are connected to programs

- taxation can be used as an instrument—as opposed to simply a mechanism to raise funds—if the intent behind the instrument is to raise or lower the costs of certain activities

- information is widely used by governments to persuade or to change attitudes; it is especially important in many social and health-related policy fields, where people have to make their own decisions about their behaviour

New Dynamics

- expenditure-based instruments are less available simply because there is less moneys; at the same time, governments are targeting what money they have left more precisely (i.e., attaching conditions), and also trying to leverage their moneys by having them supplemented by third parties

- insofar as a larger number of policy issues appear to be connected to attitudinal factors and/or the power of information, governments are increasingly relying on information-based policy instruments

- taxation instruments appear to be relying more on user charges and various fees, rather than general taxation, as a means of raising revenue

- international agreements and international standards are increasingly important to the design of policy instruments, and indeed may become the key instruments for achieving certain policy ends

REFERENCES

Aaron, H. J., Mann, T. E., & Taylor, T. (Eds.). (1994). *Values and public policy.* Washington, DC: The Brookings Institution.

Cooper, A. F., & Pal, L. A. (1996). The internationalization of rights and security policy. In G. B. Doern, L. A. Pal, & B. Tomlin (Eds.), *Border crossings: The internationalization of Canadian public policy* (pp. 207–236). Toronto: Oxford University Press.

Doern, G. B. (1995). *Fairer play: Canadian competition policy institutions in a global market.* Toronto: C. D. Howe Institute.

Doern, G. B., & Phidd, R. W. (1992). *Canadian public policy: Ideas, structure, process* (2nd ed.). Toronto: Nelson.

Doern, G. B., & Wilson, V. S. (Eds.). (1974). *Issues in Canadian public policy.* Toronto: Methuen.

Fukuyama, F. (1995). *Trust: The social virtues and the creation of prosperity.* New York: Free Press.

Government of Canada. (1996, September 30). *Building the information society: Moving Canada into the 21st century* [On-line]. Available: http://info.ic.gc.ca/info-highway/society/toc_e.html

Governor General of Canada. (1996, September 30). *Speech from the Throne* [On-line]. Available: http://www.southam.com/nmc/waves/depth/ thronespeech/throne.html

Hood, C. (1984). *The tools of government.* London, England: Macmillan.

Hood, C. (1995). *Explaining policy reversals.* Buckingham, England: Open University Press.

Howlett, M., & Ramesh, M. (1995). *Studying public policy: Policy cycles and policy subsystems.* Toronto: Oxford University Press.

Kirschen, E. S., et al. (1964). *Economic policy in our time* (3 vols.). Amsterdam: North-Holland.

Laidlaw Environmental Services. (1996, September 30) [On line]. Available: http://www.mcgraw hill.com/corporate/environeng/Laidlaw.HTM

Landy, M. (1993). Policy shapes and citizenship. In H. Ingram & S. Rathgeb Smith (Eds.), *Public policy for democracy* (pp. 19–44). Washington, DC: The Brookings Institution.

Lewington, J. (1996, July 15). University president sees stress growing in job. *Globe and Mail,* A3.

Linder, S. H., & Peters, B. G. (1989). Instruments of government: Perceptions and contexts. *Journal of Public Policy, 9,* 35–58.

Lindquist, E. (1992). Public managers and policy communities: Learning to meet new challenges. *Canadian Public Administration, 35*(Summer), 127–159.

March, J. G., & Olsen, J. P. (1995). *Democratic governance.* New York: Free Press.

McDonnell, L. M., & Elmore, R. F. (1987). *Alternative policy instruments.* Santa Monica, CA: Center for Policy Research in Education.

Mittelstaedt, M. (1996, July 15). Green issues split Harris, voters. *Globe and Mail,* A4.

Ontario drug fees will have human cost. (1996, July 15). *Globe and Mail,* A4.

Ontario Fair Tax Commission. (1996). *Fair taxation in a changing world.* Toronto: University of Toronto Press.

Pal, L. A. (1988). *State, class and bureaucracy: Canadian unemployment insurance and public policy.* Montreal: McGill-Queen's University Press.

Purchase, B., & Hirshhorn, R. (1994). *Searching for good governance.* Kingston, ON: Queen's School of Policy Studies.

Putnam, R. (1993). *Making democracy work: Civic traditions in modern Italy.* Princeton, NJ: Princeton University Press.

Ryan, P. (1995). Miniature Mila and flying geese: Government advertising and Canadian democracy. In S. Phillips (Ed.), *How Ottawa spends, 1995–96: Mid-life crises* (pp. 262–286). Ottawa: Carleton University Press.

Schneider, A., & Ingram, H. (1990). Behavioral assumptions of policy tools. *Journal of Politics, 52,* 510–529.

Schultz, R. (1994). Deregulation Canadian-style: State reduction of recasting? In I. Gow & L. Bernier (Eds.), *A downsized state? Canada and Québec compared* (pp. 129–147). Montreal: Presses de l'Université du Québec.

Sproule-Jones, M. (1994). User fees. In A. M. Maslove (Ed.), *Taxes as instruments of public policy* (pp. 3–38). Toronto: University of Toronto Press.

Statistics Canada. (1996, September 30). *Provincial and territorial government revenue and expenditure* [On-line]. Available: http://www.statcan.ca/ Documents/English/Pgdb/State/Government/govt04.htm

Thirsk, W. R., & Bird, R. M. (1994). Earmarked taxes in Ontario: Solution or problem? In A. M. Maslove (Ed.), *Taxing and spending: Issues of process* (pp. 129–184). Toronto: University of Toronto Press.

Toner, G., & Conway, T. (1996). Environmental policy. In G. B. Doern, L. A. Pal, & B. W. Tomlin (Eds.), *Border crossings: The internationalization of Canadian public policy* (pp. 108–144). Toronto: Oxford University Press.

Windsor, H. (1996, July 10). Ottawa's new information agency gets off to a rocky start. *Globe and Mail,* A5.

World Trade Organization. (1996, September 30). *Technical regulations and standards* [On-line]. Available: http://gatekeeper.unicc.org/wto/comp_ leg_wpf.html#Technical

Chapter 5 Implementation

Say implementation and you say organization. Whereas Chapter 4 dealt with policy instruments—the means or techniques of getting things done—this chapter addresses the challenges of organizing and delivering outcomes through those instruments. The policy literature is fond of saying that no one paid much attention to implementation until the 1970s, but this is wrong. Policy analysts themselves did not pay much attention to it, but the field of public administration has concentrated on implementation for most of its history, since a good deal of administrative science, or management, as it is now called, deals with harnessing personnel and other resources in order to get things done. The subject of implementation brings public administration and public policy analysis about as close as they ever come. Even then, the policy literature has paid less attention to organizational details than the political and intellectual constraints in implementation. This chapter will pick up the discussion from Chapter 4 and look at design questions (how we achieve our objectives) from the point of view of organizing services and programs. Implementation studies have the reputation of being the dismal science of policy studies, since much of the work here tends to emphasize how tough it is to get anything accomplished. However, in contrast to theory, the practice of public administration and policy implementation has been undergoing a revolution in recent years. With decentralization, partnerships, client focus, quality service standards, subsidiarity, special operating agencies, privatization, and commercialization, the list of new management practices is long. As one would expect, there is considerable debate whether these new forms of policy implementation represent improvements or decline.

Implementation and policy design are conceptually distinct, though they overlap in practice. Think of design as the blueprint for the policy, and implementation as its execution. Looked at in this way, the relationship between the two aspects of the policy process raises an interesting question: is it possible for badly designed policies to be well implemented, and good policy designs to be badly implemented? Box 5.1 illustrates a rough set of relationships that can exist between implementation and design. A well-designed policy that has good implementation is almost a definition of success: a good idea well executed. There is another degree of success however, which might be thought of as policy hope—a good idea that suffers from inadequate implementation. It must be said that this explanation of failure is the refuge of many a policy designer. The idea was fine, but the follow-through was responsible for less than spectacular results. More on this in a moment. The other two rows in the table define degrees of failure. Straight failure is a bad idea that was implemented as planned, while policy misery surely must be a combination of a bad idea plus flawed execution.

Box 5.1   **DESIGN AND IMPLEMENTATION**

Implementation	Design	
	Good	*Bad*
Good	Success	Hope
Bad	Failure	Misery

We can see from these crude categories that implementation makes a distinct contribution to the success or failure of a policy.

The study of policy implementation is crucial for the study of public administration and public policy. Policy implementation is the stage of policymaking between the establishment of a policy, such as the passage of a legislative act, the issuing of an executive order, the handing down of a judicial decision, or the promulgation of a regulatory rule, and the consequences of the policy for the people whom it affects. If the policy is inappropriate, if it cannot alleviate the problem for which it was designed, it will probably be a failure no matter how well implemented. But even a brilliant policy poorly implemented may fail to achieve the goals of its designers. (Edwards 1984, ix)

The design phase is about determining the problem, the goals, and the most appropriate instruments for a solution. Even if all that goes well, and the conceptualization of the policy problem is broadly correct, the follow-through can create failure. Knowing this, of course, the smart designer builds implementation into the policy design from the beginning, though this too can raise problems if we presume that there should be both some degree of flexibility in the way policies are implemented, as well as input from below. In this chapter we will assume that the policies are well designed, and concentrate on principles and mechanisms of implementation. The first section quickly reviews some of the conventional wisdom of the policy literature, while the second reviews the exploding world of new forms of public management and service delivery.

IMPLEMENTATION THEORY

Consider Box 4.5 in Chapter 4 listing the dozens of actions the federal government plans to undertake to build the information society in Canada. Each one of these is an instrument, and each one is contained in the broader policy framework the government has designed to deal with the issue. In implementing these instruments, what would one want to assure success?

Box 5.2 draws on Hogwood and Gunn's (1984, chapter 11) list of requirements. The image of the successful implementer that arises from this list of requirements is someone or some organization that has brains, strong planning capacity, resources, authority to act, and complete understanding of the goals. It is, in short, a world without friction, without scarcity, without confusion, miscommunication, conflict, or misunderstanding. It is also a world of hierarchy and power, where the implementor decides and those decisions cascade down to the final point of delivery without obstruction or misinterpretation. Little wonder, then, that perfect implementation never happens, and, as Hogwood and Gunn (1984) conclude, some degree of failure "is almost inevitable" (p. 198).

The Hogwood and Gunn list of requirements is developed from the administrator's or implementor's point of view. Another approach that picks up many of the same variables, but also incorporates some system-level considerations, was offered by Sabatier and Mazmanian (1981). Box 5.3 summarizes the framework. It hinges on three broad categories of variables. First, the tractability of the problem—some issues, like

Box 5.2	ELEMENTS FOR SUCCESSFUL IMPLEMENTATION

No insurmountable external constraints	• usually organizations and individuals that will not cooperate, but can include acts of nature
Adequate time and sufficient resources	• time, money, and people
Required combinations	• time, money, and people in the right order and mix
Valid theory	• good design, especially cause-and-effect relationships
Causal connections are reasonable, clear, and direct	• homelessness is doubtless related to capitalism, but rather than trying to change capitalism, find shelter
Dependency relationships are minimal	• authority is not fragmented or dispersed
Agreed objectives	• everyone sings from the same song sheet; no dispute about ends
Correct sequence of tasks	• doing first things first, and so on
Communication	• clear communication and understanding
Compliance	• no sabotage, recalcitrance, or rebellion

Source: Hogwood & Gunn (1984).

traffic congestion, are easier to deal with than others, like disposal of nuclear wastes. A good causal theory, a relatively narrow range of targeted behaviour, a small population target group, and a small desired change in behaviour as a result of policy make implementation more successful, all other things being equal. Second, Sabatier and Mazmanian also incorporate legislative and institutional variables. The statute should be clear, and the implementing agency well resourced. Linkages to cooperating agencies should be designed with a minimum of veto points and strong lines of accountability. The statute should be implemented by agencies or individuals sympathetic to its goals, and outside access to the decision-making process should be skewed toward supporters rather than critics. A third category is broad socioeconomic and political variables that determine the fate of implementation. These overlap in part with forces discussed in Chapter 3, maintaining the sense in the public and the political system that the problem to which the policy is being directed is important and requires attention. In sum, the chances of successful implementation, which Sabatier and Mazmanian define as "the translation of statutory objectives into the policy decisions of implementing agencies" are maximized if:

> the statute stipulates unambiguous objectives; assigns implementation to sympathetic agencies who will give it high priority; minimizes the number of veto points and provides sufficient incentives to overcome resistance among recalcitrant officials; provides sufficient financial resources to conduct the technical analyses and process individual cases; and biases the decision-rules and access points in favor of statutory objectives. Conformity of policy decisions with statutory objectives is also very dependent on the ability of supportive constituency groups and legislative/executive sovereigns to intervene actively in the process to supplement the agency's resources and to counter resistance from target groups. (pp. 21–22)

Even this is a daunting list, showing why the study of implementation appears to be the dismal science of policy analysis. The book that arguably kicked off interest in implementation by policy analysts was by Jeffrey L. Pressman and Aaron Wildavsky, with the appropriately pessimistic title: *Implementation: How Great Expectations in Washington Are Dashed in Oakland: Or, Why It's Amazing that Federal Programs Work at All, This Being a Saga of the Economic Development Administration as Told by Two Sympathetic Observers Who Seek to Build Morals on a Foundation of Ruined Hopes.* The book examines an urban employment scheme called the Oakland Project, announced in 1966. At the time, Oakland had an unemployment rate of 8.4 percent, concentrated among inner-city blacks. The program was to spend $23 million on a variety of public works projects, and would be administered by the Economic Development

Box 5.3   A CONCEPTUAL FRAMEWORK OF THE IMPLEMENTATION PROCESS

Tractability of the Problem

1. Availability of valid technical theory and technology
2. Diversity of target-group behaviour
3. Target group as percentage of the population
4. Extent of behavioral change required

Ability of Statute to Structure Implementation

1. Clear and consistent objectives
2. Incorporation of adequate causal theory
3. Financial rescues
4. Hierarchical integration with and among implementing institutions
5. Decision-rules of implementing agencies
6. Recruitment of implementing official
7. Formal access by outsiders

Nonstatutory Variables Affecting Implementation

1. Socioeconomic conditions and technology
2. Media attention to the problem
3. Public support
4. Attitudes and resources of constituency groups
5. Support from sovereigns
6. Commitment and leadership skill of implementing officials

Source: Sabatier & Mazmanian (1981, 7).

Administration (EDA). Some 3000 jobs were to be created through an innovative scheme whereby employers seeking EDA loans or support would have to submit an employment plan showing how they would recruit target group members. As Pressman and Wildavsky (1984) pointed out, the Oakland Project enjoyed wide political support, was well funded, with moneys in place. Yet three years later, only $3 million had been spent, most of that for a freeway overpass and architects' fees. Why did the Oakland Project fail?

From the beginning, "the success of the EDA program depended on agreement among a diverse group of participants with differing organizational objectives" (p. 30). The project had, at minimum, fifteen different sets of actors, some within the same agency. They included, among others, five different sets from within the EDA itself, the Department of Health, Education, and Welfare, the Department of Labor, the U.S. Navy, the City of Oakland, and black leaders. Beyond this there were all the private sector actors who were supposed to create jobs with the help of EDA funds. Levels of commitment, perceptions of urgency, and capacity varied enormously among these actors. Moreover, the implementation process was marked by a sequence of tasks that had to be completed or agreements struck before the process could move on. Pressman and Wildavsky call these "decision points" that required "clearance" by multiple sets of actors in order for implementation to go forward. They hypothesized that 30 decision points required a cumulative total of 70 clearances. Assuming an 80 percent probability of agreement on each clearance point, the chances of completion were one in a million. Even if one assumed an unrealistically high probability of 99 percent for each clearance, the odds for successful implementation were only about one in two. "However you look at it, the ultimate probability of success is very low" (p. 107).

One might argue that the Oakland Project succumbed to the fragmentation that characterizes the American political system. It is true that parliamentary systems like Canada's have a higher degree of executive dominance and institutional capacity to implement from the top down (Atkinson 1993; Weaver & Rockman 1993). But as parliamentary systems go, Canada's is highly decentralized because of its distinctive brand of federalism. The other notable feature of the Oakland Project was the high consensus around it. In cases where principles differ, where problem definitions are widely divergent, where actors have incentives to impede, delay, or frustrate, it could be expected that policies will face even greater odds against implementation.

Fortunately, things are not so grim. Subsequent work has shown that the probability of successful implementation increases if one adopts assumptions that are plausible, but slightly different from those held by Pressman and Wildavsky in their study. After all, things do get accomplished, however imperfectly. The Pressman-Wildavsky implementation model consists of a chain of statistically independent nodes or clearance points with an attached probability. Relax the model in five ways and the probability for clearance increases substantially (Alexander 1989). First, it is unrealistic to assume that actors will only make one attempt at clearance. They may persist in multiple tries. Second, clearance points are not always independent; they might be packaged or bundled in ways so that one clearance ripples through several others. Third, there is a bandwagon effect at times where previous clearances actually increase the probability of future clearances. This usually happens in threshold decisions where a certain number of agreements are necessary before a large payoff can be received. This puts pressure on holdouts. A good example is labour negotiations, where both sides try to "build momentum" on a series of minor issues before they tackle the larger ones. Fourth, program reduction strategies may be used to shorten the "decision chain." If the proposed program is being held hostage at one clearance point because of some feature that requires agreement from reluctant supporters, cut out that component and proceed to the next decision point. Finally, one can assume higher probabilities of clearance than 99 percent in some instances, and this has a marked effect on overall clearance probabilities.

All of these techniques, in one way or another, involve trying to make the implementation process more controlled. But what if, as Eugene Bardach (1977) wrote years ago, "the character and degree of many implementation problems are inherently unpredictable" (p. 5)? Bardach took the dynamic conceptualization of implementation first developed by Pressman and Wildavsky – dynamic in the sense that it occurs over time— and arrived at the notion of "games" as a way of understanding the essentially defensive nature of implementation:

> The idea of "games," therefore ... directs us to look at the players, what they regard as the stakes, their strategies and tactics, their resources for playing, the rules of play (which stipulate the conditions for winning), the rules of "fair" play (which stipulate the boundaries beyond which lie fraud or illegitimacy), the nature of the communications (or lack of them) among players, the degree of uncertainty surrounding the possible outcomes. The game metaphor also directs our attention to who is not willing to play and for what reasons, and

to who insists on changes in some of the game's parameters as a condition of playing. (p. 56)

In reflecting on what makes the implementation game successful, what enables implementors to deal with its inevitably unpredictable character, Bardach offered several strategies. First, avoid implementation designs that rely on complex management systems, large organizations, and lots of clearances. Implement through the market, if possible, deliver cash rather than services, and aim at smaller targets. Second, engage in scenario writing to work out different possible consequences of a string of actions and interactions. Third, and most importantly, fix the game in the sense of "repairing" it when it goes off the rails and in the sense of "adjusting certain elements of the system of games ... so as to lead to a more preferred outcome" (Bardach 1977, 274). This amounts to paying attention to the policy-formation process (Winter 1990, 25–26).

If the prospects for implementation were as bleak as some of the earlier literature suggested, then policy-making would seem a hopeless enterprise. It may be that we have unrealistically high notions of what constitutes policy success. Ironically, as perceptions of government became more negative over the 1970s and 1980s, the public sector may be presumed to be doing worse than it actually is: "by adopting new ways of looking at and evaluating public policymaking, we have ourselves constructed a significant number of the fiascoes we subsequently 'observed'" (Bovens & t'Hart 1996, 146). However, the lessons of implementation cannot be ignored. It is difficult to make things happen, and it becomes increasingly difficult the further removed the situation from the preconditions identified by Hogwood and Gunn. It can also be more difficult than it need be, if we expect perfect implementation through control. If top-down control is our standard, if we see implementation as the formal elaboration of some unitary design, then almost by definition that is unlikely to happen, given what we know about the limits of organizations and the impact of politics on decision-making. Majone and Wildavsky (1984) urge an image of implementation as evolution, not as control:

Implementation is evolution. Since it takes place in a world we never made, we are usually right in the middle of the process, with events having occurred before and (we hope) continuing afterward ... When we act to implement a policy, we change it. When we vary the amount or type of resource inputs we also intend to alter outputs, even if only to put them back on the track where they were once supposed to be.

In this way, the policy theory is transformed to produce different results. As we learn from experience what is feasible or preferable, we correct errors. To the degree that these corrections make a difference at all, they change our policy ideas as well as the policy outcomes, because the idea is embedded in the action. (p. 177)

Implementation is therefore an execution process, an elaboration, a realization of schemes and conceptions, the building of links in often long chains of decision and agreement. It can also be seen as a process of communications, an "implementation subsystem full of messages, messengers, channels, and targets" (Goggin et al. 1990, 33). It takes place in a world of multiple powers and authorities, organizations, and personalities, and therefore is inevitably a struggle. Even this fails to capture the reality, since it still implies an evolution from the design or blueprint, when in fact what may be happening is closer to the loop or cycle mentioned in the preceding quote, where implementation is a function of combined "top-down" and "bottom-up" processes. Indeed, some students of implementation have been so impressed by the degree to which the fortunes of policies are determined at the final point of delivery, that they have urged a "backward mapping" technique to work out what the policy should actually be, as opposed to more conventional "forward mapping."

> Forward mapping ... begins at the top of the process, with as clear a statement as possible of the policymaker's intent, and proceeds through a sequence of increasingly more specific steps to define what is expected of implementers at each level. At the bottom of the process, one states, again with as much precision as possible, what a satisfactory outcome would be, measured in terms of the original statement of intent ... [Backward mapping] begins, not with a statement of intent, but with a statement of the specific behavior at the lowest level of the implementation process that generates the need for a policy. Only after that behavior is described does the analysis presume to state an objective; the objective is first stated as a set of organizational operations and then as a set of effects, or outcomes, that will result from these operations. Having established a relatively precise target at the lowest level of the system, the analysis backs up through the structure of implementing agencies, asking at each level two questions: What is the ability of this unit to affect the behavior that is the target of the policy? And what resources does this unit require in order to have that effect? In the final stage of analysis the analyst or policymaker

describes a policy that directs resources at the organizational units likely to have the greatest effect. (Elmore 1982, 19, 21)

In sum, the conventional work on implementation has tended to highlight its multidimensionality, difficulty, ambiguity, and growing realization of its importance. The multidimensionality arises from the understanding that implementation can be viewed as an organizational process, something internal to bureaucracies and focused on the challenge of balancing discretion with accountability. Implementation can also be viewed primarily as a political process of bargaining among actors who, while not necessarily equal in resources, can each affect outcomes. It can also be seen from the perspective of individuals, personalities, and leadership capacities, either in organizations or political structures. The difficulty of implementation lies in the high demands for success. As Hogwood and Gunn, as well as Sabatier and Mazmanian illustrate, it is a lot easier to outline the requirements for successful implementation than to actually fulfil them. The ambiguity of implementation reflects the complex symbiosis between theory and practice: policy is initially nothing more than ideas or conceptualizations, while implementation is the specific means of execution and elaboration in practice. Theory guides practice, but practice must, of necessity, add details that were never contemplated in the origins of the policy. Finally, the importance of implementation comes through precisely this contribution of practice—it is, in effect, the test of the policy theory (assuming it goes well). By testing, we learn. So a properly designed implementation process should provide a mechanism for policy feedback, learning, and improvement.

Implementation, however, is not a matter of merely empirically deciding what works and then developing checklists of factors to consider as one plugs along. As Linder and Peters (1990, 64–65) note, looking at policy from the top down, the "implementation solution" criterion seems to be clarity, so that compliance can be ensured down the line. From the bottom up, however, the main criterion appears to be flexibility and discretion, and hence policy design should emphasize simplicity. Bardach (1977) made the same point: "even when we know what ought to be done, and can get political leaders to agree to mandate it, government is probably ill-suited to do the job. At the very least, it is likely that the bureaucratic and regulatory strategies government has traditionally relied upon are ineffective if not mischievous" (p. 4). The factors that we consider to be important in implementation, in other words, depend on the way in which we perceive governance. To take an extreme example, if the scope of government were to be reduced to its 19th-century proportions of maintaining public safety and infrastructure such as roads and sewers, it is unlikely any student of public policy would dream of implementation as a major issue. Implementation is only a concern when there are lots of complex policies to implement. Moreover, the nature of the issues and challenges we confront in implementation also depend on the modes of implementation that we characteristically use. When governments deliver services like education directly themselves, accountability and compliance are more or less presumed to flow from the line relationships that extend down from the ministry to the local schools. Imagine a situation where all educational services were delivered by third parties, and the ministry's role was to develop curricula and distribute support to parents in the form of vouchers. Key implementation issues would suddenly become related to compliance with curricular guidelines and fraud in the use of the vouchers.

Like everything else in policy-making, the world of implementation has changed drastically in recent years. The main trends have been toward decentralization, devolution of responsibilities to other government jurisdictions or third parties, and restructuring accountability relationships within government departments. There is an extensive public administration literature on these developments. Not all of it is complimentary, but it recognizes that something fundamental has been going on across the industrialized world as more and more countries join the bandwagon of new public management.

NEW PUBLIC MANAGEMENT IN CANADA

The broad outlines of the philosophical premises of the new public management (NPM) were sketched in Chapter 2. In light of the closing points in the previous section, forms of governance are being radically rethought, and that is having fundamental implications for the way in which policy is both designed and implemented. The sources of the NPM are various. Politically, the first wave of radical governmental reform came with the Thatcher regime in Britain in the late 1970s and early 1980s. According to Savoie (1994a, 231), these initiatives became one of the key inspirations for the Mulroney-era changes to the public service. The massive changes undertaken by the New Zealand government in the mid-1980s and briefly described in Chapter 2 were another harbinger of things to come. Intellectually, the management revolution has been led by gurus such as Peters and Waterman (1982) and Osborne and Gaebler (1993). While the political roots of NPM were initially in the conservative end of the political spectrum, over the last decade governments of every political stripe have accepted at least part of the message and have started to reform their internal structures and connections with social partners. In New Zealand, change was initiated by a Labour government. In Canada, the Saskatchewan NDP government was the first to balance its budget, ahead of Conservative Alberta. The British Columbia NDP budget of June 26, 1996, echoed themes that by then were commonplace:

British Columbians rightly believe the province has a leadership role in health care, in education, in assisting those in need, and in supporting jobs and economic growth. But British Columbians also know we can do this in better, less expensive ways. We do not have to fall back on old practices in running government. Government does not always work as well as it should. Government is sometimes part of the problem, instead of being part of the solution. Government does not have to be bigger in order to be better. In other words, we can cut the cost of government without sacrificing the value that British Columbians get from government ... Today, I'm announcing a comprehensive review of all government programs. We need to take a hard look at government and find a better way, a smarter way of delivering services. We need to look at every government program and ask ourselves two questions: Do we need this? And is there a better way to do it? Through this review, we will streamline bureaucracy, increase government efficiency, and cut costs. We will ensure that this government serves the public interest, not the interest of bureaucracy. We will focus our resources where they're most needed and best applied. Leaner government, not meaner government. That's our commitment. (British Columbia Ministry of Finance 1996)

The broad appeal of NPM ideas suggests that deeper forces are at work—that bundle of factors described in Chapter 2 that links globalization, technology, and shifts in postwar paradigms to the nature of the nation-state. Dobell and Steenkamp (1993) capture some of the contradictory tendencies, situating the appeal of pro-market administrative mechanisms in the 1980s, and more recent trends as a reaction to a new intensity of globalization.

Demands for consultation, responsiveness, co-ordination and integration followed as pressures on the public sector, often conflicting with the continuing demands of international institutions ... pressing their own market-oriented reform programme in the face of growing concerns about social justice and social cohesion. The public-service manager in the borderless economy, then, faces a cold impersonal world as an agent in a diverse community governed by the unforgiving rules of global markets and exposed in a global culture, vulnerable to the pressures not only of international institutions but the swings of opinion and emotion in far-flung popular movements pressing for democracy ... (p. 571)

It is important to note these conflicting pressures since they help explain some of the confusing characteristics of the NPM. On the one hand, the NPM is all about reorganization and restructuring, and relies heavily on market terminology such as quality management and client satisfaction. On the other hand, the larger debate of which the NPM is a part—redesigning our governance systems to incorporate more participation, citizen control, democracy, and responsiveness—is considerably broader in scope than the narrow maxims of the NPM would imply. We will come back to this question of the tensions that underlie the new thinking about implementation in the conclusion to this chapter.

What are the key principles of the NPM? First, as we noted in Chapter 1, it is critical of traditional bureaucracies. Bureaucracy in this perspective is inflexible, slow, rule bound, and clumsy. Second, a basic question is posed as to whether government should be involved in the policy area in the first place. This seems like much more than a management issue, and it is. But it represents a sea change in thinking that presumes that the lines between state and civil society are drawn in different ways, ways that return substantial responsibilities to nongovernmental actors. Third, if it is determined that a government policy response is appropriate to the problem, the mode of delivery or broad implementation strategy stresses a strong focus on nongovernmental actors (communities, private corporations, citizens) as primary partners in delivery. Fourth, there is greater attention to outcomes and performance than ever before, with a special emphasis on clear standards of service to which agencies can be held accountable as much as possible. Agencies are encouraged to think of service recipients as customers or clients. Fifth, organizationally, the NPM looks to new hybrid forms of delivery that have greater flexibility, and also to a sharper distinction between policy-making functions in the executive and service functions that can be delivered on a contractual basis by some entity, either at arm's length or in the department.

These principles permit a fairly wide variation in practice, and governments that have moved in this direction have done so to different degrees and in different configurations. Moreover, there are important ideological differences that still surface, whatever the similarities in approach. In Canada, for example, while both NDP and Conservative governments have been interested in decentralization and partnerships, the NDP governments have leaned more in the direction of the nonprofit NGO sector than the private, for-profit sector. It must also be remembered that the NPM itself requires implementation, and government organizations may adopt the rhetoric but not the reality of the approach. However, despite these caveats, governments of all political stripes in Canada have come to think about their role and their capacities quite differently, thereby calling into being new forms of policy implementation.

At the federal level, the inauguration of new ways of thinking about management and program delivery came with the 1989 initiative entitled PS2000. According to Paul Tellier (1990), who was then the clerk of the Privy Council and responsible for launching PS2000, the program had three core objectives: better service, improved personnel management, and flexibility. The federal bureaucracy was to become a supple, responsive organization that could quickly adapt to external changes and demands. Together, these objectives would shift public sector thinking away from a philosophy of control to a philosophy of empowerment. The process was undertaken through the establishment of ten task forces consisting of deputy and assistant deputy ministers addressing the following issues: classification; the structure of the management category in the public sector classification system; salaries and benefits; staffing; staff relations; staff training; adaptation of the work force to external changes; resource management; administrative policies and services common to departments; and service to the public.

The Task Force on Service to the Public reviewed "best practices" in the public service and with an eye to developing a "template for the model of the ideal service organization" (Rawson 1991, 491). Though it found that individual public servants were keen to provide good service, the system as a whole did not encourage it. Improved service to the public would come only from strong leadership and a commitment to empowering front-line public servants, those who deal directly with clients. Along with empowerment, there was a need to decentralize wherever possible, and to ensure that the bureaucracy actually valued high service achievements by recognizing and rewarding it. Despite this NPM rhetoric, however, PS2000 focused on management rather than structure, certainly when compared with the radical structural changes introduced in Britain under the Next Steps program. Whereas Next Steps called for a radical restructuring of government departments and agencies on the assumption that organizational change would lead to new behaviour, the PS2000 approach, even in an area like service to the public, avoided structure in favour of recommendations about management and culture.

The ten PS2000 Task Force reports submitted over three hundred recommendations, many of which dealt with minor administrative changes. Some of the others were on the pattern of the recommendations coming from the Service to the Public Task Force: broad statements of principle that called primarily for changes in the way that people think. By 1992 the entire process had bogged down. Paul Tellier had left his post as clerk of the Privy Council, and the government became preoccupied with constitutional and other policy issues, as well as the impending election. The 1992 progress report on PS2000 showed very thin results across the federal public service. In 1993, however, a major federal government reorganization was launched. Once more, the issue was efficiency and effectiveness, but this time it was to be achieved through a radical reduction and recombination of federal government departments from thirty-two to twenty-five. Despite resistance and a bumpy implementation, the reorganization went ahead and was accepted in all but a few details (for example, immigration was moved out of Public Security) by the newly elected Chrétien government in October 1993.

The 1994 federal budget announced the successor to PS2000, the Program Review (though PS2000 was never formally abandoned). Linked to a deficit reduction strategy, Program Review's "main objective was to review all federal programs in order to bring about the most effective and cost-efficient way of delivering programs and services that are appropriate to the federal government's role in the Canadian federation" (Ministry of Finance 1995, 33). As described in Chapter 2, ministers were asked to review all their programs in light of the six tests or questions: serving the public, necessity of government involvement, the federal role, scope for partnerships, efficiency, and affordability. Note that the first four of these speak directly to the issue of implementation, or how government programs are delivered to the public. Coupled with large budget cuts, the effect of the Program Review has been a major downsizing of the federal civil service. In its first sixteen months in office, the Liberal government cut fifteen thousand full-time equivalent positions. In the February 27, 1995, budget, the finance minister announced further cuts of forty-five thousand positions over the next three years (Lee & Hobbs 1996,

355–356). Figure 5.1 shows the impact of these cuts in programs and personnel on federal department budgets between 1994 and 1998. The average decline in departmental spending is 20 percent, and while a few programs have increased (elderly benefits and Indian Affairs), a large number will see cuts in the order of 30 percent to 40 percent. Transport (discussed below) will see its budget reduced by almost 70 percent.

Just as important as the financial impact of Program Review, however, is its impact on and reflection of a new way of thinking about government services. The most extensive presentation of this comes in the government's blueprint entitled *Getting Government Right: A Progress Report* (Treasury Board of Canada 1996a). The government's strategy has four objectives: (1) clarification of federal roles and responsibilities, (2) better targeting of resources on high priority social and economic issues, (3) better and more accessible government "involving clients more in decision making and using modern and practical service delivery tools," and (4) more affordable government. Overarching these goals is a fundamental rethinking of services and the best ways of delivering them.

> A central thrust of the renewal agenda has been to determine where the federal government is best placed to deliver programs or services and where these programs and services are more appropriately delivered by others. The net result is significant changes both in the services the federal government provides and in how it delivers them. The federal government is increasing its use of partnerships with other levels of government, the private sector and citizens to better manage collective and particular interests within Canada's economic and social union. In addition, by paying greater attention to how well it delivers services, the federal government is finding better ways to manage its operations efficiently and provide quality service to Canadians. (Treasury Board of Canada 1996a, 7)

Box 5.4 gives a summary of the changes this has yielded in the way Ottawa operates. It cites some of the key phrases from the document to give a flavour of the philosophical approach, and then some examples of initiatives.

The summary in this table reinforces the points made about the characteristics of the NPM at the beginning of this section. They demonstrate that the first phase of rethinking government—that of reducing expenditures and doing the same with less—has been superseded by a second phase of structural reform both about the things that governments do and how they do them (Privy Council Office 1995). The antibureaucratic tone

Figure 5.1 **Federal Department Spending, 1994–1998**

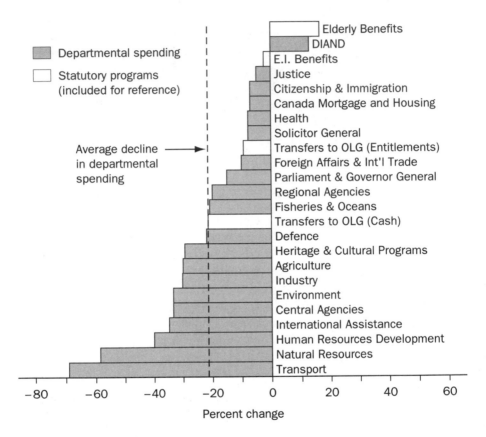

Source: Federal Budget, 1996.

is certainly there, in urging the importance of moving away from direct delivery to frameworks, the use of partnerships, and more market mechanisms to ensure quality and responsiveness. The emphasis on partnerships is particularly strong, with some variant of the word being used 37 times in a 30-page document. As well, the focus on outcomes or service, on treating the recipient as a client or customer is evident and underpins Ottawa's Quality Service Initiative. The result is a search for new organizational forms for program delivery or implementation.

Box 5.4   SUMMARY OF IMPACTS OF PROGRAM REVIEW

Clarifying Federal Roles and Responsibilities

Building the Economy

"In the transportation sector, the federal government is changing its role significantly. Instead of owning, operating and subsidizing large parts of Canada's transportation system, the federal government is focussing on its core policy and regulatory responsibilities to ensure the efficiency, effectiveness, safety and security of the system. Important components of the transportation infrastructure are being transferred from the federal government to other stakeholders."

Examples:

- sale of CN, sale of federal government hopper cars
- commercialization of the St. Lawrence Seaway and ferry operations
- elimination of direct transportation subsidies (e.g., Atlantic rail subsidies) and reduction of rail and ferry transportation subsidies
- phasing out of subsidies in the agri-food sector, such as the dairy subsidy
- end of business subsidies, so that in future, all business assistance programs will be in the form of loans and repayable contributions
- takeover of airports by communities

- transfer of regional and local ports to provincial governments, municipal authorities, community organizations, or other interests
- elimination of subsidy payments under the Western Grain Transportation Act
- transfer of responsibility for the management of freshwater fish habitat to inland provinces
- shift to more strategic business support through the generation and distribution of information, framework regulation to encourage competition

---

Social Policy

"The federal government's key objective, which is broadly shared by the provinces and territories, is to maintain universal access to a comprehensive package of publicly funded health services and to basic social services of comparable quality for all Canadians, regardless of where they live in Canada. Tackling the deficit problem is critical to meeting this objective. A federal government that is fiscally healthy is in a better position to allocate resources among individuals, families, regions and generations and to ensure that people in need are protected by social safety nets. Furthermore, despite the significant reductions in program spending, preference has been given to spending on social programs and services."

Examples:

- assumption by First Nations of responsibility for managing their health services
- use of federal spending power to create new social programs only with majority provincial consent
- replacement of previous transfers for health, post-secondary education, and social assistance with Canada Health and Social Transfer
- redesign of employment insurance to integrate income benefits with active measures to help Canadians find work
- end of federal government's direct delivery of settlement services for immigrants

Foreign Policy

"The federal government has redefined its international and defence priorities to ensure Canada's national interests are well represented in the international arena and to embrace and reflect the new realities of globalization, trade liberalization, and the expanding understanding of global security, which includes poverty and environmental degradation."

Examples:

- international trade in partnership with the provinces and the private sector
- new framework for aid policy

New Partnerships

"In affirming and strengthening its core roles, the federal government has chosen to focus its resources on those functions and activities that it is best placed to deliver. In some cases, the federal government is working in partnership with others in the federation to make its involvement more effective ... New partnerships can bring the federal government closer to communities and citizens by moving decision-making, program delivery and design closer to citizens. These measures acknowledge that the needs and preferences of local communities vary in terms of desired services and programs."

Examples:

- reduction of duplicated and overlapping services between provinces
- RCMP cooperation with communities on crime issues
- amalgamation of services of 21 federal departments through Canada Business Centres

- determination of research priorities by working with stakeholders (e.g., Agriculture and Agri-Food Canada)
- immigration cooperation with NGOs to increase settlement of refugees

Making the Federal Government Work Better

"The federal government has made and will continue to make efforts to improve the quality of its programs and services to make them effective, efficient, affordable, accessible and fair. Central to this commitment are: better use of information technology to get government closer to Canadians; more responsive and flexible approaches to program delivery; changes in the way government makes decisions; and putting government operations, where appropriate, on a results-based footing, with a client-centred focus on quality service."

Harnessing Technology

"Traditional public sectors have tended to be large and complex, delivering programs through a series of separate points of service and offices in communities and towns across the country. In the past, physical infrastructure was the most effective means of service delivery, and helped bring governments in touch with the citizens they served.

New information technologies challenge this traditional model by allowing governments to make services more accessible and affordable. Canadians can now receive, through a single location, a range of government services from several departments or levels of government. Services can be provided directly to the home or through automated kiosks."

Examples:

- call centres to deal with inquiries
- electronic filing of forms
- Internet sites
- client identification cards

- HRDC's comprehensive service delivery network combining offices, telephone and mail service centres, electronic kiosks, electronic on-line services, and community partnerships

Improving Services

"Departments and agencies are moving away from the traditional models of service delivery to explore new ways to deliver programs and services that offer the best value for taxpayer dollars."

Examples:

- integration of databases to save client time in filling forms (e.g., single Business Number)
- alternative dispute resolution
- integration of overlapping services (e.g., merging

nonmilitary fleets of Coast Guard and Oceans Canada
- commercialization of the Canadian Air Navigation System
- single food inspection agency
- employee takeovers of government services

Adopting a Results-Oriented Approach

"Canadians expect their governments to be more transparent, responsive and accountable, and they have become more informed consumers of public goods and services. In response, government must become more service oriented and productive.

Where appropriate, the federal government will take a more business-like approach to the management of its programs and services. In some cases, this will mean the government divests itself of those services that can be better provided by the private sector, as in the example of the Fishing Vessel Insurance Program.

In other areas, government activities will be subject to market tests of relevance, cost and delivery."

Example:
• Quality Service Initiative

Source: Treasury Board of Canada (1996a, September 30). *Getting Government Right: A Progress Report* [On-line]. Available: http//www.tbs-sct.gc.ca/tb/estimate/gette.html

At the same time, it is important to gauge the limits of this revolution in governance and place it in a comparative context. To begin with, the strategies discussed in *Getting Government Right* are only part of what can be a major restructuring of government itself. In all places where the NPM has been implemented, there have been moves to change the nature of executive agencies and their relations to service or delivery agencies. The logic behind this is that mixing policy development functions with delivery of services in a traditional, hierarchical, civil service bureaucracy is not conducive to efficiency and flexibility. If the point is the highest standards of service to the public, then these functions should be clarified and distinguished in some way, so that service delivery need not be hobbled by considerations that are more appropriate to policy development and advising the executive. Simply put, many of the things that enhance the neutrality and capacity of the civil service as a support for government reduce its capacity to serve the public.

The clearest and earliest example of this approach to the organization of government functions was the U.K.'s Next Steps initiative, formally launched in 1988 with the release of the report entitled *Improving Management in Government: The Next Steps* from the Prime Minister's Efficiency Unit. Greer (1994, 23) asserts that the ideas presented in this document were not in themselves radical, addressing age-old questions of how to improve the delivery of public services and what to do about accountability, but that what distinguishes Next Steps is that it actually succeeded in implementing these changes. The key change was to devolve "the delivery of most public services to *executive*, or *Next Steps agencies*, while policy roles that have traditionally been the role of the senior public service, and related administrative functions, remain the responsibility of departments" (Canadian Centre for Management Development 1996, 33). By April 1993, 89 executive agencies had been created, covering 260 000 civil servants or 45 percent of the total (Greer 1994, 1). By the beginning of 1996, 67 percent of the civil service (366 000) were employed in 97 executive agencies (Canadian Centre for Management Development 1996, 37).

The Next Steps system has several components. First, the government prefers, if possible, to devolve the service to the private sector, posing questions about alternative providers and the rationale of government involvement similar to the six questions in the Canadian Program Review. Second, once a service has been identified, an executive agency within the department is established with its own head or chief executive. Third, framework documents are drafted outlining the "agency's aims and objectives; reporting; accountability and financial procedures; pay; recruitment, training and other personnel delegations; and labour matters" (Seidle 1995, 34). Fourth, the chief executive and the minister agree on performance indicators and outcome targets. The framework documents and targets are published, thereby providing an accountability regime for the chief executive both with regards to the minister and the public. Chief executives are appointed on contract to the government for fixed terms. Fifth, Next Steps has been supplemented since 1991 by the Citizen's Charter, which stresses six broad performance principles that are to apply across the British public sector: (1) published standards for service, (2) transparency about costs and performance, (3) choice of services and regular consultation about needs, (4) courtesy and helpfulness, (5) where errors occur, putting things right, and (6) value for money (Doern 1993). These principles are designed to be specifically applied through department charters, and so by mid-1994 "there were 39, and all executive agencies serving the public directly had published or were preparing a statement of their Citizen's Charter standards" (Seidle 1995, 40).

The U.K. model restructured government through a division between policy advice or development and delivery. The agencies are retained in the departments, even though they function according to their own framework agreements. The New Zealand model, launched in the mid-1980s, is similar in principle but quite different in design. New Zealand, at the time of its reforms, had retained many more commercial and quasi-commercial functions within departmental structures than was characteristic of other Commonwealth countries, and so the first step in the government reorganization was the establishment of "state-owned enterprises" to act as commercially viable providers of government services. A group of these were later privatized in the sale of government assets in 1989 (Seidle 1995, 55). The next stage was the application of a similar model to the provision of operational services within the government itself. In all the cases, the philosophical preference was to buy these services from commercialized entities, state-owned enterprises, or the public sector. Where that was not possible, however, there was an attempt to divide groups of services and operations into distinct entities. Seidle (1995) reports, for example, the department formerly responsible for science and technology was replaced with a Ministry of Science and Technology, a Foundation for Research, Science and Technology, and ten Crown research institutes (p. 57). The latter are examples of numerous "Crown entities" that have been established to deliver certain services. They have their own executive and boards, governed by accountability agreements negotiated with the department,

The Australian approach has been different in style and substance, but with much the same effect—a focus on quality, on clients, and on service delivery, but contained within departments. The Australian model keeps policy development and operations within one organizational entity, the department, but splits the functions of purchase and provision, rather than of policy and operations characteristic of the U.K. and New Zealand approaches. Departments buy services from providers (in-house, state governments, private or nonprofit sector) on behalf of their clients. Thus, "a division between *purchase* and *provision* ensures that responsibility for outcomes stays within the portfolio, under the direct authority of the senior portfolio Minister, while allowing for *contestability* [competition among providers] in the *provision* of services" (Canadian Centre for Management Development 1996, 8).

These examples from three Westminster-style governments are only part of a larger international trend that in one form or another has taken up restructuring the public sector to more sharply define services, agencies that provide them, and accountability relationships both to government and to clients. The Organization for Economic Co-operation and Development (OECD), with a membership of twenty-five countries, reports that "consolidation of these trends is a recurring theme in most countries—many report sustained effort in key areas. Restraining the growth and adjusting the structure of the public sector remain the focus of numerous initiatives" (OECD 1995, 7). The report notes that the "campaign for down-sizing or right-sizing the public sector has not diminished" (p. 9). Canada is cited as a case in point with its federal deficit reduction strategy, but Finland is also mentioned as a government for whom the size of the public sector was a "major concern." Sweden introduced structural changes that reduced state employees by 62 000 between 1994–95. Privatization, commercialization, and corporatization lead the list of public sector changes. Decentralization and deconcentration of financial management in central governments are also important. The OECD report also notes that a "wide range of performance-oriented initiatives has been reported in 1994 as the shift of management focus from processes to results gains momentum" (p. 10).

How does Canada fare in terms of these larger trends? The list in Box 5.4 suggests a wide-ranging acceptance of many of the finer principles of the NPM, but it should be clear in examining the U.K., New Zealand, and Australian cases that the Canadian variant has been somewhat tepid on several fronts. In the earlier phases of both PS2000 and the subsequent reforms of the cabinet system, for example, there was never the same level of public political commitment and leadership to management change in Canada as there was in the other three countries. The PS2000 exercise was primarily driven by the mandarinate, with little interest from the executive. Aucoin (1995) cites the Auditor General of Canada's 1993 study to the effect that "Canadian reforms under the Conservatives had met with less than the desired success precisely because the required political and public service leadership had been lacking" (p. 13). In the other Westminster democracies, leadership on management change had come directly from the top, from prime ministers and senior cabinet ministers. In the Canadian case under the Conservatives, the willingness to raise management issues in anything but the stereotypical bureaucrat-bashing mode was rare. While Aucoin confirms that under the Liberals and the new clerk of the Privy Council, there has been a more radical approach (as indicated in federal budgets and Program Review), but that there still "appears to be no interest in mounting a comprehensive program of public management reform" (p. 16). The fundamentals of the NPM as experienced in New Zealand and the U.K. require a combination of rather radical restructuring around the separation of policy from operations, along with a determined focus on service that in turn demands the development and application of performance standards. In Canada, at both federal and provincial levels, restructuring has not gone very far, with the main organizational vehicle remaining the department or ministry, but without the change in form that was typical of Australia (Aucoin 1995, 149). Senior federal civil servants have been cool to the idea of performance measures (though the new Quality Service Initiative discussed below may indicate a shift) (pp. 197–200).

A good example of at least federal government hesitancy on this front comes from the establishment of Special Operating Agencies (SOAs), the closest Canadian equivalent to Next Steps agencies. Whereas in the U.K., special agencies were central to the government's policy on management because that policy was focused on a single overarching strategy of structural reform, the Canadian approach to SOAs was "part of a larger management improvement complex of strategies" (Armstrong 1991, 6). Five SOAs were created by the end of 1990, and by early 1991 there were fifteen. No new ones were created for another two years, at which point a "stock-taking" exercise was launched that took a year (Seidle 1995, 85). In 1995 the federal Translation Bureau became an SOA, and three others were announced. Most of the Canadian SOAs, with the visible exception of the Passport Office, provide internal services to government rather than to the public at large. Moreover, their executives have nothing close to the autonomy or broad accountability relationships characteristic of counterparts in the other Westminster democracies. Borins (1995) noted that the "British government, following Sweden, has concluded that over 60 per cent of its activities can be given over to executive agencies while a much more hesitant Canadian federal government has given over to special operating agencies less than 5 per cent of its activities" (p. 125).

The cautious approach to SOAs was embedded in their management philosophy from the beginning. As Ian Clark, the then secretary to the Treasury Board noted in 1991:

> SOAs are not quasi-Crown corporations. They remain a distinct part of the home department, albeit with enhanced operational authority. From a policy and strategic perspective, however, accountability to the Deputy is, if anything, strengthened ... This means that, while agencies are given increased administrative delegation, Deputies

should be able to spend more time in setting out and monitoring the strategic direction and performance of the agency. (p. 17)

The ultimate purpose of SOAs is better quality and more efficient public services, and so the service context within which these experiments were launched is important to gauge as well. Though there are signs that at the federal level there is a renewed commitment to quality services, Doern (1994) noted that in the mid-1990s, the existing SOAs and other agencies that were trying to renew themselves did so in the face of a commitment to quality that was "still characterized by greater caution than in some other OECD countries" (p. 87).

The NPM and its implications for implementation, of course, affect the entire public sector, not just the federal government. In fact, while Ottawa traditionally has "been the leader in the field of administrative reform in Canada" (Gow 1994, 75), it is probable that the momentum of innovation in management practices has shifted to the provinces and municipalities, or that they are at least as committed to innovation, if not more so, as the federal government. Savoie (1994b) reports, for instance, that it took four years after the inauguration of the Institute of Public Administration's annual Innovative Management Awards for a federal department (Fisheries and Oceans) to capture a prize (p. 13). Managerialism, or the NPM, "is having a strong impact on government operations at all three levels" (p. 16).

NPM AND IMPLEMENTATION

We can conclude from the previous section that something indeed has changed about the organization and delivery of public services at every level of government in Canada. Moreover, these changes echo structural reforms that have been underway for at least a decade in the other major Westminster democracies as well as the United States. The Canadian experience until the 1990s was, in comparative terms, less far-reaching, radical, or publicly debated than was true of the U.K. or New Zealand. In the first half of the 1990s, management reform, while defended in terms of higher standards of service to the public, was largely driven by fiscal constraints at both the federal and provincial levels of government. But the fiscal constraints should be given their due: as we noted in Chapter 4, without those constraints it would have been easy to continue doing business as usual.

Things have changed, and "alternative service delivery" is the order of the day. Before trying to summarize what some of these changes are, this section presents some concrete cases, both large and small, to illustrate some of the possibilities. Indeed, it is quite important to reflect on cases this way, since the NPM, while committed to several key principles, admits of a wide variety of interpretations at the level of implementation. It is precisely its emphasis on innovation that stresses fresh ways of doing things with different combinations of delivery modes (e.g., market and quasi-market partnerships).

A good source of cases and examples is the federal government's Innovation and Quality Exchange (IQE), developed to support the "Quality Service Initiative" approved by the federal Cabinet in June 1995. The IQE "presents information related to quality management, service standards, and successful investment in government re-engineering projects" (Treasury Board of Canada 1996b). The repository aims to compile an electronic database of "success stories" on benchmarking, service standards, and alternative delivery mechanisms. The following is a lightly edited list of cases drawn from the three levels of government. (Each segment consists of direct quotes from the relevant Web pages.)

Initiative: Electronic Tax Filing in Canada

EFILE, or electronic filing, is an alternative offered to individuals to file their income tax returns. Revenue Canada introduced EFILE nationally in 1993 to provide a paperless option of having individual tax information sent to the department by computer. Although the bulk of EFILE returns request refunds, some EFILE returns are to confirm tax balance owed.

In 1995, 3.9 million people chose EFILE because it was a quick way of filing. It reduces the costs to the tax filers (e.g., postage and interest) and to the government (e.g., processing time and resources, storage and handling). Every million EFILE returns save about 60 persons and thousands of square metres of warehouse space, beside being environmentally friendly.

The majority of EFILE returns are processed within two weeks (three weeks in the U.S.). Both electronic and paper returns are accepted and reviewed using the same criteria. EFILE eliminates many manual processing steps, and the fact that electronic returns are prepared using automated tax calculation software, contributes to more accurate information being presented for assessment (IQE E-File 1996).

Initiative: A Manitoba Fleet Agency

In 1934, a Fleet Vehicles Branch was created by the government of Manitoba to provide a centralized fleet management program and to capitalize on scale economies.

In 1992, in pursuit of continuous improvements to program and service delivery, the agency was approved to operate as a Special Operating Agency (SOA). It was the first provincial SOA to be created in Manitoba. Special Operating Agencies are operational organizations within existing departmental structures which deliver services. They operate as an enterprise.

The Fleet Vehicle Agency (Fleet) maintains, manages, and operates a fleet of about 2200 vehicles: sedans, light trucks, mini- and full-sized vans. Almost two-thirds of the fleet operates in rural areas from 662 different base locations. Where economical, the agency locates pools of vehicles near the work location of its major users and provides a variety of vehicles to meet seasonal program needs.

The agency offers four services: full-service fleet leases including fuel, general maintenance, and a number of management services; fleet management services (with no lease); vehicle leases (with no associated services—dry lease); and short-term rental services.

It has recently introduced a computerized Fleet Management Information System (FMIS) to provide clients with contemporary techniques for evaluating fleet and operator efficiency. Customized bills and reports allow the agency to meet customers, individual accounting and coding needs.

Agency vehicles are supplied with a fleet credit card for tracking vehicle expenses. The agency monitors, approves, and pays for vehicle repairs at private facilities. The charges are included in the variable rate, thus reducing the administrative burden of paying individual invoices (IQE Fleet 1996).

Initiative: Province of Ontario Clearing the Path for Business Success

To simplify the way business complies with Ontario government regulations, a Clearing the Path project was initiated to help businesses. The project offers entrepreneurs an easy-to-use computerized registration system to prepare, transmit, and comply with government regulations through a single window.

Clearing the Path collects essential business information only once and then sends out to each program area what is needed for processing and approval. Participating ministries and agencies agree on performance standards so that clients are aware of the time cycle and the process. In all cases, the service and time standards are dramatically improved.

For the clients, the service responds with a business name registration. This step is key when applying for the federal Business Number and for a range of other Ontario tax and Workers Compensation Board registrations. The process is electronic and signatureless. No user fees are charged now.

Planned enhancements include adding updates, renewals, and cancellations of registrations to complete the management of the full registration life cycle. Also, where possible, instant registration will be supported for business names registration, and additional federal, provincial, and municipal licences will be part of future releases.

Ontario is considering partnerships with the private sector to support these features of Clearing the Path. Registration and reporting options now available to business clients are on computer workstations, and will be expanded to other access channels including the telephone, and computer access via network service providers and the Internet in the next 12 to 18 months (IQE Path 1996).

Initiative: Peel Regional Police Child Abuse Investigations

The Peel Regional Police (PRP), serving the cities of Mississauga and Brampton in southern Ontario, with a population of 748 000, reported increased child abuse in recent years. More than 750 charges were laid in 1993 and 1994 for sexual offences where the victims were under 16. The actual reports to the Children's Aid Society were considerably higher. Increased reports support the fact that child abuse is an underreported offence. The rise is also attributable to population growth and to increased awareness of the issue.

Therefore, the Peel Regional Police aimed to improve its response to child abuse cases. A strategic plan was developed to:

• create a full-time coordinator's position to lead the child abuse program and be the liaison with other police services, the justice system, and social agencies;

- move the child abuse investigations from the Youth Bureau to specially assigned officers in the Criminal Investigations Bureau;

- certify the case investigators from the Institute for the Prevention of Child Abuse: the most intensive training ever for a Canadian police service;

- improve and standardize interview techniques which are key to the child's effectively recalling and communicating events;

- sign a protocol between Peel Regional Police, the Peel Children's Aid Society (CAS), and the Peel Crown Attorney's Office to define respective roles;

- construct "soft" interview rooms off-site for victim use. Studies have shown that children respond better when questioned in a comfortable environment;

- install videotaping equipment to aid in prosecution and reduce court appearances for the victim. The existence of the tape also encourages guilty pleas; and

- draft a new child abuse directive that formally establishes the responsibilities for members of the service who respond to suspected child abuse.

As a result of implementing this plan, the quality of child abuse investigations has improved. The interview rooms are used regularly, and cooperation between the police and social agencies has increased. The presence of a coordinator creates a focal point for continuous improvements (IQE Peel 1996).

Initiative: North York Applies Total Quality in Education

A public opinion poll that was conducted for Canada's National Quality Institute (NQI) found that more than half of all Canadians believe the quality of service in education is "poor" or "satisfactory." The North York Board of Education and its schools reacted by emphasizing the need to consult its clients, to measure its performance, and to continually improve services.

The board embarked on a total quality management and service program. It was a recognition that the school system can no longer afford to sidestep quality, service, accountability, and affordability.

The quality movement in education reflects a new reality: competition for market share and students with a keen eye for value and affordability.

The board's total quality management plan embraced the following guiding principles:

* identify and meet client expectations;
* benchmark the processes;
* continue process improvement; and
* accountability and affordability.

The board began a process in 1988 with the schools and parents, students and teachers, called "quality assurance." The board's quality assurance process is a form of an inspection by a team of parents, board and school officials and elected trustees. Between 10 and 15 schools are inspected on an annual basis. The quality assurance process aimed at identifying customers' expectations; monitoring client satisfaction; allocating resources consistent with client priorities; and sharing and communicating the results publicly.

The quality assurance process is diagnostic. It allows the board to learn and replicate what is working in the schools, and to take corrective measures. Last year, the inspection teams were broadened to include business, universities, government, and media representation (IQF North York 1996)

The preceding examples are Canadian, but the innovation networks that now appear to bind together public administrators, managers, consultants, and academics have ensured that examples of public sector innovation in program delivery are as widely available as possible. The John F. Kennedy School at Harvard University, for example, maintains a Web page entitled *Innovations in American Government* (John F. Kennedy School 1996). The fifteen winners of innovation awards by the school included projects such as: CityWork, a Louisville, Kentucky initiative that encourages city employees to work in teams to recommend changes to program delivery practices; the Hamilton Terrace Learning Centre in Louisiana, that combines educational and welfare services in a special school that brings together dropouts, welfare recipients (usually single mothers), and adults; the Civil Enforcement Initiative in New York City that allocates attorneys to police forces to combine criminal and civil remedies for crime; GENESIS, a program in Boulder, Colorado that aims to provide informational services to 95 percent of pregnant teens in the county; and Project QUEST, a San Antonio, Texas, program managed by community groups and associations to provide long-term, intensive training to unemployed persons.

These are simply the tip of the NPM iceberg. The Canadian federal government has committed itself to two framework documents on alternative services and quality, which will gradually alter the shape and delivery of many programs and services, but which also echo an emerging, shared philosophy of governance across all three levels in Canada. The *Framework for Alternative Service Delivery* (Treasury Board of Canada 1996c), for example, states:

> Governments implementing alternative program delivery try to select the best way to deliver programs, activities, services and functions to achieve government objectives, while creating a more client-oriented, affordable and innovative program delivery environment. They can do this in numerous ways, including: establishing more service-oriented and businesslike special operating agencies (SOAs) and other flexible service delivery arrangements; establishing new forms of cooperation among departments such as sharing the provision of administration services at the local level; setting up Crown corporations; negotiating partnering arrangements with other levels of government and the private and voluntary sectors; devolving programs and services to the provinces; commercializing government services to improve efficiency while protecting the public interest; and privatizing government programs and services that no longer serve a public policy purpose. (Treasury Board of Canada 1996d)

Its declaration of quality service urges that federal government services be (1) accessible, dependable, and timely, (2) clear and open, (3) fair, respectful, and courteous, (4) good value for tax dollars, and (5) responsive and committed to improvement through ongoing client consultation (Treasury Board of Canada 1996e). By summer 1995 two-thirds of federal departments had developed standards consistent with these broad principles (Seidle 1995, 89).

As Figure 5.2 outlines, the range of available modes and partners is virtually limitless, with various permutations and combinations of commercialized, voluntary, and purely public services, with every hybrid in between. Combined with the Quality Service Initiative that aims at enticing federal departments to write and publish concrete standards of performance by which they can be measured, it is clear that the world of implementation and policy instruments has changed dramatically.

Figure 5.2   **Opportunities for Program Delivery Alternatives**

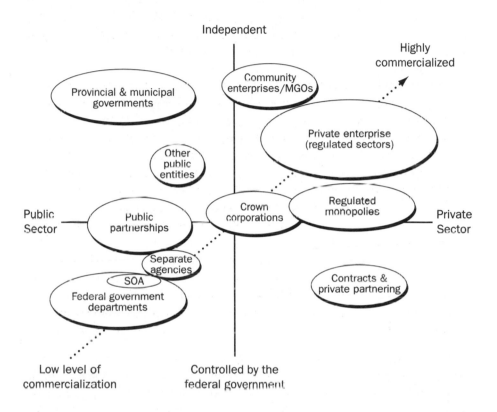

Source: Treasury Board of Canada (1996, October 2). *A framework for alternative service delivery* [On-line]. Available: http://www.tbs-sct.gc.ca/tb/pubs/pro-mgt/apd/fr/fr2-le.gif

CONCLUSION

It is easy enough to see what is different about implementation—new organizational forms, clearer standards, use of information technology, and partnerships. We have not discussed partnerships in detail in this chapter, saving that for Chapter 6. However, it is clear from Figure 5.2 that part-nering in some format is becoming a critical aspect of governance and service delivery. This poses fresh challenges for public managers and policy analysts, since our traditional paradigms of service delivery have relied on a top-down, centralized control model. When governments act as partners, providing support and frameworks rather than services directly, it changes the nature of the implementation game quite dramati-cally, for example, through highlighting accountability issues, monitoring, and learning loops. In terms of the theory discussed in the first part of this chapter, modern implementation practices seem to combine strategies of autonomy to reduce blockages in decision-making (e.g., SOAs) and strate-gies of interdependency which will actually demand greater attention to communication and cooperation (e.g., partnerships).

It should also be clear from this chapter that while the world of policy implementation has changed, the tableaux of those changes is confusing and difficult to trace. The broad principles are straightforward, and any self-respecting acolyte of the NPM can read them off the rosaries of rein-vention and reengineering. In practice, however, we saw that the range of experiments is quite broad (for the NPM, happily so, since from a thou-sand management flowers will the sweet seeds of inspiration grow), as well as varied in intensity. Currently, Ottawa seems to be undergoing a culture shift/shock that appears to be genuinely, if slowly, inducing managers and policy-makers to think differently. As one interviewee put it, the use of NPM principles now is

> *very conscious. It goes one step before performance basis, because we ask "As a Canadian, what do you have a right to expect from govern-ment; what do you feel you want to hold the federal government accountable for?" And it's this performance. So it's not the perfor-mance the government wants to give; it's the performance the client wants to get. How you give it to them becomes a technical question.*

> *Local governments are sometimes far ahead of provincial and federal counterparts, largely because they have faced the fiscal shortfalls first and perhaps most brutally, and because they are primarily in the business of service delivery.*

We have argued that many of these changes are being driven by deep forces that are difficult, if not impossible, to avoid, and that these changes in governance cut across ideological lines. The NPM is not so benign, however, that it lacks severe critics. For one thing, the NPM and the new implementation strategies it calls up are a function of a preoccupation with the deficit, and principally with its expenditure side. There are those who argue that this is merely a business agenda, not some new science of management. As well, the reason for innovation, of course, is reduced resources, and especially reduced personnel. The human cost has been in public sector jobs, with literally thousands of people being let go. Those who remain standing in the rubble of public sector institutions have little choice but to seek partners and support. A big part of the equation has already been determined: a smaller public sector, doing fewer things with fewer resources. It is only a matter of time before circumstances demand innovation.

So, are SOAs, quality initiatives, and all the talk about partnerships just whistling in the dark? Or worse, are they smokescreens for what, in fact, will be an outright attack on the virtues of the public sector? On balance, this book accepts these changes as being broadly beneficial to the citizenry insofar as service, efficiency, and effectiveness are enhanced. It also supports the idea of decentralization and devolution as much as is feasible to community groups and local entities. Partnerships can be a way of involving all of society in governance. However, as we discuss in Chapter 8, there are important questions of governance, accountability, and democracy that need to be addressed. Chapter 6 takes up some of these issues in looking at the kind of policy networks, communities, and partnerships that are rapidly becoming the basis of government-society linkages in both policy development and delivery.

SUMMARY

Implementation Theory

- policy design is the blueprint for a policy, whereas implementation is its execution

- policies can vary simultaneously in terms of design and implementation —well-designed policies can be badly implemented, and badly designed policies can be well implemented; the worst case is a bad policy with bad implementation

- build implementation into policy design

- all other things being equal, a policy will be easier to implement (not necessarily better or more successful in dealing with the problem) if it has a tractable problem, good theory, relatively clear and narrow targets, authorities with resources and commitment, and few dependency relationships

- two widely used metaphors for implementation are (1) implementation or decision "chains," with links and clearance points, and (2) games that require iterative interventions by "fixers" to keep the thing going

- forward mapping conceives implementation as the gradual elaboration down the line of the original designer's vision; backward mapping works by beginning at the end or the point of delivery, asking what the intended result or change should be, and then mapping out requirements at that level and then up the line as necessary

- implementation issues depend on the scope of government action and the vantage point from which we assess it—if government's role is small, then implementation is less crucial an issue; if we value flexibility and responsiveness over fidelity to some blueprint, then what matters in implementation (discretion, adaptability) changes too

New Public Management in Canada

- the new public management is a view of government that cuts across ideological lines and has been very visible in government reforms in many OECD countries in the last decade: it is critical of traditional, hierarchical bureaucracies; looks to a redefinition of the role of government to be more facilitator than doer; relies on partnerships and the private sector for delivery; puts a greater emphasis on performance, quality, and client satisfaction

- PS2000 was launched in 1989 as the precursor to more recent changes in the federal government under Program Review

- Next Steps: a British initiative launched in 1988 that emphasized a client orientation as well as a restructuring of government agencies into Special Operating Agencies (SOAs); now over 60 percent of British civil servants work in SOAs; other features include the Citizen's Charter and published performance standards

NPM and Implementation

- Quality Service Initiative is an attempt to publicize innovative management and service delivery modes throughout the public sector

- innovation networks: universities, think tanks, and government agencies are increasingly exchanging information among themselves about innovative management practices on the theory that there is no single formula, but rather that changes take place at the delivery points and so will vary substantially in the application of principles to meet the characteristics of each case

REFERENCES

Alexander, E. R. (1989). Improbable implementation: The Pressman-Wildavsky paradox revisited. *Journal of Public Policy, 9*, 451–465.

Armstrong, J. (1991). Special operating agencies: Evolution or revolution? *Optimum, 22(2),* 5–12.

Atkinson, M. (1993). Public policy and the new institutionalism. In M. Atkinson (Ed.), *Governing Canada: Institutions and public policy* (pp. 17–45). Toronto: Harcourt Brace Jovanovitch.

Aucoin, P. (1995). *The new public management: Canada in a comparative perspective.* Montreal: Institute for Research on Public Policy.

Bardach, E. (1977). *The implementation game: What happens after a bill becomes a law.* Cambridge, MA: MIT Press.

Borins, S. (1995). The new public management is here to stay. *Canadian Public Administration, 38*(Spring), 122–132.

Bovens, M., & t'Hart, P. (1996). *Understanding policy fiascoes.* New Brunswick, NJ, Transaction Publishers.

British Columbia Ministry of Finance. (1996, September 27). *Budget speech* [On-line]. Available: http://www.fin.gov.bc.ca/budget96/speech.htm

Canadian Centre for Management Development. (1996). *Key characteristics of departments and executive agencies in the Westminster democracies.* Ottawa: Canadian Centre for Management Development.

Clark, I. D. (1991). Special operating agencies: The challenges of innovation. *Optimum, 22(2),* 13–18.

Dobell, R., & Steenkamp, P. (1993). Preface to the symposium on public management in a borderless economy: National governments in a world of trans-national networks. *International Review of Administrative Sciences, 59*(December), 569–577.

Doern, G. B. (1993). The UK citizen's charter: Origins and implementation in three agencies. *Policy and Politics, 21*(January), 17–29.

Doern, G. B. (1994). *The road to better public services: Progress and constraints in five Canadian federal agencies.* Montreal: Institute for Research on Public Policy.

Edwards III, G. C. (1984). Introduction. In G. C. Edwards III (Ed.), *Public policy implementation* (pp. ix-xv). Greenwich, CT: JAI Press.

Elmore, R. F. (1982). Backward mapping: Implementation research and policy decisions. In W. Williams (Ed.), *Studying implementation: Methodological and administrative issues* (pp. 18–35). Chatham, NJ: Chatham House.

Goggin, M. L., et al. (1990). *Implementation theory and practice: Toward a third generation.* Glenview, IL: Scott, Foresman/Little, Brown Higher Education.

Gow, J. I. (1994). *Learning from others: Administrative innovations among Canadian governments.* Toronto: Institute of Public Administration of Canada.

Greer, P. (1994). *Transforming central government: The Next Steps initiative.* Buckingham, England: Open University Press.

Hogwood, B. W., & Gunn, L. A. (1984). *Policy analysis for the real world.* Oxford, England: Oxford University Press.

IQE E-File. (1996, September 30). [On-line]. Available: http://www.tbs-sct. gc.ca/tb/iqe/fed_inie/efilee.html

IQE Fleet. (1996, September 30). [On-line]. Available: http://www.tbs-sct. gc.ca/tb/iqe/prv_inie/manvfae.html

IQE North York. (1996, September 30). [On-line]. Available: http://www.tbs-sct. gc.ca/tb/iqe/mun_inie/nrthyrke.html

IQE Path. (1996, September 30). [On-line]. Available: http://www.tbs-sct. gc.ca/tb/iqe/prv_inie/ontpathe.html

IQE Peel. (1996, September 30). [On-line]. Available: http://www.tbs-sct. gc.ca/tb/iqe/mun_inie/peelkide.html

John F. Kennedy School of Government. (1996, September 30). *Innovations in American government* [On-line]. Available: http://ksgwww.harvard.edu/ ~innovat/index.html

Lee, I., & Hobbs, C. (1996). Pink slips and running shoes: The Liberal government's downsizing of the public service. In G. Swimmer (Ed.), *How Ottawa spends, 1996–97: Life under the knife* (pp. 337–378). Ottawa: Carleton University Press.

Linder, S. H., & Peters, B. G. (1990). Research perspectives on the design of public policy: Implementation, formulation, and design. In D. J. Palumbo & D. J. Calista (Eds.), *Implementation and the policy process: Opening up the black box* (pp. 51–66). New York: Greenwood Press.

Majone, G., & Wildavsky, A. (1984). Implementation as evolution. In J. L. Pressman & A. Wildavsky (Eds.), *Implementation: How great expectations in Washington are dashed in Oakland: Or, why it's amazing that federal programs work at all, this being a saga of the economic development administration as told by two sympathetic observers who seek to build morals on a foundation of ruined hopes* (3rd ed.) (pp. 163–180). Berkeley, CA: University of California Press.

Ministry of Finance (Canada). (1995). *Budget speech.* Ottawa: Ministry of Finance.

OECD. (1995). *Public management developments: Update 1995.* Paris: OECD.

Osborne, D., & Gaebler, T. (1993). *Reinventing government: How the entrepreneurial spirit is transforming the public sector.* New York: Penguin.

Peters, T., & Waterman, R. H. (1982). *In search of excellence.* New York: Harper.

Pressman, J. L., & Wildavsky, A. (1984). *Implementation: How great expectations in Washington are dashed in Oakland: Or, why it's amazing that federal programs work at all, this being a saga of the economic development administration as told by two sympathetic observers who seek to build morals on a foundation of ruined hopes* (3rd ed.). Berkeley, CA: University of California Press.

Privy Council Office. (1995, September 30). *Third annual report on the public service of Canada* [On-line]. Available: http://info.tc.gc.ca/pco/chap-1e.txt

Rawson, B. (1991). Public Service 2000 service to the public task force: Findings and implications. *Canadian Public Administration, 34*(Autumn), 490–500.

Sabatier, P. A., & Mazmanian, D. A. (1981). The implementation of public policy: A framework of analysis. In D. A. Mazmanian & P. A. Sabatier (Eds.), *Effective policy implementation* (pp. 3–35). Lexington, MA: Lexington Books.

Savoie, D. J. (1994a). *Thatcher, Reagan, Mulroney: In search of a new bureaucracy.* Toronto: University of Toronto Press.

Savoie, D. J. (1994b). Looking to managerialism to do better with less. *Optimum, 24*(3), 12–18.

Seidle, F. L. (1995). *Rethinking the delivery of public services to citizens.* Montreal: The Institute for Research on Public Policy.

Tellier, P. M. (1990). Public Service 2000: The renewal of the public service. *Canadian Public Administration, 33*(Summer), 123–132.

Treasury Board of Canada. (1996a, September 30). *Getting government right: A progress report* [On-line]. Available: http://www.tbs-sct.gc.ca/tb/estimate/gette.html

Treasury Board of Canada. (1996b, September 30). *Innovation and quality exchange* [On-line]. Available: http://www.tbs-sct.gc.ca/tb/iqe/mnpgen.html

Treasury Board of Canada. (1996c, October 2). *A framework for alternative service delivery* [On-line]. Available: http://www.info.tbs-sct.gc.ca/ RRXWWKDWODEKWSQUWWTYWTKWXYZKOLXQLCEUKAW/html/ TB_B4/text/files/FR.e.html

Treasury Board of Canada. (1996d, October 2). *Alternative program delivery— Setting the stage* [On-line]. Available: http://www.info.tbs-sct.gc.ca/ RRXWWKDWODEKWSQUWWTYWTKWXYZKOLXQLCEUKAW/html/ TB_B4/text/files/FR2-10E.html

Treasury Board of Canada. (1996e, September 30). *An overview of quality and affordable service for Canadians* [On-line]. Available: http://www.tbs-sct. gc.ca/tb/pubs/qual-ser/ser-stan/oqua/oqua3-4e.html

Weaver, R. K., & Rockman, B. A. (1993). Assessing the effects of institutions. In R. K. Weaver & B. A. Rockman (Eds.), *Do institutions matter? Government capabilities in the United States and abroad* (pp. 1–41). Washington, DC: The Brookings Institution.

Winter, S. (1990). Integrating implementation research. In D. J. Palumbo & D. J. Calista (Eds.), *Implementation and the policy process: Opening up the black box* (pp. 19–38). New York: Greenwood Press.

Chapter 6 Policy Communities and Networks

We are so used to the idea of interest groups in politics that we rarely realize the implications for policy-making. Is interest group politics merely about lobbying legislatures? If so, then the ultimate decisions are still made by politicians, and the implementation details are worked out by administrators. Is interest group politics determinative of the policy process? If this is the case, then the role of legislatures and administrators is considerably diminished, and more attention needs to be placed on nongovernmental actors. In recent years the policy literature has placed great emphasis on policy communities and policy networks, two concepts that try to capture the degree to which any policy field or sector is populated by a host of government agencies, interest groups, associations, social movements, and so on. It has been argued that the nature of these policy communities is crucial both to policy development and to implementation. On the development side, governments need information that nongovernmental actors possess. On the implementation side, the more coherent the interests and organizations in a sector, the easier it is to implement a decision. This chapter reviews the literature on networks, and then shows how contemporary policy-making is coming to grips with issues of consultation and partnerships. As Chapters 4 and 5 showed, constraints on policy instruments and new ideas about implementation are forcing policy-makers to rethink how they interact with relevant actors in their policy sectors. As well, globalization and communications technologies are fundamentally changing the nature of the networks themselves.

Politics without interests is an oxymoron, but for many years some major strands of the policy literature were prepared to think about policy-making as a rational enterprise consisting of priority setting, options analysis, and careful consideration of costs and benefits. Interests did not enter the picture, or if they did, it was more as a complicating and confusing factor than a constituent component of the process (Nagel 1988). The contemporary study of public policy fully acknowledges the role of interests in policy-making, and a master concept for understanding that role has come in the notion of policy communities and policy networks. These are by no means the only frameworks, but they, and a small subset of others, will be examined here in some detail. A sampling of the larger universe of ideas about interests in the policy process is provided in Box 6.1.

Box 6.1   CONCEPTUALIZING INTERESTS
IN POLICY-MAKING:
A GLOSSARY

Concept	Definition	Key Source
Advocacy coalitions	• a wide range of actors, including government from all levels, officials, interest organizations, research groups, journalists, and even other countries, who share a belief system about a policy area and over time demonstrate some degree of coordinated activity • an important feature is the idea that policy fields are marked by competing advocacy coalitions	• Sabatier & Jenkins-Smith 1993

Discourse coalitions	• a range of policy actors united by broad ideas about the policy field, ideas which include assumptions, images, rhetoric, and linguistic turns • appears similar to advocacy coalitions, but has a stronger emphasis on language and meaning	• Fischer & Forester 1993
Epistemic community	• originally developed in the field of international relations, this concept tries to capture the influence of international groups of scientific experts on policy-making, for example, in the environmental field • emphasis on the power of ideas and expertise, as expressed through professional organizations or individuals	• Haas 1992
Iron triangle	• the stable and cozy relationships among congressional committees, executive agencies (primarily regulatory), and economic interest groups	• Carter 1964 • Ripley & Franklin 1984

	• implies long-term, stable interactions among a few actors, insulated from the rest of the policy process	
Issue network	• offered as a critique of the "iron triangle" concept in that most policy subsystems were actually quite fluid and changing, with actors coalescing as necessary around issues, not policy sectors	• Heclo & Wildavsky 1974 • Heclo 1978
Policy community	• the list of actors in a policy network, presumably ones who share at least some common language, but who may be opponents on the issue • the difference from the advocacy coalition approach is that policy communities are presumed to include everyone active in a field	• Wright 1988 • Coleman & Skogstad 1990
Policy network	• current consensus is that this designates the particular pattern of interactions and relationships	• Atkinson & Coleman 1992 • Van Waarden 1992

	• the most important feature is the discerning of patterns of relations that have consequences for the development and delivery of policy	
Public interest groups	• interest groups that advocate on behalf of the public good rather than the direct self-interest of their members • emphasis is on advocacy for "causes" and the public interest rather than economic lobbying	• Berry 1977 • Pal 1993 • Stanbury 1993 • Philips 1993
Social movement organizations	• interest groups rooted in social transformations of the 1960s that led to new values, new class structures, and new social coalitions (e.g., environmentalism, feminism) • key feature is the link between organizations and their social foundations, as well as the new dynamics of participation that arise with these organizations	• Offe 1987 • Zald 1987 • Klandermans & Tarrow 1988 • Melucci 1989

Subgovernment	• a generic concept that expresses the idea that policy does not get made in a single "system" but in subsystems that consist of microcosms of all the relevant political and institutional actors • this concept was developed in the 1950s as part of pluralist analyses of policy-making	• Truman 1951 • Jordan 1990 • Pross 1992

The idea of policy networks is a relatively "new key term" (Marin & Mayntz 1991, 11), one that when joined to policy communities constitutes "two of the most important conceptual innovations to emerge" in recent studies of the policy process (Atkinson & Coleman 1992, 158). For some the concepts are at best "metaphors" (Dowding 1995), and for others the overlap and confusion of the complementary network concepts (see Box 6.1) leads to little more than a "debate over terminology" (Lindquist 1996, 219). The concerns we will raise in this chapter tap into another issue as well: the degree to which the network concept goes far enough in capturing the realities and contradictions of contemporary policy-making. On the one hand, there has been tremendous pressure in Canada and elsewhere to broaden out the policy development process to include more actors such as interest associations and various groups of experts. As well, we saw in Chapters 4 and 5, that governments are spending less and favouring alternative modes of program delivery, most of which stress partnerships. Consultation and partnering are the order of the day. On the other hand, as Lindquist points out (1996, 220), despite the policy literature's emphasis on networks and communities, it has had relatively little to offer in the way of tools to foster, develop, and manage relationships between governments and their policy communities. More troubling still, it may be that even the existing literature is inadequate to the new, emerging dynamics of networks and policy communities. One small example is the idea that "only a *few* or *not too many* actors can actually *inter-act* with each other" for a policy network to actually function (Marin & Mayntz 1991, 17). However, the Internet has the potential of making this idea obsolete: thousands of individuals and organizations can combine in something much closer to a true network or web than has ever been imagined in network analysis itself.

The next section provides background on the communities and networks literature, emphasizing (with Lindquist) the tension between the theoretical importance of the ideas and the poverty of practical insights for policy-making. The chapter then proceeds to analyze the ways in which the realities of policy communities and networks are intruding on the consciousness of policy-makers themselves and being addressed through consultation schemes and partnership models of implementing public programs. The conclusion returns to the tensions implied by these new pressures. Are our traditional forms of governance up to the challenge?

COMMUNITIES AND NETWORKS: CONCEPTUAL FRAMEWORKS

Approaches and Concepts

While there has been a harmonic convergence around the ideas of policy networks and communities, that convergence has come from several different directions. It is of more than mere antiquarian interest to explore the various sources of the network idea, since each of the origins suggests a different aspect of the policy process that was inadequately grasped by the older theoretical apparatuses. This will help us later in the chapter when we examine the contemporary changes in the policy process that are forcing even more radical conceptualizations of networks and webs of interest, cooperation, and conflict.

The broad backdrop to the various origins of network analyses is a concern with understanding the relationship between state and society, and in particular the organization of interests in society. As banal and obvious as that sounds, the early postwar history of political science and public policy wrestled with the best way of theorizing the connections. While the Marxist literature addressed itself to various ways of thinking about the importance of class, the non-Marxist literature eventually settled on the notion of "interest group pluralism" as its master concept. The pioneering postwar book on the subject was David Truman's *The Governmental Process* (1951). Truman, and others in that tradition, conceptualized society as consisting of an almost limitless array of interests that could mobilize around an almost equally limitless range of issues. If people shared interests, they would likely form groups. If issues arose that affected those interests in a policy sense, then the groups would politicize and lobby government. The success of specific lobbies would depend on resources such as personnel, finances, membership, and leadership. Though Truman himself did not subscribe to the view that public policy was simply the result of pulling and hauling among groups, and that the government was merely a "neutral force" (p. 106), the pluralist tradition as a whole tended to de-emphasize the state or policy-making institutions, and stressed the influence of lobbies and interest groups politics (Nordlinger 1981, Chapter 1; but see Almond 1990, Chapter 8). While pluralism did not use the contemporary terms of interest intermediation or associational system, it drew a distinctive portrait of each. Interest intermediation, or the way in which societal interests interact with state institutions, was sketched as a highly variable, unpredictable, unstable process that depended on the organization of interests and government institutions in each policy sector or subgovernment. The associational system— the patterns of groups and organizations—was also depicted as a rather confusing constellation of small, medium, and large groups, competing and cooperating as they felt necessary. In fact, this was an implicit portrait of the American political system itself—highly democratic, a nation of "joiners," with widely dispersed political resources and a responsive, almost transparently permeable, set of state institutions.

We can identify at least four major sources of inspiration for the broad concept of networks as it has been applied in a variety of different forms. One of the first breaks with pluralism was over its portrait of the associational system and patterns of policy-making. Empirical case studies in the period showed that patterns were much more stable, and relationships far more closed, than pluralists had suggested. Instead of a pleasing variety of political actors and multiple access points, the (American) policy system was actually organized in tight nodes, usually with cozy agreements among business, executive agencies, and congressional committees, in iron triangles. Policy-making took place, in short, not in the legislature or the executive, but in smaller clusters that truly were subgovernments in the sense that they might all be operating according to different principles, with different rhythms and often conflicting outcomes. The only coherence in the system existed at the subsystemic level. This was seen to be particularly true of regulatory policy fields, where there was a strong economic incentive for business to influence and even capture their regulators.

By the mid-1970s the notion of iron triangles seemed like a caricature too, and Hugh Heclo (1978) crystallized the growing unease by identifying what he called issue networks. Interestingly, Heclo was not arguing for a new master concept, but pointing out that the nature of the (American) policy system had changed. For one thing, the technical complexity of policy issues had increased, demanding the participation of policy experts and researchers rather than just narrow interests. There was a greater fluidity in issue generation as well, as the policy system constantly churned and produced new agenda items. Rather than the stable patterns of control that characterize iron triangles, Heclo saw issue networks as being quite permeable, with a kaleidoscope of changing faces as interest in (not a stake in) the policy issues waxed and waned. Heclo's work can be traced as the direct source of fresh inspiration to European research on subgovernments (Jordan 1981).

A second important source of work on networks came from comparative research on industrial performance and economic policy. One of the earliest uses of the term policy network was in a book edited by Peter Katzenstein, *Between Power and Plenty* (1978a). The inspiration for this work was completely different than the concerns surrounding pluralism: as specialists in foreign relations, and with a focus on foreign economic policy, Katzenstein and his colleagues were interested in the ways in which domestic political structures affected this policy field. Since "the domestic structures in the advanced industrial states differ in important ways, so do the strategies of foreign economic policy which these states pursue" (Katzenstein 1978b, 4). A key conditioning factor of foreign policy was the character of domestic interests and institutions, which could be termed the "policy network." Policy instruments were conditioned by the "character of the *policy network* spanning both the public and the private sector," and the key factors were the "differentiation of state from society and the centralization within each" (Katzenstein 1978c, 308).

This branch of research had offshoots that remain highly relevant to the work on policy networks today. Work on "state structures" argued that each state had a characteristic pattern of associational and state institutions. In a sense, this was a search for a macro variable, a single pattern at the broadest or deepest level of a given society that would affect policymaking across all sectors. For example, the work on corporatism urged that some countries were characterized by corporatist structures, centralized state agencies and highly centralized associational systems, working in tandem to develop and implement policy, and that despite variances, corporatist dynamics would be discerned in most policy fields in that polity (Schmitter & Lembruch 1979). It also suggested that corporatist political structures were more effective in the development of economic policy. This helped feed a debate about the nature of the state and its autonomy from social interests (Nordlinger 1981; Skocpol 1986), as well as a subsequent interest in political institutions (Weaver and Rockman 1993). This style of analysis has stressed the structuring effect of state institutions on associational systems (e.g., Baumgartner 1996; Coleman 1994). Other work looked more at the relation between state and society in specific (usually economic) sectors, and led directly to some of the most important contributions to network analysis. The contemporary variant or application is work on state policy capacities, especially in economic or industrial policy, where it is said that centralized administration and coherent associational systems will prove more competitive (Atkinson & Coleman 1989a; Wilks & Wright 1987).

A third source of inspiration for network analysis was the growing work on "new social movements" and "public interest groups." Phillips (1994) defines a social movement as "(a) an information network of organizations and individuals who (b) on the basis of collective identity and shared values (c) engage in political and/or cultural struggle intended to expand the boundaries of the existing system and (d) undertake collective action designed to affect both state and society" (189; see also Carroll 1992). She points out that social movement organizations rarely act alone (they are, after all, part of a social movement), and connect through various types of networks. The distinction between the movement and the organizations built upon it is important, and gives a clue as to why the network idea spontaneously arose in this field of research. Any movement (e.g., environmental, consumers', women's) is bound to spawn a variety of organizations that address different aspects of its agenda, but those organizations will have a common cause and will seek to cooperate in order to maximize their policy impact.

Public interest groups have been defined as "an organizational entity that purports to represent very broad, diffuse, non-commercial interests which traditionally have received little explicit or direct representation in the processes by which agencies, courts, and legislatures make public policy" (Schuck 1977, 133). Broadly speaking, these are citizens' organizations and typically are either very similar, or identical to social movement organizations, for example, consumers' groups and environmental organizations.

They both have a penchant for "expressive politics" or a political agenda that does not focus exclusively on material issues, and certainly not on direct political gain. While some scepticism is warranted regarding their altruism, it remains true that in structure and strategy, public interest groups differ markedly from traditional types of organizations. Most importantly, because they tend to be marginal and under-resourced when compared to large corporate interests, they too have been noted for their coalition or networking strategies.

A final source of inspiration for the network concept has been the changing nature of political reality, some elements of which are reflected in the sources described above. Kenis and Schneider (1991, 34–36) summarize these changes as follows:

1. *Emergence of organized society*: more and more of our social and political life is controlled by "organized collectivities" and as their importance and number increase, so will their interdependencies.

2. *Sectoralization*: the functional differentiation of policies, programs, and agencies.

3. *Crowded policy domains*: more organized collectivities and corporate actors means more intervention and participation within a given policy space.

4. *Scope of policy-making*: growth both in the number of policy domains and degree of intervention in them.

5. *Decentralization and fragmentation of the state*: the state increasingly consists of a host of discrete and loosely coordinated institutional entities.

6. *Blurring of boundaries between the public and private*: governments are increasingly involved at the interstices of civil society in implementing informal relationships (e.g., speech codes).

7. *Rise of private governments*: many political tasks can no longer be accomplished without the help of private organizations.

8. *Transnationalization of domestic politics*: policy issues are affected by factors at the international level and governments increasingly pursue policy objectives through international forums.

9. *The importance of information*: increased complexity demands better information and scientific expertise.

The result?

> Increasingly unable to mobilize all necessary policy resources within their own realm, governments consequently become dependent upon the cooperation and joint resource mobilization of policy actors outside their hierarchical control. Policy networks should therefore be understood as those webs of relatively stable and ongoing relationships which mobilize dispersed resources so that collective (or parallel) action can be orchestrated toward the solution of a common policy problem. (Kenis & Schneider 1991, 36)

Peters and Barker (1993) emphasize information requirements of the modern polity as well as the new demands for openness and participation as key ingredients forcing governments to engage in networks and communities.

> But the multiplication of interest groups produces multiple sources of information that have become increasingly difficult to exclude from policy-making. Any official attempt to exclude unwanted information runs up against the increasing (sometimes legally mandated) openness of governments, as well as the increasing information needs of governments when making policy about complex topics. So governments experience political and perhaps legal trouble if they are exclusionary while also denying themselves potentially important information. The 'cozy little triangles' that once dominated policy-making now have become 'big sloppy hexagons.' (p. 9)

We will return to the question of how reality bites in the policy process and generates network dynamics. To this point, it should be clear why the network/community concept is as important as it is: it has filtered through both policy studies and the broader study of government and politics because it reflects some important shifts in our forms of governance. The increasing complexity of both society and government; the importance of information and expert knowledge; the reliance of government on nongovernmental actors to both formulate and implement policy; shifts in class structure, values, and social groups: these are some of the forces that underpin an interest in networks and communities. All of these changes continue to exercise an important influence on modern policy-making, but they have been supplemented and reinforced by the factors described in Chapter 2.

In all the variants of network analysis, the central questions are, first, how to conceptualize the relationships between civil society and the state, and second, what difference certain patterns of relations make to policy outcomes. A third question of more relevance to the practitioner is rarely raised in this work, but will be the focus for the second half of this chapter: how to manage and nurture relations between government agencies and their policy constituencies. But first, we will briefly examine the state of the art in conceptualizing policy networks.

Policy Network/Community Analysis

It is one thing to say that policy networks and communities are important; it is another thing to conceptualize those networks. Paul Pross (1995) offered an early definition as well as a diagrammatic portrait of policy communities. Policy communities are "groupings of government agencies, pressure groups, media people, and individuals, including academics, who, for various reasons, have an interest in a particular policy field and attempt to influence it" (p. 265). Figure 6.1 displays what Pross calls his "bubble diagram" of policy communities. Note that it divides the policy community in any given policy field into the "subgovernment" and the "attentive public." Actual decision-making takes place in the subgovernment, which is dominated by large institutions, groups, and core government agencies. Players in the subgovernment, Pross argues, work to limit participation from outsiders. The attentive public are the outsiders whose main influence on the process is to generate ideas and discussion through conferences, publications, and occasional lobbying. In Pross's view, the policy community is actually an insulating device to keep a grip on the process; indeed, he argues that most of the inside players in a policy community try to keep debate within the realm of the technical and routine. Figure 6.1 shows a policy community in which the federal government is dominant, but the basic structure of core agencies in the subgovernment surrounded by other groups and agencies is generic.

There are several limitations to this way of thinking about policy communities. For one thing, it is largely static (though Pross is careful to argue that, in fact, policy communities are constantly in flux). For another, it does not travel well across policy fields. Some areas are indeed dominated by government agencies, and largely insulated from outside pressures—finance comes to mind. But many others are increasingly open to pressures from the attentive public, and that public is not prepared to be polite and keep policy-making at the level of routine. In social policy, for example, fundamental assumptions about the role of government are constantly being posed. In information policy, as we saw in the previous chapters, some huge issues of both community and communication are at stake. Another problem is that in this model, foreign governments and foreign pressure groups are relegated to the margins of the model. This metaphor is increasingly obsolete in a globalized world. Finally, the model does not capture varying relations among the actors. The bubbles are large or small, but the figure as a whole gives no idea of the connections (or lack thereof) among the players.

Some of these limitations have been addressed in more refined models of policy networks (to which Pross's work is an important contribution). In a tradition that descends directly from Katzenstein's framework, this approach focuses on two variables: the nature of centralization in the state and the centralization or organization of the associational system. This is often termed a "structural approach" to network analysis because it focuses on patterns of relations among actors, patterns that can be mapped and are to some degree distinct from the beliefs or ideas that the actors themselves carry in the policy process. If we take a simple dichotomy of high organization/low organization, then we have a straightforward group of four categories to start with. In his excellent survey of the policy network literature, Lindquist (1992) draws on work by Atkinson and Coleman (1989a; 1989b) and Coleman and Skogstad (1990) to neatly summarize the network types in a chart, reproduced below as Figure 6.2 (with five types). The degree of organization here means things like: analytic capacity, access to important data and information, ability to act unilaterally, coordination, focus on long-term or short-term issues, and a reactive or anticipatory policy stance (Lindquist 1992, 134). Figure 6.3 offers another graphic representation of these networks, accompanied by brief definitions.

This depiction of policy network types has the advantage of variety. It is clear that there will be variation in policy networks across policy fields (though why that is, and if there are any underlying patterns to network organization in a specific political system, is a tougher question). Governments, or more precisely, the core agencies in the subgovernment, can be either well organized, strong, and policy capable, or weakly organized without much policy capacity. Atkinson and Coleman (1989a, 80–81) identify four conditions for what they call "state autonomy at the sectoral level": the bureau should have (1) a clear conception of its role and a value

Figure 6.1 **Policy Community "Bubble Diagram"**

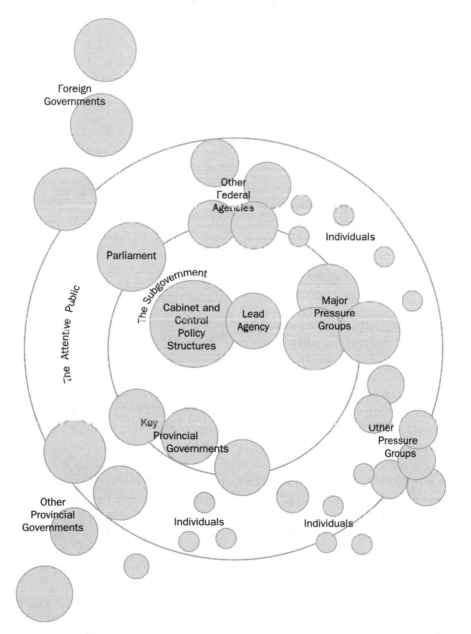

Source: Pross (1995, 267).

Figure 6.2 **Policy Network Categories**

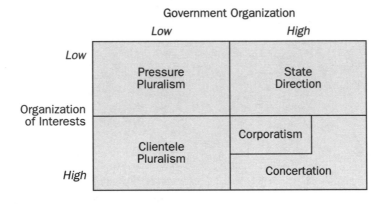

Source: Lindquist (1992, 135).

system that supports its mandate, as well as support from the minister, (2) a distinct professional ethos from its clients, (3) a body of law and regulation that it firmly administers, and (4) the capacity to generate its own information related to its mandate. In addition, they argue that state agencies are distinguished by their degree of concentration, by which they mean that strong, informal alliances between the political executive and officials. By the same token, associational systems can be weak or strong. Atkinson and Coleman (1989a, 82–83) identify six conditions for a "highly mobilized sector." Business groups (their focus) should have: (1) separate associations representing different products and producers, without overlap or competition, (2) only one association that speaks for the sector as a whole, (3) a high proportion of firms represented in the sector's associations, (4) large firms that demonstrate leadership in the sector, (5) in-house capacity to generate information among firms and associations, and (6) associations that can strike deals with government and make them stick with members.

The Atkinson and Coleman schema actually yields eight categories of networks. The more criteria one adds, of course, the more types of networks one can generate. Van Waarden (1992), for example, argues that the major dimensions of policy networks are: "(1) actors, (2) function, (3) structure,

Figure 6.3   **Definitions of Policy Networks**

TYPE	CHARACTERISTICS

Pressure Pluralist Network

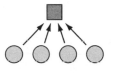

State agency is autonomous; associational system is dispersed and weak. Many groups compete for state agency's attention. Groups advocate policies rather than participate in policy-making.

Clientele Pluralist Network

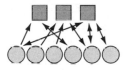

State agencies arc both weak and dispersed, as are associational systems. Agencies rely on associations for information and support and allow them to participate in policy-making.

Corporalist Network

State agency is strong and autonomous; associational system comprises a few large and powerful groups, usually representing consumer and producer interests. Groups and agency both participate in policy formulation and implementation.

Concertation Network

State agency is strong and autonomous; associational system is dominated by one organization that represents it. Agency and organization are equal partners in long-term planning and policy-making.

State-Directed Network

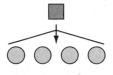

State agency is strong and autonomous; associational system is weak and dispersed. State dominates policy sector and associational system.

■ = State Agencies   ◯ = Organizations

Source: Pal (1992, 112).

(4) institutionalization, (5) rules of conduct, (6) power relations, and (7) actor strategies" (p. 32). He further subdivides each of these dimensions to arrive at a list of thirty-eight criteria defining thirteen different types of policy networks! Recognizing that this is unmanageable, Van Waarden recommends concentrating on three criteria: the number and type of societal actors involved, the major functions of networks (e.g., negotiation, consultation, coordination, cooperation in policy formation, or implementation), and the balance of power between state and societal interests.

Apart from pretty diagrams, what do policy networks tell us about policy-making? Most of the network literature has been applied to economic policy fields, and assumes that concentration plus organization equals policy capable systems. Atkinson and Coleman (1989a), for example, bemoan Canada's weak industrial policy capacity, which they argue is due to a tradition of pressure pluralist networks and weak state capacities. The implication is that the more that state and associational actors emulate the "strong" end of the continuum, the better policy will be. While this makes some intuitive sense, it needs to be treated cautiously. For one thing, it has a vaguely undemocratic flavour. The more hierarchical, coordinated, and tidy the policy sector, the fewer opportunities there will be for the "attentive public" to get into the act. As well, in light of the discussion in Chapter 5, governments increasingly see their role as the development of policy frameworks within which private actors can pursue their goals. Current policy thinking is that the wider the networks and the more competition among players, the better policy outcomes will be. Finally, as policy sectors get more complex and more globalized, the demands for information from all sectors and connections among the players rise exponentially. The tightly coordinated policy networks recommended in this literature may not be adequate to the new dynamics of modern policy process.

Advocacy Coalitions

A relatively new entry in the network literature is sufficiently well articulated to deserve separate treatment. The advocacy coalition framework (ACF) shares many of the insights of the policy community/subgovernment literature, but approaches networks completely differently from the work discussed above.

As Paul Sabatier (1993) describes it:

The advocacy coalition framework (ACF) has at least four basic premises: (1) that understanding the process of policy change—and the role of policy-oriented learning therein—requires a time perspective of a decade or more; (2) that the most useful way to think about policy change over such a time span is through a focus on "policy subsystems," that is, the interaction of actors from different institutions who follow and seek to influence governmental decisions in a policy area, (3) that those subsystems must include an intergovernmental dimension, that is, they must involve all levels of government (at least for domestic policy); and, (4) that public policies (or programs) can be conceptualized in the same manner as belief systems, that is, as sets of value priorities and casual assumptions about how to realize them. (p. 16)

A distinctive feature of the ACF is its emphasis on the role of ideas and values in the policy process. The ACF assumes that both policy actors and policies themselves can be understood in terms of the structure of their belief systems. These systems have three key elements. The first is the deep or normative core, which consists of fundamental axioms about human nature, justice, and priorities among values such as security, health, and love. These ideas are very difficult to change through policy arguments. The second set of ideas is the near (policy) core, and it comprises notions about the proper scope of government activity, distributions of power and authority, orientations on substantive policy conflicts, and basic choices about policy instruments. These are difficult to change, but can be altered if experience seriously differs from theory. The final set contains secondary aspects, and consists of instrumental decisions needed to implement the policy core such as decisions about administrative rules, budgetary allocations, and statutory interpretation. These are comparatively easy to shift or change, and constitute the bulk of technical policy argumentation.

Figure 6.4 illustrates the main elements of the ACF. Note that it has both a strong dynamic quality as well as a contextual dimension that places policy subsystems into the larger socioeconomic and political situation of the polity. The relatively stable parameters are system variables that change only slowly over time, but set the stage in terms of institutions as well as resources for policy actors. The external events embrace both unpredictable shocks to the subsystem, as well as the interaction effects with other subsystems. Together, these provide constraints, resources, and opportunities for the policy subsystem, which in the ACF, is dominated by a number of advocacy coalitions, "composed of people from various governmental and private organizations who share a set of normative and

Figure 6.4 **The Advocacy Coalition Framework**

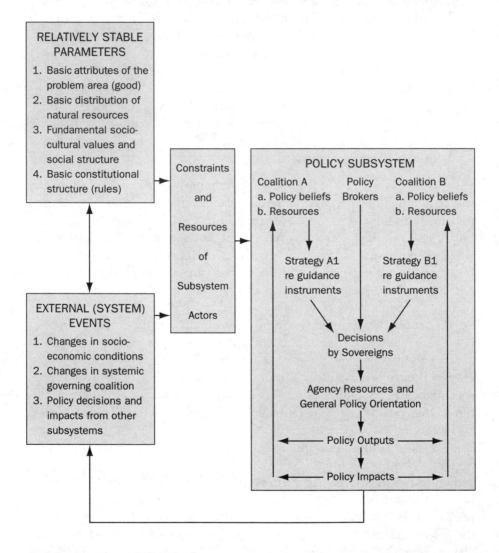

Source: Sabatier (1993, 18).

causal beliefs and who often act in concert" (Sabatier 1993, 18). These coalitions pursue competing strategies to achieve their policy objectives, a conflict which is usually mediated by policy brokers interested in compromise. At any given time, the policy sector will be dominated by a winning coalition. The framework is interested in what it calls "policy-oriented learning" or "relatively enduring alterations of thought or behavioral intentions that result from experience and are concerned with the attainment (or revision) of policy objectives" (Sabatier 1993, 19). Most change in policy subsystems occurs because of external shocks, but instrumental learning is important, especially if the goal is better public policy.

The ACF also has several distinct hypotheses about how policy subsystems operate. Among them are: (1) in any subsystem, the lineup of allies and opponents is stable over periods a decade or so, (2) there is more consensus within coalitions on core beliefs than on secondary ones, (3) government policies rarely change if the original sponsoring coalition is still in power, (4) policies for which there are quantitative data are more amenable to policy learning than areas distinguished by qualitative data, and (5) policy learning across belief systems is more likely when there exists a prestigious forum that forces professionals from all sides to participate.

The ACF is a useful framework for mapping out, in a dynamic fashion, the players, issues, and debates in a policy subsystem. Its incorporation of ideas and values, as well as the impact (usually limited) of expertise and scientific professionals, is welcome. Also, the idea of a coalition gets around the more rigid and insular conceptualization in the network literature that divides subsystems into decision-makers and attentive, but impotent, publics. Unlike the structural approach to policy networks, however, it does not provide any a priori typologies. Indeed, it is relatively weak in describing patterns of relationships either among the coalitions themselves or among brokers.

POLICY COMMUNITIES AND POLICY MANAGEMENT

The various approaches to policy networks discussed above give us the ability to map actors, understand their relationships, and possibly make some predictions about policy processes characterized by different types of networks or coalitions. But do these theories go far enough in capturing the contemporary complexities of the policy process? As we argued, the network idea itself can be seen as a response to changing political realities. If the realities continue to change, should the concept of networks be refined as well?

The Contemporary Importance of Policy Networks and Communities

It is no coincidence that the concepts related to policy communities and networks began to multiply and develop just around the time that associational systems were becoming more complex. We saw earlier that Heclo's idea of "issue networks" was explicitly designed to capture the idea of a more fluid, information-based policy system in which government departments and industry players (what Pross calls the subgovernment) were no longer entirely dominant. Khayyam Paltiel (1982) noted that the "1960s were characterized by an explosion of self-awareness among consumers, students, women and native groups and ... by Québécois nationalism and ethnic group self-consciousness. These social movements were accompanied by a bursting forth of clientelist groups, created in response to the elaboration of the welfare state during the same period" (p. 205). In the case of the United States, Jack Walker (1991) noted: "over half of the citizen groups were created in the past 25 years, in a dramatic surge of growth that has changed the nature of interest-group politics in America. Profit sector organizations have not shown such a surge in growth ..." (p. 34). While there are no reliable data on broad trends in the last decade, there is no doubt that groups continue to multiply across most sectors, though not likely at the same pace that marked the 1970s and early 1980s. Most citizens' organizations and nonprofit associations depend on sponsors of one sort or another, such as private foundations or government (Pal 1993; Walker 1991, Chapter 3), and these sources of support have been drying up or shifting their emphases. The complexity, intensity, and importance of the associational system and policy networks/communities for policy-making continues to be affected by the various factors outlined in Chapter 2, along with several others that define the new mode of governance that is emerging in Canada and elsewhere.

For one thing, the rights revolution in Canada, the United States, and to a lesser extent in Europe, continues to multiply the types of claims made against the state. In the American case, for example, Melnick (1994) traces the development of what he calls "programmatic rights" that the American judiciary has over the past twenty years discovered in federal statutes, such as the right of disabled children to free, appropriate public education. "The new understanding of rights, in contrast, has led the judiciary to enlarge public responsibilities and to increase the power of the national government" (p. 17). In the Canadian case, Cairns (1993) has remarked on the increasing diversity of interests and identities in Canada, and the difficulty for politicians of "representing, accommodating, and transcending the diversities of Canadian society" (p. 201). He also succeeds in tying this increasing diversity to the problem of representation. Groups and associations today, at least those founded on an identity as opposed to an interest, demand to represent themselves in order to have an authentic voice speaking on their behalf. This limits the capacity of the associational system to aggregate interests and streamline the consultative process.

> This difficulty reflects the convergence of three phenomenon. (1) The ethnic, social, and cultural diversity of Canadian society is increasing. (2) These diversities, based on gender, ethnicity, lifestyle, and so on are now politicized and indeed, in some cases, constitutionalized. (3) The politicized identities and group self-consciousness building on these diversities support the assertion that 'X' cannot represent 'Y,' if 'X' does not share/possess the characteristics that Y considers essential to his/her identity and as necessary for the vigorous pursuit of Y's political goals. (Cairns 1993, 201)

Globalization and increasingly sophisticated forms of communications also continue to change the nature of policy networks. With the exception of the notion of epistemic communities (see Box 6.1)—which draws explicitly on international connections among experts—most of the communities/networks and associational literature presumes a national or domestic framework. As policy issues increasingly get driven upward to the international level, and as NGOs increasingly respond by connecting to counterparts everywhere around the globe, the idea that policy networks are primarily domestic needs rethinking. Domestic human rights groups, for example, now are routinely connected to international networks. Sikkink (1993) points out that over the postwar period there was an "explosion of NGOs" in this field, as well as the "formation of coalitions and communications networks designed to link those groups together" (p. 418). It is widely acknowledged that "both the organizational structures and the communications facilities are expanding to bring together the forces of like-minded individuals and interest groups across national boundaries" (Dobell & Steenkamp 1993, 574). By one estimate, for example, in 1909 there were 176 international NGOs—defined as operating in at least three countries—whereas by 1993 there were 28 900 (Commission on Global Governance 1995, 35).

Some see the possibility of an emerging global civil society in the practices and perspectives of new social movements (Falk 1987; Walker 1988).

If true, this emergence is possible only because of communications technologies that are linked in what Deibert (1995) calls the "hypermedia environment": "a planetary 'central nervous system' composed of a web of webs of communications devices—telephones, televisions, computers, camcorders, personal digital assistants, satellites—all increasingly linked together into an integrated network of digital-electronic-telecommunications" (p. 6). Deibert argues that although "hypermedia do not generate these new social movements, they do create a communications environment in which such activities flourish dramatically" (p. 14). Stanbury and Vertinsky (1994) outline some of the potential impacts of the new communication and information technologies on interest groups:

> The new information technologies are making it less expensive for interest groups to operate. They enable organizations to seek out more easily others with similar interests and to communicate with them more often and for longer periods of time. The new technologies also make it easier to raise funds, to acquire information, monitor issues, communicate views, and mobilize constituents to a threat or opportunity for group action. (p. 91)

As an illustration of the growing importance of international networks of communications, consider the following groups drawn from the international human rights movement. Some of the groups, such as the Association for Progressive Communications and the Institute for Global Communication, weave together other sectors such as feminists and environmentalists.

1. *The Association for Progressive Communications (APC)* is one of the most important and best-known networks. It claims to have member networks in 19 countries, partner networks and local hosts in 133 countries, linking together over 28 000 individuals and organizations. Information is available through the APC, of course, but the purpose of the APC itself is to provide communications and information-sharing capacity to organizations and individuals. The Canadian partner is Web Canada, which consists of partner networks: the Environment Intern-Network, Women'sWeb, Access to Justice Network, International Development, Human Rights and Peace, Education and Youth, Social Policy and Social Services, and Faith & Justice.

2. *The Contact Directory to Nonprofits on the Web* is designed to "help people think globally and act locally," and lists thousands of organizations by region. Under International Civil Liberties Resources, it lists

twenty-two organizations, thirteen guides and directories, and a host of publications.

3. *The Global Democracy Network* is a project of the Parliamentary Human Rights Foundation that "works with Members of Parliament worldwide to protect human rights and strengthen democracy." It also lists resources, but has a section on its page with direct links to human rights home pages and human rights organizations.

4. *World Citizen Web* is dedicated to the development of a world government. The organization is linked to other organizations as well, but has its own documents and resources dedicated to its project.

5. *PeaceNet* is part of the Institute for Global Communication, which includes LaborNet and several other networks of organizations dedicated to progressive issues. PeaceNet bills itself as a resource for human rights activists to "alert the online community to abuses, and to network on issues of concern, and to make important documents and reports available." It provides a sample list of forty-seven organizations that use PeaceNet, such as Africa Watch, Amnesty International, Americas Watch (Chile), Article 19, Asia Watch, East Timor Alert Network, Human Rights Internet, Human Rights Watch, International Burma Campaign, Quaker United Nations Office, and the Body Shop.

6. *OneWorld Online* provides informational resources through its guides and its list of partner organizations, which include a cross section of organizations dealing with human rights, the environment, education, and development. Among these organizations are: Amnesty International, CARE, Charter 88, Friends of the Earth, the International Institute for Sustainable Development, the International Planned Parenthood Federation, the Open University, OXFAM, the Save the Children Fund, and UNICEF.

Along with rights, identities, and globalization, science and science-related issues are increasingly important in policy-making. The greater the scientific dimension of a policy issue, the greater the importance of scientific or specialized information and those who possess it. The concept of epistemic communities captures both the new prominence of scientific specializations and their international connections. Scientific expertise in this context means more than the physical sciences; it embraces the growing importance of such social science disciplines as economics, psychology, criminology, social welfare, and management. The burgeoning field of environmental policy depends on scientific assessments, many of which are not much more than "guesstimates," but which are crucial nonetheless for coming to terms with problems such as ozone depletion and the impact of toxic substances. The Canadian Environment Protection Act, for example, is the basis for a classification effort by Environment Canada of a large subset of over 28 000 substances in terms of their toxicity (Leiss 1996, 131; though see Toner 1996). This project cannot be completed without expertise and time! The same is true of a host of social, health, and economic problems. A knowledge-dependent policy process poses several challenges for policy-makers. One is the need to somehow balance expertise with democracy. Scientists and experts make claims and recommendations based on notions of truth, not majority wishes. This balancing act has been at the core of what Chapter 1 described as the postpositivist revolt in the policy sciences. The fear is that an overly rational policy process will be driven more by small cliques of experts than by the democratic desires and participation of the public. Another challenge for public managers is how to connect with communities of scholars and researchers who possess the specific expertise required in a policy field. As government departments are downsized, some of them may lose crucial analytical capacities, and as a consequence become more dependent on outside knowledge producers. In short, policy networks are not merely about interests, but about information and expertise that should be a foundation for policy development and implementation.

Another aspect of communities and networks that is changing in the current policy climate is their alignment with levels of government. As governments devolve more of their policy responsibilities to jurisdictions that are closer to the people or closer to the policy problem (even as they shift some responsibilities upward), policy communities change to reflect the new "core" in the subgovernment. A prime example of this change is the Canadian Health and Social Transfer, which abolished the cost-shared Canada Assistance Plan and thereby got Ottawa out of the social service sector. Previously, the social services policy community was strongly oriented to the federal level, since Ottawa not only spent money in the field but was seen to be a leader. Now, as the core responsibility shifts to the provincial level, the corresponding policy communities will fragment and focus more on local/provincial dynamics. As we noted in Chapter 4, governments are keen on devolution or "subsidiarity," the principle of lodging policy responsibilities at the lowest feasible level of government. When a shift of gravity like that occurs, policy networks tend to realign their orbits as well. Ironically, at least in some economic policy fields, this

Table 6.1 Differences Between Lobbying, Representation, and Consultation

	Lobbying	Representation	Consultation
Direction of communication	• primarily one-way, from interest groups to government	• primarily one-way, from interest groups, associations, elected politicians, and experts to government	• primarily two-way, from government to groups or clients, and from those groups and clients to government
Objective	• to change legislation or policy to suit the interests being represented	• to convey views, information, perspectives, and interests of a broader community into the policy process	• to improve service as well as support for services and policies through communication with clients and stakeholders
Government	• viewed primarily as key decision-makers, politicians, and senior officials	• viewed primarily as the political executive	• viewed primarily as the department or agency delivering services
Nongovernment	• viewed primarily as interest groups and associations representing relatively narrow or specific interests	• viewed primarily as citizens with fairly general interests and values that need to be reflected in the policy process	• viewed primarily as clients and stakeholders with respect to a specific policy or program
Examples	• industry association meetings with minister	• elections, polling, task forces, and royal commissions	• roundtables, extended workshops that involve discussion and analysis of policy issues and program design and delivery

decentralization of policy communities is linked to globalization. Take regional development policy. When national governments controlled trade policy through tariffs and other means, they could also determine regional development strategies, since they held the main policy levers. The relevant policy communities tended to be hierarchically organized and focused on the federal and provincial governments. Local and regional interests were relatively bit players. It is unclear, however, what direct role the federal government has in regional development policy in a global, free trade environment. When local actors can make their own decisions about attracting international investment or appealing to international markets, the local synergies and connections become much more important.

Finally, we also noted in Chapter 4 that governments are increasingly attracted to the idea of partnerships and framework policies. Partly this is due to lack of money, and shifting responsibilities onto third parties is a way of offloading expenses. However, the broad consensus that appears to be emerging about the limitations of governments and the virtues of setting frameworks within which private actors can pursue their interests, places greater emphasis on partnerships between the public and private/nonprofit sectors. Policy communities and networks are important today not only because they represent interests that have to be integrated into the policy process, or information that is crucial to analysis, but because they are relatively untried sinews for implementation and delivery. The concept of working partnerships for the development and delivery of services implies a very different set of relationships than is typically envisaged in the communities/networks literature. That literature focuses more on the political dynamics of interest representation, whereas the challenges of partnerships focus more on the logistics of joint action to achieve common goals.

The preceding suggests a somewhat confusing array of forces that serve to make policy communities and networks even more important than they have been in the past, but also perhaps more challenging to integrate into the policy process. The associational system shows no signs of shrinking, and some elements of it, such as those involved in the delivery of public services, may face considerable pressures to expand in the next few years. The rights revolution and salience of identity politics encourage people to expand the number of communities and networks to which they belong. Information technologies make possible even wider, global connections of interests and communities. Movements like human rights, environment, and women's issues are truly global in scope. At the same time, some policy issues get driven further down, and so some networks that would have had

Box 6.2 **PRINCIPLES FOR CONSULTATION**

1. Consultation between government and the public is intrinsic to effective public policy development and service to the public. It should be a first thought, not an afterthought.

2. Mutual respect for the legitimacy and point of view of all participants is basic to successful consultation.

3. Whenever possible, consultation should involve all parties who can contribute to, or are affected by, the outcome of consultation.

4. Some participants may not have the resources or expertise required to participate, and financial assistance or other support may be needed for their representation to be assured.

5. The initiative to consult may come from inside government or outside—it should be up to the other to respond.

6. The agenda and process of consultation should be negotiable. The issues, objectives, and constraints should be established at the outset.

7. The outcome of consultation should not be predetermined. Consultation should not be used to communicate decisions already taken.

8. A clear, mutual understanding of the purpose and expectations of all parties to the consultation is essential from the outset.

9. The skills required for effective consultation are: listening, communication, negotiating, and consensus building. Participants should be trained in these skills.

10. To be effective, consultation must be based on values of openness, honesty, trust, and transparency of purpose and process.

11. Participants in a consultation should have clear mandates. Participants should have influence over the outcome and a stake in implementing any action agreed upon.

12. All participants must have reasonable access to relevant information and commit themselves to sharing information.

---

13. Participants should have a realistic idea of how much time a consultation is likely to take and plan for this in designing the process.

14. Effective consultation is about partnership. It implies a shared responsibility and ownership of the process and the outcome.

15. Effective consultation will not always lead to agreement; however, it should lead to a better understanding of each other's positions.

16. Where consultation does lead to agreement, wherever possible, participants should hold themselves accountable for implementing the resulting recommendations.

Source: Privy Council Office (1993, Figure 4-4).

---

their centre of gravity at the national level, now become truly local or regional. Finally, the information and organizational capacities of policy communities are being viewed in a different light by policy-makers; these are resources they need, and they have to think of new ways of linkage.

We can conclude then that contemporary importance of policy networks and communities has not diminished, indeed, it has grown. However, the realities of the policy process continue to change the nature and dynamic of those communities, posing substantial challenges for policy-makers. Lindquist (1992; 1996) offers the concept of "stewardship" to capture what these challenges entail. Assuming that policy communities and networks are crucial components in the development and implementation of public policy, a core responsibility for any public manager is the improvement of learning and adaptive capacities, leading to higher levels of policy debate and relevant policy expertise. What this entails in practice depends on the type of policy community in question and its specific needs. Capacity-building for intellectual communities may mean enhancing informational resources and communication abilities. For communities involved in policy delivery, it may mean development of organizational capacity through training. Whatever it means, thinking about the policy networks and communities relevant to one's policy responsibilities is a key responsibility for the public manager in the 1990s.

Consulting and Partnering

The two big trends in policy community relations (though this term is not itself used to describe what is going on) have been public consultations and, more recently, partnerships. Both of these can be viewed cynically. Consultations can be seen as empty theatrics where interest groups rant predictably while decision-makers watch the clock, waiting for it all to be over so that they can then go and make the decisions they were going to make anyway. Partnerships can be viewed as an attempt to get out of key areas of government responsibility by shifting delivery (but not adequate financial or logistical support) over to the private/nonprofit sector. There is a strong element of truth in both of these critiques, but it captures, at best, only half of the reality. Policy-makers realize the limitations of these strategies (and sometimes manipulate those limitations to their own ends), but they also genuinely believe that consultation in policy design and partnership in policy delivery are important aspects of their jobs. They may not always like it, but they will engage. There are real puzzles in this engagement, however, challenges that have to be recognized and addressed if governance is to evolve into the next decade. With consultations, the challenge is balancing public demands with the realities of hard decisions. With partnerships, the challenge is balancing accountability with autonomy. We pick up these themes later in Chapter 8.

Consultation

The dictionary definition of consultation is simply to ask for advice or opinion, and is a subset of communication between two or more parties. Any government that purports to be democratic, one would think, is intrinsically a government that consults. The recent emphasis on consultation therefore seems a bit puzzling from this perspective. If governments have not been consulting when making and implementing policy, then what have they been doing? In fact, there is a more specific meaning to consultation in the current context, one that reflects the forces described in Chapter 2. Table 6.1 summarizes some key differences between lobbying, representation, and consultation. Almost any form of communication can be seen as a consultation, if by that term we mean only the exchange of information or views. Government polling, for example, might be seen as a form of consultation since it probes for the views of citizens on a wide variety of subjects. The same might be true of task forces, royal commissions, parliamentary committees, referendums, and even elections, all of which are often described as consultations with the public. Using the term this broadly, however, wrings out almost any of its usefulness.

Table 6.1 should make clear what distinguishes consultation from broader or different forms of communication. First, it is focused on the operational and programmatic level, as opposed to broad values or directions for policy development. One can still consult about broad values, but these should be clearly connected to specific issues and programs. The interlocutors, therefore, are the agencies responsible for program design and delivery, and direct clients or stakeholders in the relevant policy community or network. This distinguishes consultation as a policy management activity from broader forms of political representation, such as parliamentary committee hearings on a piece of legislation, for example. The objective is ongoing development and management of the policy or program in question, not the establishment of parameters for political discussion and debate.

Within this broad definition, there can still be various types of consultation being pursued. The PS2000 Task Force on Service to the Public, for example, outlined a continuum that depended on the degree of information exchange and joint participation in problem solving: (1) listening, (2) dialogue, (3) debate, (4) joint analysis, and (5) jointly agreed solutions (Privy Council Office 1993, Chapter 4). The Task Force also provided a useful list of principles for effective consultation, reproduced in Box 6.2. The list makes clear that effective consultation is actually an ongoing relationship, not a one-off exchange of views. This accurately reflects the emphasis in the policy communities/networks literature on stable patterns of interactions over time to establish clear communications and some shared language. The list also makes clear the key ingredients of successful consultation: mutual respect and trust by participants, clarity on objectives, shared decision-making about the parameters of the consultation, and adequate information resources.

It is easier to list principles than to put them into practice. Whereas consultation at all levels of government has become a sort of policy mantra, the realities and challenges are more complex. For one thing, consultations are only one stream of information and advice into the policy process, but those who are consulted naturally want to see their efforts reflected in policy outputs. As well, the openness demanded by consultation can run against the organizational grain of government. As one NGO representative put it: "*And that's one of the difficulties ... the departments operate quite secretly in many areas, and are not very quick to share their information. We have a great deal of difficulty getting information often times, and that makes it difficult to develop some of this material, to do our own work, and judge anyone else's capacity."* Consultation also has a potentially threatening side from the officials' point of view. It can become less an information and advice exercise than a festival of complaints and attacks on policy-makers. Referring to the Spicer Commission process of 1991 that was deliberately designed to elicit national critical debate about the constitution, one official said: *"I can't tell you how often I've heard 'Spicer' as an epithet—several people in a room, and the director will say 'Well, OK, as long as it's not a Spicer process."* Some officials approach this possibility more pragmatically, seeing it as an opportunity to anticipate criticisms: *"I would say a good half of our consultation is really to hear what people have to say, and the other half is to figure out where they're going to attack us so we can prepare."*

It is sometimes easy to forget how time-consuming consultation can be, especially as government gets downsized. A senior official described the challenges this way:

Frankly, we still don't have it [time needed to do analysis]. I see that as one of the biggest tensions in the policy process right now—it's like everything in the world, it's speeded up so much and everyone wants it done yesterday, but at the same time they want consultation and they want input from stakeholders or the general public, but it takes a lot of time to do that properly, without people feeling manipulated. The time dimension of it, in my judgment, is not something that we as policy advisors in government or ministers in cabinet or the government itself have really wrapped our minds around.

You can't bluff it when you're in a world where you know you are going to have to go out there and defend this ... I don't think often in the past that public servants actually were in any kind of public environment to defend or explain what they were doing. It was more behind closed doors, you had to convince your minister and then help your minister convince cabinet and help the government explain it to the world. It wasn't very often that public servants were actually put on the front line to explain themselves. I see that happening more and more, and it requires more rigour in the analysis ... There are more sorts of priors that can be taken for granted when you're working internally, because you've got a context, a political agenda, you've got a political leaning that you know that you're dealing with. There's a certain level of thoroughness that is required in having gone from A to Z and every little angle you can possibly imagine when you're dealing with a more public environment. It's harder to say "Good question, I'll get back to you." You have to have thought it all through.

There is always the suspicion that government officials are manipulating the consultative process to pursue their own agenda. Interviewees candidly admitted that this was sometimes true, but in ways that can actually help, not hinder, the policy process, reflecting to some degree Lindquist's notion of stewardship.

When I was in [department X] I used to complain about the "good governance lobby"—because it didn't exist! You're always ticking everyone off because no one is looking for good governance, everyone is looking for their narrow interest. But when I came here, I realized that these guys had already figured that out, and what they would do is create these multi-stakeholder groups, who were in effect a good governance lobby, because you'd have the [various interests] all on the same committee, and they had to agree on something. What they'd agree on is some sort of balancing of social interests. Now occasionally what they agreed on is some absurd product of compromise, occasionally what they agreed on was a good, balanced decision.

Looking at it from the narrow interest of the minister or the policy, it wouldn't be bad to have someone say you did the right thing, when you do the right thing. But who's going to say it? No one, because the right thing rarely satisfies any of the stakeholders. So what this does it gets you approval, from a group, and the reason why the group approves if you're doing a balanced thing, is because the group is balanced. It doesn't always work, and it's very painful, but in some areas it can be very, very powerful.

All of the preceding examples and comments suggest that one of the most difficult things in a partnership is reaching consensus, rather than mere compromise. As governments get more interested in partnerships, they also are forced to get more interested in tools that facilitate a different form of decision-making. A good example of this is the increasing attention being paid to formats for consensus decision-making itself, and the use of Alternative Dispute Resolution (ADR) in some policy fields. ADR has been described by one of the leading Canadian practitioners as "a process whereby all parties in a dispute can voluntarily come together to discuss the issues and develop solutions which the parties can themselves create to meet each other's interests" (Tannis 1993, 2). As the name implies, the technique is used primarily to resolve family, community, and local disputes that might otherwise end up in a highly adversarial, lengthy, and expensive legal battle. But ADR is increasingly being used in what are essentially policy-related disputes among stakeholders around environmental issues, regional planning, and broad consultations that are designed to encourage stakeholders to come up with their own policy recommendations. Indeed, perhaps the most dramatic and large-scale example of ADR is NAFTA itself, with special committees to resolve trade disputes.

ADR is a species of consensus decision-making models such as round-tables. While to the hardened policy veteran, consensus decision-making may seem to have about as much substance as cotton candy, it is grounded in some clear methodological principles (Hansen 1995). It requires a paradigm shift from adversarial, interest-based lobbying to negotiation grounded in rules the participants themselves design, shepherded by a mediator, and aimed at shared interests rather than compromises that give a little piece of something to everyone. As a recent Department of Justice document notes, increasingly, "stakeholder groups are being formed to assist government in setting public policy, determining rights, establishing corporate or government direction, and employing consensus decision-making for many programs" (Department of Justice 1996, 6). In this environment, new institutional mechanisms for generating agreement are on the policy table.

Partnerships

There is some overlap between the concept of consultation and of partnership. As Box 6.2 indicates, to consult is to consider the other party as a partner in policy development. Indeed, Kernaghan's (1993, 62–65) classification of partnerships has consultation as one end of a continuum of power sharing over decisions and implementation: (1) consultative partnerships: exchange of advice and information, (2) contributory partnerships: money or other forms of support for projects managed by a third party, (3) operational partnerships: share work together in achieving goals, but the main decisions are still made by one partner, usually government, and (4) collaborative partnerships: sharing both work and decision-making. Seidle (1995) notes that in most definitions " 'joint action,' 'power sharing' and 'mutual benefits' are essential elements of true partnerships" (p. 141). While it seems puzzling that public officials would willingly relinquish some of their autonomy, Seidle discerns a rising interest in partnerships, both with private sector entities and nonprofit, noncommercial organizations such as those in the social services sector. The reasons reflect our earlier arguments in this chapter. Government wants to save money, and partnerships can be a way of offloading services. But governments also recognize some of their own limitations in directly delivering services, and so partnerships can be a means of improving service delivery, getting better feedback, and encouraging civic engagement (Seidle 1995, 144–145).

Rodal and Wright (1994) also note that "the drive to forge partnerships in the 1990s is greater than it has ever been, and there is readiness to experiment with a variety of new types of partnerships that are more bold and complex than past arrangements" (p. 19). Lindquist (1994), however, points out that at one level, partnerships have always been a routine element of governance. What is different today is the fiscal context of restraint, as well as the multilateral nature of contemporary partnerships: "In addition to government-to-government or government-business negotiations, many partnerships now are likely to involve non-profit, community and labour groups" (p. 23). This leads to a bewildering array of types of partnerships that easily outstrip attempts at clear classification, such as Kernaghan's above.

> Partnerships may involve many combinations of participants (different governments, private sector organizations, and nonprofit and community organizations) who, in turn, may coalesce to take up simple or very complex tasks. Partnerships may involve small or large projects which can be local, regional or national in scope. Moreover, the partnership may revolve around particular aspects of project development and include developing the guiding policy framework, working out the specifics of program design, assuming responsibility for financing or program delivery, and evaluating the performance of those arrangements. Then there are the peculiarities of each policy domain, and the degree of comfort and experience of the partners working with each other in partnership arrangements. (Lindquist 1994, 23)

Despite the variety of partnership forms, work in the field has identified some salient considerations for public managers. Perhaps the preeminent one is accountability. When governments enter into partnerships, of necessity they relinquish power and control. In cases of substantial loss of control, however, the government agency is still in some measure responsible for the expenditure of public funds and for outcomes, yet those expenditures and outcomes may be determined more by the partner than by the government agency. Government organizations are used to operating in a hierarchical, top-down fashion, but partnering implies spheres of autonomy as well as coordination for the different partners. How to combine that autonomy, the prime contribution of the partnership agreement, with accountability for performance and results?

Alti Rodal (1994) has provided some additional benchmarks for thinking through the nature of partnerships. She identifies the following challenges for public managers (pp. 49–51):

1. *Heavier requirements for coordination*: With more players there is a greater need to coordinate activities both within government and between government and its partners.

2. *More extensive consultation*: This is required to ensure that stakeholders' interests are incorporated and there is consensus over objectives.

3. *Structural/organizational change:* New accountability relations probably require redesigned organizations and procedures.

4. *Human resource management*: The delegation and joint responsibility that characterize partnerships require a different, more cooperative, and sensitive management style.

5. *Communications*: Trust and clear understanding of the nature of the relationship depend on clear communications.

6. *Identification of constraints and obstacles*: Among these are government's reluctance to share power; short-term political horizons overwhelming the necessary long-term commitments; mistrust of government by other players; and culture gaps between government and the private, nonprofit, and for-profit sectors.

7. *Managing risks and maximizing benefits*: Government agencies that enter into partnerships should be aware of risks and benefits and be prepared to deal with them.

8. *Development and training*: This means fostering the right attitude and skills, many of which are not found in the traditional public sector organization which is used to a more bureaucratic, command-and-control approach.

Rodal (1994) also provides a useful framework for thinking about the "partnership cycle" (pp. 51–54). She argues that there are specific management challenges at each of the stages in the cycle: initiation, planning, implementation, monitoring, and evaluation. In the first stage of initiation, Rodal cautions that partnerships are not a panacea, and that a primary question to ask is whether collaboration in this specific field will enable partners to do together what they cannot do (or do well) alone. Are there similar levels of commitment and compatible agendas? Once a partnership is accepted in principle, the planning phase is launched: "identifying opportunities and potential partners; assessing the competence of potential partners in assuming responsibility for functions transferred to them … and assessing the potential risks to and impact on individual stakeholders, the government and the country" (p. 52). A critical issue at this stage is ensuring that the government's partners indeed have the capacity to carry through on their commitments. The implementation of a partnership involves negotiating the partnership agreement and managing the relationship. The agreement is crucial since it sets parameters for responsibilities, discretion, reporting requirements, accountability relationships, and so on. Finally, monitoring and evaluation involve an agreement among the partners on how to measure outcomes, who conducts the evaluation, designing performance indicators, as well as decisions about ongoing as opposed to wrap-up evaluation.

CONCLUSION

This chapter has examined the two sides of policy communities and networks: (1) the academic side with its emphasis on the explanation and description of patterns of associational-state linkages in policy domains, and (2) the public management approach to consultation and partnerships. The two overlap in important ways, but are also distinct. They share the insight that contemporary governance entails a substantial degree of private/nonprofit/public cooperation and interaction at every phase of the policy process, and that the quality of policy outcomes often depends on the nature of these interactions. However, the emphasis in the policy communities and networks literature has been on describing the actors and evaluating the implications of the broad character of their relationships in terms of associational and organizational cohesion. The work on consultation and especially partnerships has had a more microscopic and management orientation: how do we get these things to work at the level of a specific program or policy issue?

In keeping with the theme of this book, both streams converge on the same idea: modern policy-making cannot be directed by government, supplemented by representations from the public or interest groups. That model died years ago, as analysts and practitioners realized the importance of new social movements, public interest groups, more complex associational systems, and the strategic value of information. As we argued in this chapter, networks are, if anything, more important now than before, even as their fundamental characteristics have changed in light of globalization and other forces. Government has less money, and a more sober assessment of its own capacities. It cannot monopolize information anymore, and in many policy areas, is heavily dependent on the specialized expertise or experience of its partners. The image of a towering Leviathan has to be replaced with that of a prone Gulliver, tied with myriad strings to interests and policy sectors.

Does that mean that government is necessarily weaker? In some ways, yes. In other ways, however, it actually suggests a broadening and deepening of government influence through its leverage in policy networks and partnerships. As Rodal and Mulder (1994) suggest, a crucial question is the degree to which government remains a leader in these networks and partnerships (p. 37). Also, we sometimes forget the other powers and instruments that governments have at their disposal to encourage private/public partnerships. Gratias and Boyd (1995) highlight the ways in which government may use legislative and regulatory powers to nudge both the for-profit sector and the nonprofit sector into mutually beneficial relationships that would not have happened in the absence of that strategic intervention.

If policy communities and networks are as important to the policy process as we suspect, then policy analysis, as well as policy management, have to change considerably. Analysis has to come to terms with the fact that policy outcomes depend crucially on the actors in the community and the nature of the network. Policy management has to shift its attention to new organizational forms of public sector and private sector cooperation and interaction. Both have to come to grips with what all this means for judging performance. We turn to this question, the question of policy evaluation and its new importance, in Chapter 7.

SUMMARY

Communities and Networks: Conceptual Frameworks

- definitions of different ways of conceptualizing interests in the policy process: see Box 6.1

- a key question in discerning the character of interests in a policy field is to determine whether they are (1) directly self-interested in the outcomes of the policy decision, (2) oriented to public interest or advocacy, (3) knowledge-based, or (4) what mix of these three

- another key question in understanding the policy community is how open or closed, how fluid or stable are the coalitions of governmental and nongovernmental actors

- the change in the broad character of policy communities that we have seen in the last decade is due to changes in social and political structures—policy fields have become more complex, crowded, decentralized, and transnationalized

- while the policy literature has a slight bias toward centralized, structured policy communities and networks (it sees them as more policy capable), it is not clear that more fluid, decentralized systems might not be more appropriate for some policy fields (e.g., information technology)

- policy communities and networks alert us to the way in which policy is organized in subgovernments or subsystems, with their distinctive configurations of actors, ideas, values, and terminology

Policy Communities and Policy Management

- the importance of policy communities, and particularly NGOs, has increased in recent years: the rights revolution has encouraged new groups and new claims, and these groups are more internationalized than ever before

- consultations run a continuum from mere exchanges of views to jointly agreed solutions to policy problems

- partnerships also run a continuum from sharing information (consultative partnerships) to sharing both decision-making and delivery of programs

- a central issue in managing partnerships is accountability: where does the government's responsibility end, where does the partnering agency's begin, and how do they mesh?

REFERENCES

Almond, G. (1990). *A discipline divided: Schools and sects in political science.* Newbury Park, CA: Sage.

Atkinson, M. M., & Coleman, W. D. (1989a). *The state, business, and industrial change in Canada.* Toronto: University of Toronto Press.

Atkinson, M. M., & Coleman, W. D. (1989b). Strong states and weak states: Sectoral policy networks in advanced capitalist economies. *British Journal of Political Science, 19,* 47–67.

Atkinson, M. M., & Coleman, W. D. (1992). Policy networks, policy communities and the problems of governance. *Governance, 5*(April), 154–180.

Baumgartner, F. R. (1996). Public interest groups in France and the United States. *Governance, 9*(January), 1–22.

Berry, J. M. (1977). *Lobbying for the people: The political behavior of public interest groups.* Princeton, NJ: Princeton University Press.

Cairns, A. C. (1993). The Fragmentation of Canadian citizenship. In W. Kaplan (Ed.), *Belonging: The meaning and future of Canadian citizenship* (pp. 181–220). Montreal: McGill-Queen's University Press.

Carroll, W. K. (Ed.). (1992). *Organizing dissent.* Toronto: Garamond.

Carter, D. (1964). *Power in Washington: A critical look at today's struggle in the nation's capital.* New York: Random House.

Coleman, W. D. (1994). Banking, interest intermediation and political power. *European Journal of Political Research, 26*(July), 31–58.

Coleman, W. D., & Skogstad, G. (1990). Policy communities and policy networks: A structural approach. In W. D. Coleman & G. Skogstad (Eds.), *Organized interests and public policy* (pp. 14–33). Toronto: Copp-Clark.

Commission on Global Governance. (1995). *Our global neighbourhood: The report of the Commission on Global Governance.* Oxford, England: Oxford University Press.

Deibert, R. J. (1995). *Social forces in the hypermedia environment: Changing communications technologies and world order transformation.* Unpublished manuscript.

Department of Justice (Canada). (1996). *Justice research notes* (No. 9, April). Ottawa: Research, Statistics and Evaluation Directorate of the Department of Justice.

Dobell, R., & Steenkamp, P. (1993). Preface to the Symposium on Public Management in a Borderless Economy: National governments in a world of trans-national networks. *International Review of Administrative Sciences, 59*(December), 569–577.

Dowding, K. (1995). Model or metaphor? A critical review of the policy network approach. *Political Studies, 43,* 136–158.

Falk, R. (1987). The global promise of social movements: Explorations at the edge of time. *Alternatives, 7,* 173–196.

Fischer, F., & Forester, J. (Eds.). (1993). *The argumentative turn in policy analysis and planning.* Durham, NC: Duke University Press.

Gratias, F. X. A., & Boyd, M. (1995). Beyond government: Can the public sector meet the challenges of public-private partnering? *Optimum* (Summer), 3–14.

Haas, P. M. (1992). Introduction: Epistemic communities and international policy coordination. *International Organization, 46*(Winter), 1–35.

Hansen, J. (1995). *Table manners for round tables: A practical guide to consensus.* Summerland, BC: The Green Group/Juergen Hansen.

Heclo, H. (1978). Issue networks and the executive establishment. In A. King (Ed.), *The new American political system* (pp. 87–124). Washington, DC: American Enterprise Institute for Public Policy Research.

Heclo, H., & Wildavsky, A. (1974). *The private government of public money.* London, England: Macmillan.

Jordan, G. (1981). Iron triangles, woolly corporatism and elastic nets: Images of the policy process. *Journal of Public Policy, 1,* 95–123.

Jordan, G. (1990). Subgovernments, policy communities and networks: Refilling the old bottles? *Journal of Theoretical Politics, 2,* 319–338.

Katzenstein, P. J. (1978a). *Between power and plenty: Foreign economic policies of advanced industrial states.* Madison: University of Wisconsin Press.

Katzenstein, P. J. (1978b). Introduction: Domestic and international forces and strategies of foreign economic policy. In P. J. Katzenstein (Ed.), *Between power and plenty: Foreign economic policies of advanced industrial states* (pp. 3–22). Madison, WI: University of Wisconsin Press.

Katzenstein, P. J. (1978c). Conclusion: Domestic structures and strategies of foreign economic policy. In P. J. Katzenstein (Ed.), *Between power and plenty: Foreign economic policies of advanced industrial states* (pp. 295–336). Madison, WI: University of Wisconsin Press.

Kenis, P., & Schneider, V. (1991). Policy networks and policy analysis: Scrutinizing a new analytical toolbox. In B. Marin & R. Mayntz (Eds.), *Policy networks: Empirical evidence and theoretical considerations* (pp. 25–59). Boulder, CO: Westview Press.

Kernaghan, K. (1993). Partnership and public administration: Conceptual and practical considerations. *Canadian Public Administration, 36*(Spring), 57–76.

Klandermans, B., & Tarrow, S. (1988). Mobilization into social movements: Synthesizing European and American approaches. *International Social Movement Research, 1,* 1–38.

Leiss, W. (1990). Governance and the environment. In T. J. Courchene (Ed.), *Policy frameworks for a knowledge economy* (pp. 121–163). Kingston, ON: John Deutsch Institute for the Study of Economic Policy.

Lindquist, E. A. (1992). Public managers and policy communities: Learning to meet new challenges. *Canadian Public Administration, 35*(Summer), 127–159.

Lindquist, E. A. (1994). Taking a step back: Partnership in perspective. *Optimum, 24*(3), 22–26.

Lindquist, E. A. (1996). New agendas for research on policy communities: Policy analysis, administration, and governance. In L. Dobuzinskis, M. Howlett, & D. Laycock (Eds.), *Policy studies in Canada: The state of the art* (pp. 219–241). Toronto: University of Toronto Press.

Marin, B., & Mayntz, R. (1991). Introduction: Studying policy networks. In B. Marin & R. Mayntz (Eds.), *Policy networks: Empirical evidence and theoretical considerations* (pp. 11–23). Boulder, CO: Westview Press.

Melnick, R. S. (1994). *Between the lines: Interpreting welfare rights.* Washington, DC: The Brookings Institution.

Melucci, A. (1989). *Nomads of the present: Social movements and individual needs in contemporary society.* Philadelphia: Temple University Press.

Nagel, S. (1988). *Policy studies: Integration and evaluation.* New York: Praeger.

Nordlinger, E. A. (1981). *On the autonomy of the democratic state.* Cambridge, MA: Harvard University Press.

Offe, C. (1987). Challenging the boundaries of institutional politics. In C. S. Maier (Ed.), *Changing boundaries of the political: Essays on the evolving balance between the state and society, public and private in Europe* (pp. 63–105). Cambridge, England: Cambridge University Press.

Pal, L. A. (1992). *Public policy analysis: An introduction.* Toronto: Nelson Canada.

Pal, L. A. (1993). *Interests of state: The politics of language, multiculturalism and feminism in Canada.* Montreal: McGill-Queen's University Press.

Paltiel, K. Z. (1982). The changing environment and role of special interest groups. *Canadian Public Administration, 25,* 198–210.

Peters, B. G., & Barker, A. (Eds.). (1993). *Advising West European governments: Inquiries, expertise and public policy.* Pittsburgh: University of Pittsburgh Press.

Phillips, S. D. (1993). Of public interest groups and sceptics: A realist's reply to Professor Stanbury. *Canadian Public Administration, 36*(Winter), 606–616.

Phillips, S. D. (1994). New social movements in Canadian politics: On fighting and starting fires. In J. P. Bickerton & A. G. Gagnon (Eds.), *Canadian politics* (2nd ed.) (pp. 188–206). Peterborough, ON: Broadview Press.

Privy Council Office (Canada). (1993). *Task force report: Service to the public.* Ottawa: Minister of Supply and Services.

Pross, A. P. (1992). *Group politics and public policy* (2nd ed.). Toronto: Oxford University Press.

Pross, A. P. (1995). Pressure groups: Talking chameleons. In M. S. Whittington & G. Williams (Eds.), *Canadian politics in the 1990s* (pp. 252–275). Toronto: Nelson Canada.

Ripley, R. B., & Franklin, G. A. (1984). *Congress, the bureaucracy and public policy* (2nd ed.). Homewood, IL: Dorsey.

Rodal, A. (1994). Managing partnerships. *Optimum, 24*(3), 49–63.

Rodal, A., & Mulder, N. (1994). Partnerships, devolution and power-sharing: Issues and implications for management. *Optimum, 24*(3), 27–48.

Rodal, A., & Wright, D. (1994). A dossier on partnerships. *Optimum, 24*(3), 19–21.

Sabatier, P. A. (1993). Policy change over a decade or more. In P. A. Sabatier & H. Jenkins-Smith (Eds.), *Policy change and learning: An advocacy coalition approach* (pp. 13–39). Boulder, CO: Westview.

Sabatier, P. A., & Jenkins-Smith, H. (Eds.). (1993). *Policy change and learning: An advocacy coalition approach.* Boulder, CO: Westview.

Schmitter, P. C., & Lembruch, G. (Eds.). (1979). *Trends towards corporatist intermediation.* Beverley Hills, CA: Sage.

Schuck, P. H. (1977). Public interest groups and the policy process. *Public Administration Review, 37*(March/April), 132–140.

Seidle, F. L. (1995). *Rethinking the delivery of public services to citizens.* Montreal: The Institute for Research on Public Policy.

Sikkink, K. (1993). Human rights, principled issue-networks, and sovereignty in Latin America. *International Organization, 47*(Summer), 411–441.

Skocpol, T. (1986). Rediscovering the state: Strategies of analysis in current research. In P. B. Evans, D. Reuschemeyer, & T. Skocpol (Eds.), *Bringing the state back in* (pp. 3–37). Cambridge, England: Cambridge University Press.

Stanbury, W. T. (1993). A sceptic's guide to the claims of so-called public interest groups. *Canadian Public Administration, 36*(Winter), 580–605.

Stanbury, W. T., & Vertinsky, I. B. (1994). Information technologies and transnational interest groups: The challenge for diplomacy. *Canadian Foreign Policy, 2*(Winter), 87–99.

Tannis, E. G. (1993). *Alternate dispute resolution re HIV positive litigation and related issues: General outline of preliminary report.* Ottawa: c/o Tannis, Leclair, Reid, Solicitors and Advocates in Dispute Resolution.

Toner, G. (1996). Governance and the environment: An alternative perspective. In T. J. Courchene (Ed.), *Policy frameworks for a knowledge economy* (pp. 165–183). Kingston, ON· John Deutsch Institute for the Study of Economic Policy.

Truman, D. (1951). *The governmental process: Political interests and public opinion.* New York: Alfred A. Knopf.

Van Waarden, F. (1992). Dimensions and types of policy networks. *European Journal of Political Research, 21*, 29–52.

Walker, J. (1991). *Mobilizing interest groups in America: Patrons, professions and social movements.* Ann Arbor, MI: University of Michigan Press.

Walker, R. B. J. (1988). *One world, many worlds: Struggles for a just world peace.* Boulder, CO: Lynne Rienner Publishers.

Weaver, R. K., & Rockman, B. A. (1993). Assessing the effects of institutions. In R. K. Weaver & B. A. Rockman (Eds.), *Do institutions matter? Government capabilities in the United States and abroad* (pp. 1–41). Washington, DC: The Brookings Institution.

Wilks, S., & Wright, M. (Eds.). (1987). *Comparative government–industry relations.* Oxford, England: Clarendon Press.

Wright, M. (1988). Policy community, policy network, and comparative industrial policies. *Political Studies, 36,* 593–614.

Zald, M. N. (1987). *Social movements in an organizational society: Collected essays.* New Brunswick, NJ: Transaction.

Chapter 7   Evaluation

Consult any text on policy analysis and you will find passages extolling the indispensability of program evaluation. It could hardly be otherwise, given that program evaluation is primarily about trying to figure out how successful a policy has been, whether it met its objectives, how far it fell short, and what might be done to improve its impact. The same passages that extol evaluation, however, are usually complemented by ones that say that it is expensive, difficult, rarely conclusive, and politically unpopular. Precisely because evaluation is so potentially crucial to the fortunes of a policy or program, opponents and supporters work hard to get the evaluation results they need to strengthen their case. That is, if evaluation takes place at all. Not only is it politically sensitive (who wants to hear bad news?), it can seem secondary to the really important job of designing and implementing solutions to public problems. Policy evaluation therefore has enjoyed more theoretical than practical popularity, and in Canada at least, has not been enthusiastically supported either as a government or a third party (i.e., foundations or think tanks) activity. This is changing. The new emphasis on results, coupled with a gradual shift to special operating agencies, contracted-out services, and partnerships, increases the need for evaluation because it places new pressures on governments to be accountable. Not only does evaluation have a higher profile, but different forms of evaluation (such as client satisfaction) are becoming increasingly important. Thus, what is happening in this field directly reflects developments described in Chapters 4 to 6.

Policy analysis, defined as the disciplined application of intellect to public problems, encompasses everything from reading a newspaper to careful scientific research. In practice, much of what passes for professional policy analysis is called policy evaluation. It is conducted by governments as well as private firms, assumes a mastery of certain quantitative and qualitative techniques, and is aimed at the improvement or betterment of public policies and programs.

Its central questions are: Does this program do what it is supposed to be doing? If not, why not? What should be done? It is openly prescriptive, and serves to monitor government activities. Policies attempt to solve public problems; at some point governments (and citizens) need to know whether interventions are making a difference and are worthwhile. Since most government services are on a not-for-profit basis, there are no clear market signals (i.e., profit, loss, increase or decrease in demand) to measure performance.

Policy evaluation seems deceptively simple, but determining whether a program has its intended effect, in a world in which every effect has multiple causes, and every cause a vast stream of effects, is always difficult, if not impossible. Information is sometimes faulty or nonexistent, people uncooperative, policies vague, or measuring instruments weak. As well, evaluation is by its nature unpopular. Who wants to be told their program is a failure? Evaluation often delivers unpleasant truths, creating great temptations to shoot, or at least ignore, the messenger. However, despite these built-in limitations and liabilities, as well as a history of, at best, tepid support from most policy managers, evaluation is once again coming into its own. There are several reasons for this. First, evaluation is typically championed by the management consulting industry, since that is where a great deal of its claims to expertise lie (Saint-Martin 1996). As governments in recent years have tried to borrow more management practices from the private sector, they have also tended to import a greater profile for evaluation. Second, fiscal pressures have made it necessary to use old money for new projects, forcing evaluations of areas where policy results are relatively weak and moneys can be reallocated. A third, related reason is that many of the new techniques of governance discussed in Chapters 4–6 on design, implementation, and policy communities, demand better accountability mechanisms. That, therefore, means evaluation or assessment. When public agencies used to be largely responsible for the delivery of public programs, public managers assumed that accountability for performance was built into the organization of delivery. Once delivery and design are severed, or once policies and programs are coproduced with the private and nonprofit sectors, government is primarily either writing cheques or setting frameworks. If it is not to do this blindly, it needs to clarify what it wants out of a relationship, and how it will be monitored and measured. As Pollitt (1993) describes the U.K. case:

> the current spate of reorganizations in the public service sector appear likely further to increase the need for evaluatory skills. The

emerging panorama of this sector displays a formidable array of relatively autonomous service providers (NHS [National Health Service] trusts, grant-maintained schools, 'Next Steps' departmental agencies and many others) whose performance will require systematic monitoring and assessment. Equally important, the rapid and widespread substitution of contractual or contract-like relationships for what were previously integrated bureaucratic hierarchies implies a need for the creation of units which can perform sophisticated contract design and compliance monitoring functions—clearly a form of evaluation. (p. 353)

The 1995 OECD update on public management developments in twenty-five countries notes a similar development: "A wide range of performance-oriented initiatives has been reported in 1994 as the shift of management focus from processes to results gains momentum. Those mentioned here cover two main aspects: a drive for better reporting of performance; and increased emphasis on setting targets for service quality levels and measuring results against them" (p. 10).

This chapter has two primary objectives. The first is to introduce some of the main techniques used in evaluation research, as well as some of the benchmarks and rules of thumb for successful evaluations. This section is merely an overview of the logic of the techniques, and does not pretend to be comprehensive. The second objective is to review the history of federal government evaluation efforts in the last twenty years, and provide a sense of context about the state of evaluation in this country, and the potential for its new and enhanced status. To date, Canadian practice has restricted evaluation to more of a management tool than a real challenge to government programs. The chapter closes with a discussion of the place of evaluation both in policy analysis and in democratic governance.

TECHNIQUES

Michael Patton (1987) argues that the "practice of evaluation involves the systematic collection of information about the activities, characteristics, and outcomes of programs for use by specific people to reduce uncertainties, improve effectiveness, and make decisions with regard to what those programs are doing and affecting" (p. 15). Rossi and Freeman (1989) define evaluation as the systematic application of social research procedures for assessing the conceptualization, design, implementation, and utility of social intervention programs. In other words, evaluation researchers (evaluators) use social research methodologies to judge and improve the ways in which human services policies and programs are conducted, from the earliest stages of defining and designing programs through their development and implementation. (p. 18)

Several features of the two definitions which are broadly representative of the field should be noted. First, the definitions refer to "practice" and "application" of techniques. Second, they both identify "improvement" of public policy decision-making processes as the ultimate goal of evaluation. Third, they both highlight the "systematic" character of evaluation research. Evaluation presents itself, in short, as a scientific, systematic, empirically oriented, applied discipline or set of disciplines that analyzes current programs in order to generate intelligent information that can be used to improve those programs or the decision processes that produced them. The creative and intuitive aspect of evaluation should not be understated: Patton (1987, 98–205) lists one hundred different types of evaluation, and argues persuasively that each one demands creativity. As noted in Chapter 1, one of the most deceptively simple things about a policy is what its goals are. Before a program can be evaluated, its underlying problem definition and its goals must be understood, and so evaluators spend a good deal of time in what is usually termed the pre-evaluation phase, talking to program administrators and piecing together what people think they are doing. This is closer to cultural anthropology than regression analysis. Nonetheless, it is fair to say that of all the subfields within policy analysis, that of evaluation has remained closest to the traditional empiricist model. Evaluators are the accountants of the policy profession, and like balance sheets, their reports on effectiveness and impact can sometimes be received with glum resignation.

While these definitions appear to give evaluation a wide scope of application in policy-making, indeed to the point that it seems synonymous with policy analysis itself, a careful reading shows that evaluation is almost always linked to existing programs, either through the analysis of those programs themselves or of information relevant to them. Because of their expertise, evaluators are also often involved in generating and analyzing data that are relevant to problem definition, trend forecasting, and program design aspects such as target populations. Rossi and Freeman (1989, chap. 2) term these "diagnostic procedures" that entail, for example, the use of census data, existing social indicators such as literacy or crime rates, and surveys to determine the nature and scope of a problem. Needs assessment can be even more specific, for example, the health needs of a small rural community, and would depend on specially designed surveys and reviews of existing data. This is certainly a respectable and important component of evaluation (but as we shall see below, a fairly small part of what evaluators and policy analysts actually do), but is not its core. The core of program evaluation "includes the measurement of program performance—resource expenditures, program activities, and program outcomes—and the testing of causal assumptions linking these three elements" (Wholey 1994, 15). Figure 7.1 illustrates these three categories with some illustrative questions.

Impact

A central evaluative question is whether a policy or program makes a difference, whether it has an impact. Evaluating outcomes is critical to determining whether a program is successful or not in terms of its intended effects. Impact evaluation takes the program as the independent or causal variable, and tries to isolate its effect from other influences in the environment. This assumes that goals are clear, but sometimes they are not.

Impact evaluation tries to isolate causes and effects, but this is no easy task since any single cause or effect is (or may be seen to be) intimately bound to numerous other causes and effects. A single effect may conceivably have several causes, and the policy intervention is only one of them. Figure 7.2 provides a schematic diagram of the assumption and the problem. It helps to begin with a simple model of policy impact: here, some policy P is intended to affect some casual variable C, which will then have a desired effect on some outcome O. Note that a policy or program never has a direct influence on behaviour; it is always targeted on some factor that is assumed to influence behaviour, and by influencing that factor, in turn yields desired outcomes. Speed limits, for example, assume that accidents are in part caused by driving too fast. Accident rates are the O or outcome, while speeding is C. A program to either set lower limits or enforce them more rigorously could be two examples of interventions. But now consider the more complex model in Figure 7.2. It adds variables to the C and the O categories. Speeding itself can be regarded as a dependent variable, something caused by other factors. Speeding is affected by such things as weather conditions, road congestion, safety quality of cars, and so on. If an antispeeding campaign were found to be associated with

Figure 7.1   Core Categories of Program Evaluation

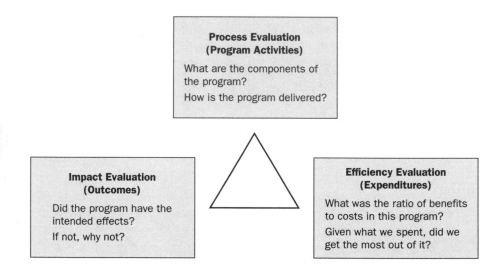

lower accident rates, would that mean that the program was successful? Not at all, since it may be that there were fewer speeders about, or that other conditions were responsible for the diminution of accident rates.

Various strategies have been developed to deal with this problem. They all rely on statistical techniques to a greater or lesser degree, and all strive to control or neutralize the extraneous causal variables that might have produced the effect. In cases where these preferred strategies are unavailable, too expensive, or time-consuming, a technique called "meta-analysis" is sometimes used. Instead of gathering new data, evaluators review the existing literature on a specific program, treating each evaluation study as a case. This "pooling" of evaluations requires a fairly large set, however, often in the hundreds, in order to be valid.

The ideal method is the classic experimental design. In this design, people are randomly assigned to one of two groups, measures are taken of target variables before the program is introduced and again afterward. The program is applied to only one group, the experimental group. The second group is the control group. If there is a sufficiently large difference in post-program scores, then the program or intervention is deemed to have caused it. The random assignment of individuals to the two groups controls for alternative explanations or causes, since the odds of being in either group are the same. In aggregate, the groups are identical in every respect except for the policy intervention (Nachmias 1979, 21–29). Experimental designs are frequently used in the educational policy field, where, for example, a new reading program might be tested on two groups of students. Pre-program reading scores for the experimental group and the control group would be gathered, the program administered, and post-program scores compared to see if they are statistically different.

Despite their statistical superiority as a measure of impact, experimental designs are rarely used in policy evaluation. They are costly and usually time consuming; decision-makers frequently want quick answers. There are also political and ethical problems with separating people into experimental and control groups. Many public programs deliver benefits to the populace, and from a political perspective it might be imprudent to deliberately withhold a benefit from some group simply to meet testing requirements. As Rossi and Freeman (1989) point out, randomized experiments can only be used with what they call "partial-coverage programs" (p. 274). Yet ethical dilemmas also arise with these, as in the controversy over withholding potentially beneficial AIDS drugs. In the medical field, for example, there are periodic debates about the efficacy of new, expensive drugs until they have been thoroughly tested. They appear to assist some patients, but do they have an appreciable impact on national health? Finally, some important policy variables cannot be disaggregated to observe differential effects on separate groups. Interest rates, the value of the dollar, and the budget deficit are examples of policy variables that apply nationally or not at all. Classic experimental designs are useless in trying to determine their impact.

In the face of these difficulties, rigorous experimental design often gives way to other, quasi-experimental forms of impact evaluation. One technique is to use time series data to establish pre-program and post-program comparisons. Another, weaker form of impact evaluation is the single observation or pre-experimental design. In this method, a program or policy is implemented, and then measurements are taken of outcomes. Assume, for example, that a government job creation program allocates $300 million for employment in depressed regions. Within a year it is found that 80 percent of program participants are regularly employed. This actually says little about the real program impact however, because the participants might have been self-selecting (i.e., only motivated individuals participated) or because the economy might have improved generally. A variation of the single observation technique is the pre-program/

Figure 7.2   Causal Model of Policy Impact

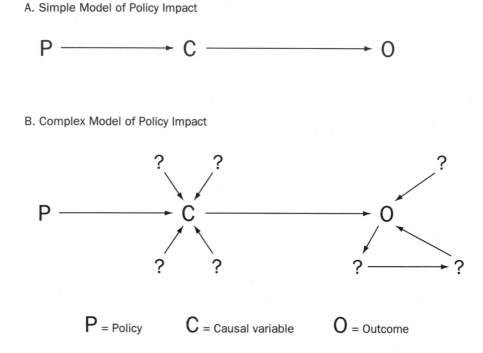

A. Simple Model of Policy Impact

B. Complex Model of Policy Impact

P = Policy   C = Causal variable   O = Outcome

post-program scheme, which does try to compare scores before and after an intervention, but only for a single group. Without a control group, it is impossible to tell whether any differences in the scores are due to the program intervention or some other cause. A final, widely used, but not very powerful, design for determining impact is contrasted groups. In this design, program recipients are compared to non-recipients, and the differences are ascribed to the program. To return to our speeding example, a 1994 study of the impact of radar cameras compared traffic patterns on a Vancouver street in which cameras had been installed with that of another street without cameras (Pedersen & McDavid 1994). Radar was determined to have made a significant difference, and while other explanations are available, these results are consistent with findings from similar studies across North America.

Process Evaluation

Process evaluation monitors an existing program to assess the effort put into it (Posvac & Carey 1980, 12). This is not the same as measuring success. As Patton (1990) puts it, process evaluation "is a focus on *how* something happens rather than on the outcomes or results obtained" (p. 94). Typically, reporting systems are developed to provide agencies with information about target populations, extent of coverage, and delivery mechanisms. Process evaluation can review program guidelines, the organization of field offices, staff training, communications systems, and even staff morale to improve organizational performance. It takes the program for granted and aims at improving the process whereby goals are met. This may sound a tad pedestrian, but is both conceptually important, and in practical terms, accounts for a great deal of what actually passes for program evaluation:

> Process evaluation is the use of empirical data to assess the delivery of programs … [P]rocess evaluation verifies what the program *is*, and whether or not it is delivered as intended to the targeted recipients and in the intended "dosage." In order to undertake process measurement, the program itself must be specified in detail. For this reason, process evaluation forces clear thinking and planning during program development—about what the program is, why it is expected to produce its results, for what types of people it may be effective, and in what circumstances. In short, process evaluation opens up the "black box" behind a program label to reveal the realities of its day-to-day program delivery. (Scheirer 1994, 40)

Process evaluation is clearly linked to implementation, and can be thought of as the evaluation of implementation procedures. This helps clarify the importance of process evaluation to program evaluation as a whole, as well as its link to impact analysis. In Chapter 5 we pointed out that the quality of implementation is quite distinct from the quality of a program—bad programs can be well implemented, and vice versa. Process evaluation is a natural complement to impact evaluation, since we need to know whether observed outcomes are the result of the program intervention as it was planned, or are due to quirks in the delivery. In other words, program design (the causal links and interventions sketched in Figure 7.2) may be fine, but the execution is flawed. If we can assure ourselves that execution is as planned, then any failures will be due to program design.

This, of course, makes it sound as though implementation and impact can be neatly severed, and they cannot. But they do represent different orientations in evaluative work.

Scheirer points out that the full description of "program components" is the foundation of process analysis, though a similar concept of "program logic" is sometimes used to sketch out the causal links for impact evaluation (Framst 1995). She defines program components as "strategies, activities, behaviors, media products, and technologies needed to deliver the program, along with a specification of the intended recipients and delivery situations" (Scheirer 1994, 45). This is tougher than it sounds, and requires extended interviews with both program administrators and clients to see what the components are and how well they are being implemented. The next trick is to determine what good or effective implementation entails. It is not directly linked to desired outcomes, which is the realm of impact evaluation. Rather, it tries to determine what the desired outcome is, and then asks what steps or mechanisms the program itself envisions in delivering the intervention to achieve that outcome. A training program for middle-aged unemployed workers, for example, assumes that better training will lead to jobs. This is questionable in many cases, but the process evaluator takes it as given. She then asks what program components go into the delivery of that training: classrooms, syllabus, materials, staff, and equipment. It should be possible to develop criteria that let us measure whether a training program is being delivered well or badly (e.g., rundown facilities, disorganization, unqualified instructors, broken equipment). If delivery quality varies, then assuming that the program is properly designed, the path to improvement is to work on better implementation. If the quality of implementation is generally high across a range of sites, but outcomes are still poor, then the problem would seem to be in program design.

As we will see in the next section of this chapter, the general field of process evaluation has grown dramatically in the last twenty years. Evaluation as a whole has become more important as governments are under pressure to be more results oriented. Impact evaluation, the analysis of results, is not easy or cheap, and there is a natural inclination to assume the design is fine, and that disappointing outcomes must be due to inadequate effort. At the same time, governments are looking more to consumer or client satisfaction as a key program outcome, and this often has more to do with delivery parameters than with the causal modelling underlying program design. Finally, management consulting firms, which do a great deal of the process evaluation demanded by government, are more adept at organizational analysis than social science techniques required for impact evaluation or efficiency evaluation. These, and other forces, have conspired in recent years to raise the profile of process analysis quite significantly.

Efficiency Evaluation

Even if the precise impact of policies could be known, this might be achieved only at exorbitant cost. Having the desired impact means a policy is effective, but if it is achieved only at great cost, it may not be efficient. Two major techniques are typically used to address this sort of concern: cost-benefit and cost-effectiveness analysis (Carley 1980, chap. 7; Rossi & Freeman 1989, chap. 7, 9; Thompson 1980; Poister 1978, chap. 11). Both techniques focus on the problem of resource allocation, since the issue of efficiency in public programs is really the issue of alternative and superior allocations of scarce resources.

Cost-Benefit Analysis

The logic of cost-benefit analysis is quite simple. The question is not only whether a policy or program has an impact, but at what cost. Policymakers want to relate costs and benefits in some way. Private businesses do this by measuring profits, though they also monitor other indicators such as productivity. Profit equals income minus expenses, both of which are calculated in monetary terms. As well, business firms measure income (or benefits) from their own perspective, not from the perspective of the consumer using a given product. Government services rarely yield revenue, and since they are services to the community, what counts as income is the benefit from the point of view of the community. The translation of these social benefits into purely monetary terms is sometimes difficult, compared to a private firm which simply bases its calculations on a market price. Thus, profit, or net benefit, is usually an inappropriate measure for most government services. The preferred measure is a ratio of benefits to cost. Table 7.1 gives a simplified example of three policy choices for which costs and benefits have been calculated. Both choices A and B have higher net benefits than choice C, but each of them is less efficient in terms of the ratio of benefits to costs. In other words, each dollar of expenditure in choice C purchases two dollars of benefits while choices A and B purchase only one dollar and fifty cents of benefits.

The table also illustrates some of the problems of program choice. Alternative C is clearly the most efficient, and would be chosen on that basis. But it also delivers the least net benefit, $1 million compared to

Table 7.1   Net Benefit and Cost-Benefit Calculations

Alternative	Benefit	Cost	Benefit Minus Cost	Benefit Divided by Cost
A	$9 000 000	$6 000 000	$3 000 000	$1.50
B	$6 000 000	$4 000 000	$2 000 000	$1.50
C	$2 000 000	$1 000 000	$1 000 000	$2.00

$3 million and $2 million for alternatives A and B respectively. One technique is to try and combine net benefit and ratio measures in some way, for example, by comparing the gain in net benefits to the loss in efficiency. The proportional loss in efficiency by moving from C to A (25 percent) is outweighed by the gain in net benefits (200 percent) so that from this perspective, A might be the preferred alternative. A is also preferred over B since, while the ratios of benefits to costs are the same, the net benefits of A are greater than those of B. These examples show that the selection of alternatives is not a mechanical process that follows easily once costs and benefits have been determined. While in the abstract it may seem easy to choose efficiency over net benefits, in the real world, decision criteria are less sharp.

It may appear that a cost-benefit ratio greater than one is self-evidently good, since there is some net gain for an investment of resources. But benefits and costs affect different categories of people, and thus may involve equity considerations, or the proportional distribution of benefits and losses equally to similar groups. Cost-benefit analysis, however, is not concerned with distributional or equity issues; it relies on a social welfare criterion known as Pareto optimality. This criterion states that a change is worthwhile if at least one person is made better off while no one else is worse off. It is not the same as an increase in total benefits, if that increase depends on someone else's loss. For example, consider a string of ten rural homes, nine of which have barely adequate road access and the tenth none at all. A tax levy on all ten homes to build a new road connecting them could possibly be Pareto optimal, as long as the benefits of improved access for the nine homes equalled the levy. The tenth home would of course be much better off. In this example, everyone is at least as well off as before, and one person may be much better off. Few policy decisions are this clear. The limitations of the Pareto criterion led economists to develop another, more flexible one: the Kaldor-Hicks criterion which identifies potential Pareto improvements as those which, assuming that net gainers could compensate losers, would leave at least one person better off without anyone else worse off. The redistribution is hypothetical, and so in effect the Kaldor-Hicks version of Pareto optimality is a criterion of net benefits. Potential Pareto improvements, it is argued, will increase total societal benefits (for both winners and losers) over time.

Practising evaluators normally leave these arcane matters of social welfare functions to academic economists. From a practical perspective, the tough issues in cost-benefit analysis are the determination and quantification of costs and benefits. Two such general problems are the selection of the accounting unit and the issue of intangibles. The accounting unit problem is about whose costs and benefits are to be measured. Three basic choices are the individual, the government, and society. Consider an employment agency decision on whether to provide counselling services to its clients. One way of assessing costs and benefits is to focus on the individual program participants: costs might include less time for leisure or job search, while benefits might be increased job skills. From the governmental or agency perspective, costs would be the budgetary ones of mounting the program, while benefits might be increased hiring rates and tax revenues as former clients get jobs. The societal perspective is the most comprehensive, weighing costs and benefits for total national income. Benefits, for instance, might include the value to the national economy of the jobs that clients get. The estimates of benefits and costs will differ depending on the accounting unit chosen.

The problem of intangibles concerns the difficulty of placing monetary values on some costs and benefits. Aesthetic considerations in town planning, the value people place on leisure, the sense of security provided by universal health care: all are presumably important in determining costs and benefits, but are difficult to quantify. It is arguable that cost-benefit analyses of public programs tend to estimate costs (program or budget costs) more accurately than benefits, many of which are intangible. Educational policy evaluation, for example, has trouble measuring such benefits as civility and cultural breadth, and tends by default to concentrate on job-related benefits. Cost-benefit calculations usually avoid quantifying intangibles, preferring instead to simply mention them as considerations. A related issue is that even if costs and benefits can be monetized, not all of them have an equal chance of occurring. Evaluations thus sometimes attach probabilities to costs and benefits.

The careful classification and treatment of different types of costs is the first step in competent cost-benefit analysis. One important category is opportunity cost, or the foregone benefits of doing one thing and not another. Assuming scarce resources, doing one thing always means foregoing something else. Cost-benefit analysis, insofar as it tries to facilitate comparisons across alternatives, tries to address the issue of opportunity cost. Other common distinctions are made in determining costs. External versus internal costs and benefits refer to indirect or unintended spillovers from a program. For example, polluting industries sometimes create jobs at home (internal benefit) while generating environmental costs elsewhere (external costs). Incremental versus sunk costs is another important distinction. Sunk costs are those incurred in the past; incremental costs are additional or future costs expended to mount or continue a program. A final distinction is between total and marginal costs. The total costs of a new counselling program for unwed mothers, for example, would include the proportion of total costs of the agency (e.g., clerical services, furniture, building, heat, light, etc.) accounted for by the program. But since these costs would occur anyway, the marginal cost of the program would be the additional resources devoted to it.

Costs and benefits usually do not occur immediately, and each may flow in different streams. In the case of capital projects or pensions, it may take many years before benefits are realized. This raises a problem of measurement, since most people prefer their benefits to come now and their costs to come later. The element of time therefore has to be assessed in estimates of future costs and benefits. The usual procedure is to apply a discount rate to the present value of costs and benefits incurred in a project. The trick is in selecting an appropriate rate. The predominant method assesses the opportunity costs of capital, meaning the rate of return if program sums were invested in the private sector. If the economy were uncluttered by monopolies or by taxation regimes which alter pretax rates of return and restrictive foreign trade, then market rate of interest could be taken as the discount rate. Because rates of return are affected by these institutional features, economists make numerous and contentious adjustments to arrive at estimates of the real discount rate.

Cost-Effectiveness Analysis
Cost-effectiveness analysis is closely related to cost-benefit analysis, and shares many of its concepts. It is a somewhat simpler and more limited technique, but one which acknowledges the shortcomings of cost-benefit approaches. Cost-effectiveness analysis restricts itself to comparing differ-

ent program alternatives for achieving a given set of goals. It thus differs from cost-benefit analysis, which purports to compare programs with different goals in terms of a common denominator of benefits. Cost-effectiveness analysis refrains from efforts to monetize benefits. It simply takes program goals as given, and then assesses different strategies for achieving those goals. It assumes that the least-cost strategy is the preferred alternative. Cost-effectiveness techniques can also be applied in reverse by assuming a fixed budget and choosing alternatives which provide the highest rate of goal achievement—the "biggest bang for the buck."

Typical cost-effectiveness analysis relates the monetized costs of a program to a nonmonetized measure of effects. A fisheries department, for example, may want to increase the fish stock in a lake by 30 percent over five years, or by 100 000 fish. It can choose between restricting fishing licences and stocking the lake. Restricting licences would require greater surveillance expenditures in the amount of $30 000 per year, while restocking the lake might incur a one-time expenditure of $100 000. Over five years, the first alternative yields a cost-effectiveness ratio of $1.50 per fish, while the second costs $1.00 per fish. It would appear that the second alternative would be more efficient or cost-effective.

Cost-effectiveness analysis poses the same problems as cost-benefit analysis. Which costs to consider? In the fisheries case, only departmental costs were counted, but the first alternative should also include foregone fishing by those excluded from licences. Defining the different types of costs and their relationship would also be necessary, as would discounting for the project over the implementation period. But cost-effectiveness analysis makes no judgments of relative benefits; it passes these considerations on to decision-makers who apply other criteria. A cost-effectiveness analysis may help determine the cheapest way to build a fighter jet, but is incapable of showing whether other uses of those funds would be of greater benefit to society.

POLICY EVALUATION IN CANADA

The tone of the first part of this chapter certainly conveys the impression that program evaluation is an essential part of any reasonable approach to policy-making: how could we presume to make policies and programs, trying to solve policy problems, if we had no idea of impact or efficiency? As odd as it may sound, however, evaluation as it is currently understood and practised is a relatively recent development in governance. Its first golden age was in the 1970s, after which it went into slight decline, though another golden (or at least, silver) age may be dawning. This relatively late start, however, coincides with the rise of the policy analysis movement itself. Both, as Chapter 1 showed, were postwar phenomena associated with the rise of more activist government, particularly in the 1960s. Program evaluation, for example, depends on the application of social science tools that themselves were only developed in this period. More subtly, program evaluation depends on viewing what government does in program terms. We do that now, because after a quarter century of public policy development and the assumption that governments have a wide horizon of responsibilities to deal with social problems, we simply take it for granted that government activity can be understood in terms of numerous clusters of programs, which, after all, are interventions to solve social issues. There was a time when the scope of government was considerably narrower, and its activities could be understood more simply in terms of concrete activities like building roads or bridges, or providing relatively uncomplicated services like education. If everyone gets the same basic education, and the presumption is that the content of that education should adhere to well-established guidelines (e.g., the three Rs, the literary canon), then there is not much point in talking about programs. The type of policy evaluation that goes on within this framework is typically a financial audit, to ensure that moneys are spent appropriately. When, however, the different needs of different students (e.g., recent immigrants, the disabled, the gifted, girls, boys, adults, the illiterate) have to be addressed, and when different educational goals are targeted (e.g., occupational, academic, life skills), then suddenly what once passed as simply education now needs to be understood in terms of programs. The type of evaluation that goes on in this context shifts from financial audits to program evaluation of outcomes and efficiency.

As Sutherland (1990) points out, the term "program" first came into "formal use in the Canadian federal government's estimates of expenditure only after 1971" (p. 140). Previously, a program "could be anything from the whole effort and apparatus of unemployment insurance to a regrouping of activities to realize a short-term special project" (p. 140). The change was due to the introduction and implementation of the planning-programming-budgeting system (PPBS), pioneered in the United States (and ironically, abandoned the same year that the Canadian federal government succeeded in applying it across all departments and in the expenditure budget process). PPBS was foreshadowed in 1969 with the

Treasury Board's release of its PPBS Guide (Government of Canada 1969). The idea was that PPBS would be gradually introduced into the Canadian budgetary process, eventually encouraging all departments to state their activities in programmatic terms, that is, in terms of goals and objectives, specific costs associated with programs designed to achieve those goals, and resources devoted to each program. Ideally, this would permit comparisons across all government agencies of related goals and their related programs. Moreover, the 1969 Guide presumed that once goals and associated programs and resources were identified, then the work of evaluation (principally cost-benefit) could go forward almost automatically. Again, to quote Sutherland (1990): "It was thought that both alternative ways of delivering the same program and different programs could be compared with one another in productivity terms—output per input unit. Analysts would be able to compare strategies for reaching given goals within a given program, but also to compare programs/goals with one another in terms of their expensiveness" (p. 143).

As Savoie (1990) notes, at the time, PPBS was thought by most practitioners and observers to hold "great promise, and few dissident voices were heard" (p. 57). Some provincial governments swiftly followed suit, most notably New Brunswick, which introduced PPBS in 1970. However, by the mid-1970s, the bloom was off the PPBS rose. Some of the wilting had to do with the failure of PPBS to help manage expenditures. In the Canadian context, PPBS had been introduced as part of the budget system, on the assumption that rigorous analysis and comparison of objectives and programs would automatically generate information that would clarify planning as well as facilitate reallocations of resources to more efficient and effective programs. That did not happen, in part because the logic of PPBS was entangled with another agenda at the time to reduce central agency control over departments. Given that PPBS did not produce a lot of good analysis, the result was less overview and more spending (Savoie 1990, 60–61). The second problem was that, even with substantially new resources being devoted to analysis, evaluation, and consulting, the results of cost-benefit and performance analysis "could generate only a drop in the ocean of analysis that would be required if every identified purpose-oriented spending entity was to be tracked" (Sutherland 1990, 144).

There were two responses to this. The first was from the Treasury Board, and consisted of an odd blend of both extending and limiting the scope of program evaluation. In 1977 it issued Treasury Board Policy Circular 1977-47, which reiterated, but actually for the first time formally stated, the requirement that all federal government programs periodically undergo an evaluation (Leclerc 1992, 51). The 1977 circular was followed in 1981 with a formal guide to evaluation that remained in place for a decade (Treasury Board of Canada, Office of the Comptroller General 1981). However, whereas the earlier PPBS framework had implicitly assumed that evaluations would take place automatically, rely principally on cost-benefit analysis, and generate comparative information across programs, the new policy left the evaluation cycle (three to five years) and the selection of programs to be reviewed up to administrators; it did not recommend any specific form of evaluation, and eschewed comparison (Sutherland 1990, 144–145). Thus, with a kind of logic that would delight Lewis Carroll, program evaluation became both universally mandated for all federal government programs over time, and yet was left up to the discretion of departmental managers as to targets and techniques of evaluation. We will come to some assessments of the scope and impact of program evaluation in the federal government as a result of these policies, but it should be clear that the context had been set for ad hoc, politically inspired and relatively insipid evaluation. Evaluation as it came to be understood and institutionalized in Canada evolved into a "strategic management tool for departments and agencies" (Segsworth 1992, 305). Program evaluation sunk into the soft folds of the bureaucratic underbelly, and became an information source for managers to improve programs rather than a real tool of accountability and comparison. In itself, there is nothing objectionable to the use of program evaluation for management purposes, but its almost exclusive dedication to this end falls far short of its potential.

The second response to the failure of PPBS came from the Auditor General of Canada. J.J. Macdonnell was appointed Auditor General in 1973, and began to press for the establishment of a comptroller general for the government of Canada. (A position by that name had existed previously but had been abolished in the mid-1960s.) Macdonnell was a private sector accountant, and wanted to establish private sector accounting practices in the government (Saint-Martin 1996, chap. 4). He tried to persuade senior cabinet ministers of the idea, but they balked at the duplication of existing Treasury Board functions. Macdonnell then dropped a verbal bomb in his 1976 report when he stated that "I am deeply concerned that Parliament—and indeed the Government—has lost, or is close to losing, effective control of the public purse" (Auditor General of Canada 1976, 9). The media seized on this, and the government was forced to announce a Royal Commission on Financial Management and Accountability as well as negotiate with Macdonnell on the establishment of the Office of Comptroller General. The office was indeed established, with "full responsibility for the coordination of evaluation planning, for policy guidance, and for assessing the quality of evaluation findings in studies carried out by departments" (Savoie 1990, 114). However, it was more a political sop than an indication of commitment to evaluation. Nonetheless, it happened that "program evaluation did indeed develop into a growth industry and that it grew around the Office of the Comptroller General" (Savoie 1990, 114). The special link through program evaluation was thus established between the Comptroller General, the Auditor General, and departments. The Comptroller General provides guidelines and advice on evaluation, but evaluations themselves are conducted by departments. The Auditor General cannot independently conduct evaluations, but reports on the success or failure of evaluation across the government.

The 1981 evaluation guide was updated and altered in 1991 as a result of a policy shift to reflect the logic of PS2000. This change, and the 1994 amendment discussed below, both illustrate the degree to which evaluation is a reflection of the institutional and policy environment, and not simply a bundle of techniques that can be generically applied. The key change was a new emphasis on evaluations that would focus on quality of service to the public. In a document entitled *Into the 90s: Government Program Evaluation Perspectives*, the Comptroller General explained the new approach:

PS2000 is about reorienting the Public Service. One of the reforms it calls for is the restoration of the preeminence of service to the public when carrying out the functions of government. Establishing a consultative, client-centred corporate culture requires research, and program evaluation offers a unique range of skills and experience to improve the delivery and cost-effectiveness of programs. A sample of recent evaluations shows that a variety of service issues were addressed and that some of them led to better quality of service to the public.

But, program evaluation offers more than just balanced, analytic methods and a digest of lessons learned. Many evaluators employ client-based consultations to carry out and market their studies. With a little broadening and some deepening of the stakeholder base, this approach could become an effective conduit for program managers not only to assess the quality of their service to the public but also to create a receptive environment for change. (Treasury Board of Canada, Office of the Comptroller General 1991, 1–2)

What did this new evaluation industry achieve between 1977 and the early 1990s? First, the quantity of evaluations began to rise dramatically. In 1980 there were only seven program evaluations in the government of Canada that met the definition in the guidelines. By 1984–85, thirty-seven federal departments were conducting them and there were over one hundred studies (Savoie 1990, 114). The annual number of evaluations has settled around that level. The Auditor General reported that in 1991–92 there were eighty evaluations conducted across the federal government, compared with ninety-nine in 1987–88 (Auditor General of Canada 1993, 247). The Auditor General conducted wide-ranging reviews of the evaluation function in the federal government in his annual reports in 1983 and 1986, and was generally critical of their quality. The 1993 report, based on data from forty-two program evaluation units, noted that both the annual number of evaluations and the resources devoted to them were in decline (p. 244–245). Examining a sample of these, the report noted that "in only about half of the programs did evaluation deal with program relevance and cost-effectiveness" (p. 230).

> Evaluation managers attached the greatest importance to helping management resolve operational issues and improve programs. They placed a much lower priority on the role of evaluation in challenging existing programs to support resource allocation decisions, and on evaluating large program units to support accountability to Parliament. (p. 245)

Hollander and Prince (1993) note the importance of distinguishing between organizational labels and analytical functions, since "evaluators may conduct classical evaluation activities, but may also engage in a variety of other activities" (p. 203). Policy units in federal and provincial governments, for example, include among their functional activities: policy development, program design, program evaluation, policy firefighting, coordination and liaison, socioeconomic research and forecasting, external scanning of the environment, needs assessment, legislation, executive assistant support, and policy advice (Hollander & Prince 1993, Table 2, p. 205).

What of the impact of evaluation studies? The evidence is mixed. Certainly, the Auditor General has consistently crabbed about the low quality and general ineffectiveness of program evaluation. However, some other studies suggest that evaluations do have an impact. In a study of two hundred evaluations conducted between 1983 and 1989, it was found that almost half (45 percent) led to operational improvements in programs, with the next largest category (26 percent) used to "improve understanding of program cost-effectiveness and to improve monitoring" (cited in Leclerc 1992, 52). While many studies (16 percent) influenced program redesign or implementation, only about 4 percent had no impact. Segsworth (1992) concurs that there has been an impact, but that it has been limited more to program operations rather than live-or-die decisions about program continuity: "Evaluation research is utilized in Canada. The policy suggests that the primary users would be senior managers in departments and the Executive Branch. This has happened. It is also true that Parliament has not used evaluation studies to any great extent over the past 15 years since the policy on program evaluation was introduced" (p. 308). Savoie (1990), on the other hand, noted that there "are few supporters in Ottawa of program evaluations" (p. 114) and that "one would be hard pressed to point to even a handful of programs that have been reduced or eliminated as a result of an evaluation study" (p. 115).

If this indeed were the end of the story, then we might conclude that evaluation in the government of Canada plays a relatively minor role in operations and review, with periodic harping from the Auditor General to maximize the potential of program evaluation for policy decision-making. However, events over the last three years suggest that evaluation, or at least policy reflection of a more fundamental sort, is beginning to enjoy greater prominence. We have outlined the key changes in the 1995 budget and the Program Review in previous chapters, and here need only bring out two key points: (1) budgets have to be seriously cut, and Ottawa and all other jurisdictions have grappled with this reality, (2) decisions have to be made about what to continue and what to terminate. Politics will always come into this process, of course, but the Program Review and equivalent exercises at the provincial and municipal level have been remarkable less for the routine and expected political manoeuvring that has gone on, as for the injection of evaluative questions (i.e., What are the benefits relative to costs? What are the results? Can we improve service?) into the debates.

This happened almost immediately after the submission of the Auditor General's typically glum assessment of the scope and impact of evaluation in 1993. The Public Accounts Committee of Parliament reviewed the Auditor General's recommendations on program evaluation during hearings in late 1994, and submitted its report in November of that year broadly supporting the Auditor General's approach. A few months earlier the Treasury Board released its new policy framework for review, internal audit, and evaluation. The 1994 framework superseded the 1991 document, which itself had been designed to reflect the new goals of service to the public trumpeted by PS2000. By 1994, PS2000 had been submerged in a broader agenda of Program Review, and the new guidelines aimed to integrate the evaluation function with this new agenda. One of the most important features of the new framework is that it is a framework. It brings together guidelines for program review, internal audit, as well as evaluation under one roof. Program Review goals set the parameters for the other functions, all of which are to be harnessed to "support the principles of managing by results" (Treasury Board of Canada 1994, 1-1-2). Another key feature is the attempt to integrate the evaluative function more closely with management. In characteristic Canadian fashion, evaluation still remains a management tool, but whereas it has tended to be marginalized in the bureaucratic structure, the new Treasury Board policy urges a "productive alliance between managers and review professionals that will link review more visibly to management decision-making and innovation, as well as accountability" (Treasury Board of Canada 1994, 1-1-2). Given the government-wide scope of Program Review, the policy gives somewhat enhanced power to the Treasury Board itself to initiate some evaluations and reviews, and to serve as a central point of inspiration in the review process.

The ways in which the forces discussed in Chapter 1 have changed the context for review and evaluation can be gleaned by looking closely at the new rationales for these activities in the 1994 policy statement. The statement on review policy stresses results, and links the importance of results to deficit control:

> The main reason for conducting reviews is to find out whether policies, programs and operations are working well. Results achieved are a fundamental aspect of the performance of government policies, programs and operations. The need for credible information on results is greater than ever. The fiscal burden carried by Canadian taxpayers, pressures to control and reduce the cost of government programs and operations, and management reform within the Public Service are all factors that make it essential to have information on results. Among other benefits, having this information enables the government to provide Canadians feedback on the value obtained with their tax dollars. (Treasury Board of Canada 1994, 1-2-2)

The complementary statement on evaluation (which the manual is careful to link to the policy on review) highlights performance, service, clients, and decentralization—all shibboleths of the new thinking on management:

> Evaluation is seen as focusing on what is really working, what isn't and on finding innovative ways of achieving government goals more cost effectively. It is also seen as providing value-added support to policy and line managers on matters such as performance frameworks and monitoring, establishing client-oriented service standards, accountability reporting, rethinking regulatory activities and emerging issues, such as the performance and accountability aspects of managing decentralized programs and those delivered by organizations outside the government. Finally, evaluation is seen as promoting organizational learning within government, for example, by communicating benchmarks for using and managing policy instruments and program delivery mechanisms. (Treasury Board of Canada 1994, 3-1-2)

In November 1995, the President of the Treasury Board submitted his annual report to Parliament entitled *Strengthening Government Review*. Art Eggleton noted that:

> To deliver better programs and services, the federal Public Service must move from a culture of rules and processes to one that also focuses on innovation and results. Changing how people think and how they carry out their work is a long term process. But we cannot improve the way government works unless we have a good idea of how well it is performing now. Knowing what works and what does not requires credible information on performance. Strong review, focusing on serving Canadians, helps ensure programs meet their objectives and are responsive to the people they serve. I see review as a set of methods for finding answers to crucial questions, such as how well are we doing and could we do better? Of course we have to use the right method for the right job. We have to train our managers to use results information, but we also have to put in place the right incentives for continuous learning. This is where strong review and our quality services initiatives set a course for positive change. (Treasury Board of Canada 1995a)

The report included an update on reviews that had been conducted in the past year connected to the Program Review, budget cuts, and reordering of government policy priorities. It paints a picture of substantial activity. Box 7.1, for example, lists major policy reviews that were undertaken between 1993 and 1995. Between 1991 and 1995, it was reported that slightly over three-quarters of departments had reviewed their programs in a "significant" way. "Since 1992 virtually all federal regulations have been reviewed. By June 1995, more than 150 regulations had been revoked and 170 revised. By the end of 1996, 100 more regulations are expected to be revoked, and significant revisions are expected to be made to an additional 200" (Treasury Board of Canada 1995a). In the same time period, there had been over 600 reviews of administrative, financial, and management policies.

The 1996 annual report of the Auditor General, while noting that the context for evaluation in the federal government had changed quite dramatically in three years since its last review of evaluation, still found the government's efforts wanting (Auditor General of Canada 1996, Chapter 3). In examining four departments in detail, the Auditor General found that evaluations still focused on smaller operational details of greater interest to administrators than to Parliament or the public. While Program Review posed certain fundamental questions about program rationale and cost-effectiveness, the report argued that these questions had not figured in the evaluations undertaken by the departments. However, large programs (defined as expenditures over $1 billion) had been subject to more scrutiny than before. On balance, there had been some improvements, but the Auditor's conclusions were still mixed.

> The need for good information on the effectiveness of programs remains strong. At the same time, the government continues to commit resources to evaluation, particularly in the larger departments. We noted in our audit that a changed, and still changing, environment for planning and conducting evaluations creates challenges for many departments. Evaluations have had to be planned and conducted in an environment dominated by reorganizing, restructuring and downsizing of government programs. Changes to departments and programs involve changes to the structure for evaluation. At the same time, Treasury Board policies governing evaluation and related work have changed. They now include sources of effectiveness information other than the work of evaluation units, but do not make clear the quality standards that apply to effectiveness measurement and analysis conducted as part of reviews other than evaluations.

Box 7.1   MAJOR POLICY REVIEWS 1993–1995, FEDERAL GOVERNMENT

Review	Processes
Social Security Reform	• Parliamentary Committee and Advisory Panel hearings
National Forum on Health	• panel of 24 Canadians doing research and consultations
Preparing for an Aging Population	• Finance and Human Resources departmental papers
Clarifying Federal-Provincial Roles	• with provinces
Small Business Policy	• report from Finance and Industry departments with business representation on two committees
Science & Technology	• Industry departmental discussion paper
Goods and Services Tax	• Parliamentary Committee
Transportation Policy	• departmental study
Sustainable Development	• Finance and Environment departments on task force
Defence	• Parliamentary Subcommittee report; departmental response
Foreign Policy and International Development Assistance	• Parliamentary Committee; hearings; departmental response
$500 000 capital gains exemption	• Department of Finance task force
Taxation of Family Trusts	• Parliamentary Committee; report

Tariff Simplification	• Department of Finance review task force
Special Import Measures Act	• Department of Finance review
Efficiency Review	• government-union joint studies
Infrastructure Works (Framework)	• multidepartment committee
Atlantic Groundfish Strategy (Framework)	• Treasury Board Secretariat advice to responsible departments
Program Review	• Cabinet review of departmental action plans

Source: Treasury Board of Canada 1995a.

In this context of change and uncertainty, some of the improvements we recommended in 1993 to key systems and procedures for managing evaluation in departments and agencies are not yet in place. We still see weaknesses in planning, in monitoring action in response to the findings of evaluation studies, and in implementing systematic approaches to assessing the performance of evaluation units. In audits carried out by this Office over the past three years, we have continued to find problems with the scope and quality of evaluations. (Auditor General of Canada 1996, Chapter 3)

CONCLUSION

Program evaluation has always enjoyed support, in principle, from policy-makers. The logic of policy analysis, as described in Chapter 1, emphasizes careful definition of policy problems, consideration of options, and interventions that lead to amelioration or improvement. Policy as intervention depends on some idea of causal connections. In this sense, every policy or program is a guess, a hypothesis about social problems. Evaluation serves the vital function of providing empirical feedback on those hypotheses in action: did they work, what impact did the intervention have, at what cost? It is for this reason that public policy theory urges the integration of policy evaluation into every stage of the policy process; since evaluation in a sense is the collective memory of what worked and what did not, integration of that information can save errors and effort.

But just as evaluation has been granted this pivotal role in theory, in practice it has been viewed sceptically and often marginalized in the policy process. The reasons are not hard to understand. Even the strongest partisans of evaluation acknowledge the often severe methodological limitations of answering impact and efficiency questions. More art than science, it is always possible to find reasons why positive or negative evaluation results are flawed. These very limitations, as well as the sheer expense of doing thorough evaluations, have usually limited evaluation to routine monitoring or process studies. Also, as we noted, there is the paradox that while evaluation seems essential in theory, in practice it can appear to be a frill when compared to direct program responsibilities and delivery. Thus, evaluation has been the poor cousin of the policy process, often relegated to small policy shops divorced from direct policy management responsibilities. "By the early 1980s analytical units were reported to be in decline. Few new units were being established and existing units had declined in organizational influence and importance" (Hollander & Prince 1993, 196). Insofar as evaluation tends to be the dismal science of policy analysis—showing that impacts are weak or dubious, and often much more expensive than first anticipated—nobody really appreciates the bad news.

To these generic reasons for the limited impact of evaluation should be added some specific Canadian twists. First, as we noted in the brief history of the Office of Comptroller General, the establishment of evaluation guidelines and institutions in the Canadian federal government in the early 1980s was done partly to placate the Auditor General, and was implemented without much enthusiasm. Second, the Canadian practice, and this is true of the provincial level of government as well, has been to use evaluation as a management tool. Evaluation units have been embedded in departments, and departmental managers have been responsible for the evaluation function, governed by loose central agency guidelines. This contrasts with the United States, where congressional committees aggressively sponsor evaluation of programs within their policy fields as a challenge to the executive, and where independent think tanks and policy groups abound. Though the number of Canadian think tanks grew in the early 1970s and again in a second wave in the late 1970s and 1980s (Lindquist 1993, 548), there are less than ten major nongovernmental, noncommercial policy institutes (e.g., C.D. Howe Research Institute,

Canada West Foundation, Conference Board of Canada, Canadian Tax Foundation, Fraser Institute, Institute for Research on Public Policy, Canadian Institute for Economic Policy, and Canadian Energy Research Institute). No one has done a careful analysis of university-based centres and institutes, but given that there are about sixty degree-granting institutions in Canada, and each will have at least two or three such entities, there are likely to be around 200 university-based centres. The judgment of the work done by major think tanks has not been kind. Tupper (1993), in a review of the fiscal analyses of two Canadian think tanks (C.D. Howe Research Institute and the Canadian Centre for Policy Alternatives), concludes that they "have commissioned little theoretical, comparative, or impressive interdisciplinary work. Governance issues, which are at the heart of the debate, are not systematically or rigorously examined. The value of their policy prescriptions is undermined by their flimsy research base and their overtly political character" (p. 545). Lindquist (1993) concurs: "My research indicates that institute studies are often of limited use to policy-makers and are more geared to educating the attentive public, while aiming to move certain issues higher or lower on the agenda ... Ideology aside, producing truly innovative work does not constitute the central mission or core values of institutes" (p. 575).

Canadian parliamentary committees have shown scant interest in evaluation studies. Evaluation reports are usually kept within departments as part of their policy development process, and public inquiries about particular studies are usually discouraged by claiming that these studies are sensitive or secret. Public debate about evaluation results of policies or programs is rarely stimulated by the media, and Canada lacks serious, wide-circulation media, such as *The Atlantic Monthly*, which act as vehicles for debating and evaluating public policy issues.

Despite this gloomy assessment of evaluation and its potential to influence policy-making, this chapter has shown that evaluation may be enjoying a renaissance of sorts. The pressures are contradictory. As the Auditor General remarked, and this is undoubtedly true for most other jurisdictions in the country, downsizing has seriously affected the evaluation function. Most evaluation shops were small to begin with, and personnel cuts can have a dramatic impact. One interviewee noted:

> *Clearly, the big change is the privatization of the policy analysis/policy development capacity, not just in the federal government but also in the provinces. I mean the downsizing of the policy shops in government and the growth of private sector public policy agencies and consultants who provide services to government. What you'll see quite frequently*

is basically what was once a policy shop is now basically a contract management group. And that's worrisome because you don't know how the people at the other end judge your product, and in a sense I think it leads to a fragmentation, at least a fragmentation in terms of policy-making because you can't be systematic and you can't have a corporate ethos running through a policy shop when you're working that way.

On the other hand, these same fiscal pressures are associated with a more serious regard for results. In a sense, governments have been talking about fiscal reductions, greater efficiency, and greater policy effectiveness for years, but since the mid-1990s have begun to match actions to their rhetoric. The result is that while evaluation in the narrow, technical sense described in the first section of this chapter may not be enjoying any greater prominence, there is a growing emphasis on policy reflection, on thinking about what one is doing. One interviewee said:

If you think of it as the evaluation bureaucracy, then in some departments they've been marginalized to the point of not existing. If you think about it as being reflective, on the impacts of what you do, and being reflective about what you do, I think it's stronger than it's ever been ... What's happened in the last little while is that many managers are re-absorbing evaluation functions (or absorbing them for the first time). Because you didn't have to be a lot smarter when you could always get another million dollars. Management used to consist of spending.

The new expenditure management system adopted in the federal government has no general policy reserve, so that departments have to find moneys from within their own budgets for new programs. Whereas policy battles would formerly take place among ministers, to be decided in large part by political clout, the battles are now on bureaucratic turf, which is obviously not immune to politics, but which places greater emphasis on evaluative questions and data. Program Review, whatever the Auditor General's reservations, did force departments to think about virtually each and every program in a way that had never happened before. Another interviewee remarked on the fact that Program Review forced a consideration of programs in his division in terms of fundamental questions like impact and effectiveness, and led to program revisions that were more closely aligned with key priorities. Indeed, sorting out priorities had rarely been done before.

Evaluation may not only be getting marginally more important in government, but the nature of evaluation itself may be changing as well. For example, the new emphasis on results of performance management means that the goals of outcomes of policy and programs are defined more broadly than ever before, and evaluation is supposed to find indicators and measures, something that practising evaluators are not always sure is possible:

> *We are moving into performance-based management, and the tradi-tional audit and evaluation functions therefore are going to become more significant. How? Because the evaluation functions are going to report on result achievement, and the audit functions are going to be concentrating on the larger delivery framework within which these results are to be achieved ... The trouble with it is that the results statements keep getting more and more macro... examples are "youth employment" or "access to culture." These are highly reified results that traditional evaluation techniques couldn't respond to anyway ...*

A focus on results will encourage impact-oriented evaluations. However, current policy paradigms stress client satisfaction and a service orientation as outcomes. This means that the old division between process and impact analysis might be blurring, and increasingly the key impacts sought by policy-makers are satisfaction and support of the process and program itself. This is abetted by the new information resources available to policy-makers.

> *Because of the fact that huge databases can be assembled and manip-ulated ... it's quite easy now to do computer runs that will tell you how many winners and losers there are... You couldn't do that fifty years ago, you could get only crude estimates. It means that the polit-ical calculus can be done in a much more precise way.*

Or as another interview put it when describing a new program information system:

> *We're putting a lot of emphasis on accountability frameworks, but what they effectively are is as close as we can come to real-time eval-uations. So that we have a tool that we probably couldn't even have contemplated five years ago, because information systems just weren't sophisticated and fast enough. We're trying to put into place a system that will allow us to do results-oriented tracking of all of our programs, what people have done, and do follow-up surveys, so that*

we can get a sense of how we are doing in our program delivery with about a three- to six- month lead time.

When one thinks like a client or a customer, one is thinking in terms not only of concrete results of a program intervention, but of how one was treated in the process that led to that intervention. Critics of the new public management described in Chapter 1 are rightly cautious about the shift from citizen to customer in contemporary policy talk. At one level it may indeed represent a diminished sense of the public purpose and public role of citizens in policy-making. But that shift also has some empowering aspects—a "program recipient" is a potentially more passive category than "customer." As evaluation stresses customer satisfaction, we can expect more resources to flow to client polling, focus groups, and other feedback mechanisms to guide policy and program development. As the federal government's Quality Services Initiative states: "A key component of a quality service culture is client satisfaction measurement" (Treasury Board of Canada 1995b, 1). As well, the kind of impact or results governments are looking for today are different from what they looked for previously, and that changes the nature of evaluation:

> *Evaluation is changing a lot, from input-based to outcome-based evaluation. It's part and parcel of the redefinition of what government is all about. When you're focusing on detailed programming, say how many women's shelters you can provide, you look at very precise activities, and evaluate on the basis of these program parameters. Now we're more focused on outcomes, not inputs. You're less interested in the number of shelters for women than in, say, intact families, or rather than curriculum you look at school leaving rates, and so on. We're moving away from being accountable for micro-details.*

There is a great deal to be sceptical about in policy and program evaluation, but we prefer to end on an optimistic and uplifting note. Yes, in practice, evaluation studies can seem so insipid, qualified, and immersed in murky politics as to appear either useless or even downright evil. Some critics dismiss evaluation as a policy sideshow, a carnival of dubious methodological handsprings and somersaults that rarely yield serious results. For other critics, such as those in the postpositivist tradition discussed in Chapter 1, insofar as evaluation is dominated by expert discourse, it threatens democracy by drawing debate away from ordinary citizens and entrapping it in a closed universe of language only a few can speak. This fear is surely overdrawn, particularly given the limited role that evaluation has played in Canadian policy-making. We are tempted to make the opposite argument, though well aware that it holds certain dangers as well. The basic questions that form the foundations of program evaluation are vital to any democratic discussion of public policy—what works, and at what cost? These are not the only questions that one can pose about policy, but they are important ones, which if seriously addressed can only benefit policy discussion. Canadian efforts should continue to emphasize the importance of broad evaluation of policy, as well as the wider exposure and dissemination of evaluation results.

SUMMARY

Techniques

* evaluation presents itself as a scientific, systematic, empirically oriented, applied discipline that generates information geared to program improvement

* evaluation is almost always linked to existing programs and focuses on three elements—resources and expenditures, program activities, and program outcomes

* impact evaluation takes the program as the independent or causal variable and tries to isolate its effect from other influences in the environment

* classic experimental designs are the best way of measuring the specific impact of a program intervention (since they randomly assign subjects to an experimental and control group), but they are rarely used in policy analysis because of feasibility problems

* pre-program and post-program designs, as well as single observation designs, are "second-best" strategies to determine impact; they both share the weakness of not being able to clearly rule out alternative explanations

* process evaluation measures program efforts, organization, and implementation procedures, focusing on "program components," such as strategies, activities, publications, technologies and infrastructures, to deliver the program

- cost-benefit and cost-effectiveness analysis are the two types of efficiency evaluation; both look to the relationship between outcomes and resources expended to achieve them

- cost-benefit analysis attempts to quantify, in dollars and cents, the costs of a program, as well as its benefits, and then to determine the relationship between them (usually as a ratio)

- a condition is considered Pareto-optimal if no one person can benefit at the expense of someone else

- cost-effectiveness restricts itself to comparing different program alternatives with achieving a given set of goals

Policy Evaluation in Canada

- the policy evaluation movement coincides with the development of the policy analysis movement, and both in turn are linked to the massive expansion of government activity and programming in the postwar period

- program evaluation entered into Canadian federal government practice with the adoption of PPBS in 1969, and became a formal requirement through Treasury Board fiat in 1977

- while the quantity of evaluations rose in the federal government after the late 1970s, there have been perennial complaints that evaluation studies are used more as a management tool than as a publicly discussed standard of policy performance

- new federal evaluation policies passed in the last three years have tried to bring together guidelines for program review, internal audit, and evaluation

- the new federal guidelines emphasize results links between results and deficit control; performance, service and clients; and decentralization

- current evaluation thinking stresses results and often defines those results in terms of client satisfaction, thus merging, to some degree, the categories of impact and process evaluations

REFERENCES

Auditor General of Canada. (1976). *Annual report 1976*. Ottawa: Information Canada.

Auditor General of Canada. (1993). *Annual report 1993*. Ottawa: Minister of Supply and Services.

Auditor General of Canada. (1996, October 2). *Annual report 1996* [On-line]. Available: http://www.oag-bvg.gc.ca/oag-bvg/rep96/1996e/html/menu3e.html

Carley, M. (1980). *Rational techniques in policy analysis*. London, England: Heinemann Educational Books.

Framst, G. (1995). Application of program logic model to agricultural technology transfer programs. *Canadian Journal of Program Evaluation, 10*(October/November), 123–132.

Government of Canada. (1969). *Planning, programming and budgeting guide*. Ottawa: Information Canada.

Hollander, M. J., & Prince, M. J. (1993). Analytical units in federal and provincial governments: Origins, functions and suggestions for effectiveness. *Canadian Public Administration, 36*(Summer), 190–224.

Leclerc, G. (1992). Institutionalizing evaluation in Canada. In J. Mayne, J. Hudson, M. L. Bemelmans-Videc, & R. Conner (Eds.), *Advancing public policy evaluation: Learning from international experiences* (pp. 49–58). Amsterdam: North Holland.

Lindquist, E. A. (1993). Think tanks or clubs? Assessing the influence and roles of Canadian policy institutes. *Canadian Public Administration, 36*(Winter), 547–579.

Nachmias, D. (1979). *Public policy evaluation: Approaches and methods*. New York: St. Martin's Press.

Organization for Economic Co-operation and Development. (1995). *Public management developments: Update 1995*. Paris: OECD.

Patton, M. Q. (1987). *Creative evaluation* (2nd ed.). Newbury Park, CA: Sage.

Patton, M. Q. (1990). *Qualitative evaluation and research methods* (2nd ed.). Newbury Park, CA: Sage.

Pedersen, K. S., & McDavid, J. C. (1994). The impact of radar cameras on traffic speed: A quasi-experimental evaluation. *Canadian Journal of Program Evaluation , 9*(April/May), 51–68.

Poister, T. H. (1978). *Public program analysis: Applied research methods.* Baltimore: University Park Press.

Pollitt, C. (1993). Occasional excursions: A brief history of policy evaluation in the UK. *Parliamentary Affairs, 46,* 353–362.

Posvac, E. J., & Carey, R. G. (1980). *Program evaluation: Methods and case studies.* Englewood Cliffs, NJ: Prentice-Hall.

Rossi, P. H., & Freeman, H. E. (1989). *Evaluation: A systematic approach* (4th ed.). Newbury Park, CA: Sage.

Saint-Martin, D. (1996). *Reforming state bureaucracies: Accountants and the politics of managerialism in Britain, Canada and France.* [Doctoral dissertation]. Ottawa: Carleton University.

Savoie, D. J. (1990). *The politics of public spending in Canada.* Toronto: University of Toronto Press.

Scheirer, M. A. (1994). Designing and using process evaluation. In J. S. Wholey, H. P. Hatry, & K. E. Newcomer (Eds.), *Handbook of practical program evaluation* (pp. 40–68). San Francisco: Jossey-Bass.

Segsworth, R. V. (1992). Public access to evaluation in Canada. In J. Mayne , J. Hudson, M. L. Bemelmans-Videc, & R. Conner (Eds.), *Advancing public policy evaluation: Learning from international experiences* (pp. 301–312). Amsterdam: North Holland.

Sutherland, S. L. (1990). The evolution of program budget ideas in Canada: Does parliament benefit from estimates reform? *Canadian Public Administration, 33*(Summer), 133–164.

Thompson, M. S. (1980). *Cost-benefit analysis for program evaluation.* Beverly Hills, CA: Sage.

Treasury Board of Canada. (1981). *Guide on the program evaluation function.* Ottawa: Minister of Supply and Services.

Treasury Board of Canada. (1991). *Into the 90s: Government program evaluation perspectives.* Ottawa: Office of the Comptroller General.

Treasury Board of Canada. (1994, July). *Treasury Board manual—Review, internal audit and evaluation* (Amendment RIE/94-1). Ottawa: Treasury Board of Canada.

Treasury Board of Canada. (1995a). *Strengthening government review: Annual report to Parliament by the President of the Treasury Board* [On-line]. Available: http://www.tbs-sct.gc.ca/tb/reps.html

Treasury Board of Canada. (1995b). *Quality services, guide II: Measuring client satisfaction.* Ottawa: Treasury Board of Canada.

Tupper, A. (1993). Think tanks, public debt, and the politics of expertise in Canada. *Canadian Public Administration, 36*(Winter), 530–546.

Wholey, J. S. (1994). Assessing the feasibility and likely usefulness of evaluation. In J. S. Wholey, H. P. Hatry, and K. E. Newcomer (Eds.), *Handbook of practical program evaluation* (pp. 15–39). San Francisco: Jossey-Bass.

Chapter 8 Conclusions

Readers who made it this far will probably have a mixed reaction to the arguments in this book. Some of you will be impressed at the deep changes that governments and the policy process are undergoing, and generally supportive of a more quality-centred, client-focused policy-making system. Others (perhaps even the same ones who are impressed!) will be dismayed or at least uneasy with the portrait drawn in this book. Governments are becoming more businesslike, and policy is arguably more responsive to clients and stakeholders. But is businesslike government the zenith of democratic aspiration? Decentralization seems fine, but how far can it go before we lose a sense of common standards and shared community? Client satisfaction is laudable, as is responsiveness to stakeholders. But are we merely customers and interests, or is there a richer role that we play in the public sphere as citizens? All of these questions should have occurred to you as you considered the previous chapters. Another set of questions probably came to mind as well. What about the content of policy, as opposed to the process? Is there such a thing as "good" public policy that transcends ideology, or that might be broadly accepted by people of different political persuasions? By the same token, what does "bad" policy look like? What skills should the contemporary policy analyst have to make good policy and avoid bad? This chapter briefly summarizes the main arguments and findings from previous chapters, and then addresses these deeper questions of policy and democratic governance.

POLICY ANALYSIS IN THE REAL WORLD

The first chapters of this book argued that both policy analysis and the context within which it is practised have fundamentally changed in the last decade. The evidence from the policy analysis literature is quite clear. For many years there has been an internal debate about its efficacy, relevance, and its role in democratic politics. The question of efficacy asks whether analysis has any influence over policy-making. At first blush, it would seem absurd to suggest that it does not, but empirical studies of the impact of analysis and the institutional location of policy shops cast doubt on any determinative influence. Of course, that is perhaps as it should be; no one wants eggheads to have the last say. But even a more benign model where policy analysis is a handmaiden to decision-making may be too robust—in practice, as perverse as it sounds, much of the effort (and expense!) that goes into policy analysis is wasted. The data, the studies, the models, and the recommendations have relatively little impact on ultimate choices. The question of relevance springs directly from this. If analysis is only a minor ingredient in the policy mix, then what is its specific contribution? This leads inevitably to the issue of democracy: policy analysis is a discipline with certain conventions and practices. If not just anyone can be an analyst, then what is the balance between democratic processes (nonexpert) and policy analysis (expertise)?

These and other questions have encouraged several strands in the discipline. One is a fairly conventional defence of the traditional rationalist, empirical approaches to analysis. Another is the postpositivist position that rationalism and empiricism are very limited ways of knowing, and that in practice decisions depend on arguments crafted from a variety of materials including "facts," values, and linguistic terms. The danger, from this perspective, is that the conceit of rationalist policy models will lead to a domination of the democratic process by self-styled experts who ignore the shaky foundations of their own recommendations.

Chapter 1 of this book took a sceptical stance toward both these positions. First, while there are indeed examples of highly formalistic policy analysis, analysis in the real world is acutely aware of its own limitations. The postpositivist theoretical critique has been absorbed by most practising policy analysts and decision-makers: they know the limits of rational models, the importance of democratic participation, and the dangers of expert dominance of the process. Second, we concluded that a good deal of the traditional tools of the trade are in fact useful to the analytical enterprise. Chapter 7, for example, outlined some techniques for impact and efficiency evaluation. Despite all the caveats, these techniques are helpful in disciplining our thinking about policy issues. By the same token, despite its obvious artificiality, the phase model of the policy process helps us get a grip on key stages or elements of decision-making. Third, we argued in Chapter 1 that both of the broad streams in the analytical literature have failed to come to terms with the changes in modern democratic governance driven by the powerful forces of globalization, technological change, and shifts in political culture.

It is, of course, important not to exaggerate the impact of these changes. On the issue of globalization, for example, one of our interviewees pointed out:

> *I think at one level there has possibly been less change than one would imagine, and at another level a great deal of change in terms of assessing the impact of big global changes. At one level ... in the 1960s, the senior officials in the government of Canada came disproportionately from the trade policy community. They were the people who grew up in a world where the refashioning of public policy that was going on in that post–World War II, Keynesian, GATT [General Agreement on Trade and Tariffs], IMF [International Monetary Fund] context. In fact, it's arguable that we had a larger, external vision and that the kind of work that went on in the bureaucracy was more sensitive to a lot of that stuff than it is today, in spite of a lot of verbiage today about these things.*

But the same interviewee then went on to say: "*The other side of the argument would be that thirty years ago, or even twenty years ago, the line of demarcation between foreign policy and domestic policy was far, far clearer than it is today. There are now huge chunks of what were once considered domestic policy that are increasingly becoming foreign policy as well (or foreign-economic policy or foreign-something policy!).*" The same pattern emerged in many of the interviews conducted for this book: a caution that the changes everyone talks about may be overblown and hyped, but a grudging admission that something indeed is different about policy-making and governance in the mid-1990s. Those changes are summarized in Chapter 2, but the subsequent chapters have demonstrated their impact across the full spectrum of the policy process. The traditional categories of problem definition, design, implementation, policy communities, and evaluation, certainly continue to apply, and continue to be applied by policy-makers themselves to make sense of what they do. But the content of those categories has shifted in important ways.

Chapter 3 showed how the nature of problem definition has shifted in recent years. First, fiscal constraints have encouraged people to focus on government budgets as a key policy problem. In addition, however, those constraints have made it very difficult to articulate policy problems in terms of solutions that require more spending. This new conceptual context has been institutionalized through the dominance of treasury or finance departments in the policy-making machinery. As guardians of the fisc, they wield enormous influence in defining policy problems in light of deficit reduction/elimination strategies. The reasons for their dominance are rooted in the globalization of financial markets, and the increasing inability of governments to insulate themselves from the harsh and fickle judgments of their creditors. Globalization has also shifted the context of problem definition in another way: increasingly, we see the causes of, as well as the solutions to, our policy problems outside our boundaries.

Chapter 4 carried this analysis forward to look at instrument choice and policy design. The new context is clear: spending instruments are out, as is regulation and public ownership. Governments around the world now prefer to design policies around self-regulative instruments, or set framework regulations that look to results rather than micro-management of behaviour. There is more reliance on individual responsibility. Governments are relying more on partnerships and third-party delivery of programs and services. At the same time, however, there are signs that there is a new interest in values and character as a policy target. Concerns about crime, TV violence, and pornography are driving governments to be more, not less, robust in their interventions. The impact of globalization on jobs and communities is also forcing governments, even very conservative ones, to bridle their enthusiasm for market mechanisms in favour of economic and social policies that try to insulate their populations to some degree. On other fronts, as Chapter 2 outlined, profound value shifts in Western countries have also contributed to demands that governments address broad issues like the environment.

Chapters 5, 6, and 7 expressed the same themes. Implementation of public policy is changing everywhere to be less top-down and more explicitly designed around partnerships, with a clearer division between policy design and delivery. Policy communities have accordingly become more important in the policy mix. As governments get smaller and leaner, they depend more on their partners, both for policy advice and implementation. Modern policy cannot be directed by government, and merely supplemented by other actors in respective policy communities. Evaluation has changed as well. It has enjoyed a renaissance of sorts as governments have emphasized results, performance, and client satisfaction. With the new focus on results and clients, however, have come new emphases in evaluative techniques, harnessing them more closely to program review and the use of innovative implementation techniques.

We argued repeatedly in the previous chapters that characterizing these changes as smaller government is simplistic. The shifts in some cases are dramatic, as are the consequences: the pressures of deficit reduction, for example. On the other hand, there are some areas where government activity has increased: securing international agreements and standards, for example, or in the area of information technology. Our synopsis of the federal government's policy framework on the information highway in Box 4.5, for example, demonstrates that significant policy interventions can be consistent with downsized government. Another equally mistaken inference from the previous chapters is that policy analysis is less important today than it was before. In fact, it is probably more important than ever. While the changes described in previous chapters have been driven by a certain consensus around a core of ideas, they do not amount to a clear or coherent public philosophy. Governments are changing, sometimes in dramatic ways, without really understanding the implications of these changes. As well, the new contexts for policy-making, both international and domestic, demand fresh policy thinking. If the line between foreign and domestic policy is blurring, how do we distinguish the domestic and international aspects of policy? If policy fields are blending into each other (e.g., social and economic policy), how do we design horizontal policy? If partnerships are the new mode of delivery, what kind of accountability regimes should apply? If client satisfaction matters, then how do we measure it and ensure that the results are integrated into policy development? As Jocelyne Bourgon, the Clerk of the Privy Council, put it in her 1995 annual report on the public service of Canada: "The changing policy environment has created a restored demand for high-quality policy advice from the Public Service" (Privy Council Office 1995). More effort has to be put into long-term and strategic policy development.

> The Public Service must develop ways to better address horizontal, cross-cutting issues, including implementing the right system of incentives and accountability, which is one of the major challenges. Finding ways to effectively address horizontal issues is a difficult task, and all western nations are trying to do a better job of it. To date, public service practice in this area has not lived up to the concepts of interdepartmental collaboration that are professed, and a better job must be done.
>
> The dominance of horizontal and cross-sectoral issues where no single department has the exclusive expertise and resources required to address contemporary policy issues and many departments must be involved in developing the best policy advice demands that public servants co-operate on policy development to a greater degree than in the past. Departmental boundaries and vertical accountability must not impede effective policy development in the Public Service.

In the future, departments need to work in a different manner, such that collaboration, partnerships and consultation to build consensus are paramount. (Privy Council Office 1995)

The real world of policy analysis is an increasingly challenging one where conventional categories have to be rethought, institutions retooled, and skills sharpened in the service of different modes of governance.

GOOD POLICY, BAD POLICY, AND GOVERNANCE

Many books about policy analysis cheat their readers by saying nothing substantive about policy itself. Everything is process, and skills and techniques are directed at highly abstract and obviously contentious goals such as economic stability. Democratic governance is clearly about working through differences, and contemporary societies are indeed marked by sharp differences in values and perspectives that inevitably translate into different policy priorities and different definitions of what constitutes good policy. But democratic politics is also about working through those differences, or reaching beyond them to some common ground. In that light, there might, in fact, be more consensus about what is "good" and "bad" policy than we think.

Three events dominated the news as the final pages of this book were being written, and they provide some guidance (as negative examples!) of the elements of good policy. The first was the Republican Party convention in the United States to nominate Bob Dole and Jack Kemp as its 1996 presidential ticket. This was the first political convention designed almost exclusively for television. Every speech was carefully vetted to ensure a consistent "message." Video vignettes of hardworking Americans who had overcome poverty and disadvantage in the teeth of bungling government intervention peppered the broadcasts. Members of minorities (who were very much in the minority of delegates, among whom one in five reportedly was a millionaire) were conspicuously placed near the cameras to give the TV audience the impression of diversity. Apart from tax cuts, smaller government, and stronger defence, the entire affair was devoid of policy content. The candidate for the highest office in the land invoked God and the American dream, his own character and his personal struggles, but said nothing of substance on the major policy issues confronting the nation. The impact was paradoxical: more people watched *Home*

Improvement than the convention, but the Republicans enjoyed a bounce in the polls.

The second event was the Canadian inquiry in the Somalia affair (pertaining to serious military misconduct during a peacekeeping mission in 1993). After months of silence, General Jean Boyle, the Chief of Defence Staff, finally appeared before the commission to answer questions about document tampering in the public affairs branch of the Department of Defence. General Boyle had been associate assistant deputy minister in 1993 in charge of policy and communications, but under questioning claimed that he had never been told about document tampering. Apparently, such activities were common knowledge in the branch, but not to the man in charge. General Boyle accused some of his senior officers of a "lack of integrity," and refused suggestions that he might have a responsibility to resign: "If CDSs [Chiefs of Defence Staff] or senior officers resigned every time their subordinates made an error ... there would never be any leadership" (Koring 1996, A1). In an unrelated but telling event the same day, a former minister of health deliberately sought out personal responsibility with another inquiry. In a legal decision, the Krever inquiry into Canada's blood system had been instructed that it could lay blame on senior officials and volunteers, but not on politicians or very senior bureaucrats. Monique Bégin, who had been a minister of health from 1976 to 1984, was one of thirty-seven former federal and provincial ministers who were absolved of blame. She took the extraordinary step of writing the Krever Commission to ask that she be included in those "named" to answer questions about the affair. Ms. Bégin argued that her action was a "matter of personal morality and integrity" as well as an issue of parliamentary principle: "The notion of 'ministerial responsibility' is the cornerstone of our executive government ... Politicians must definitely be accountable, and I am therefore prepared to join the 'named' people to answer the inquiries of your commission" (Picard 1996, A1).

The third event was the annual meeting of provincial premiers. Gathering in Jasper, Alberta, under the chairmanship of Premier Ralph Klein, the provinces worked through an agenda of social and economic issues, the prime one being a rebalancing of federal and provincial responsibilities for social policy. But the conference attracted as much attention for its organization as for its content. The conference had corporate donations of about $150 000 to help cover the approximately $250 000 cost. Major corporations such as Canadian Airlines, CN Rail, Nova, and Telus were joined by twenty or thirty smaller companies to sponsor meals, cocktails, prizes, and even casual vests with a company logo (Tibbetts 1996, A1). Corporate sponsorship had been tried previously at the G-7 summit in Halifax, but this went considerably further, causing substantial media discussion about conflicts of interest and undue influence by corporate donors.

The thread that runs through these episodes is integrity. It has at least four senses which, if respected, can help build good public policy.

Integrity of Persons

The Boyle and Bégin examples illustrate the importance of personal integrity in the policy process. General Boyle prefers to blame his subordinates, while Ms. Bégin demands to be held accountable. In public policy terms, integrity means several things. First, it means that one acts in full accordance with the duties and responsibilities of one's office. Second, it means having a regard for the truth. Third, it means being responsible for one's actions, and accountable. Finally, it means behaving with civility and sympathy. Most, if not all, scandals in government could be avoided if people behaved according to these maxims. But even smaller mistakes could be corrected. For example, a high standard of personal integrity would demand only the most professional conduct.

An emphasis on personal integrity has a moralizing aspect to it which may strike some as irrelevant to the larger questions of machinery and governmental process that apparently dominate policy discussions. In fact, the issue of personal responsibility and ethics is seen by many as increasingly important for modern organizations. Theorists tell us that organizations today have to be flexible, decentralized, adaptive, and always learning. This more fluid and organic view of organizations—a view, incidentally, that finds reflection in a great deal of thinking about how policy should be designed and delivered—cannot rely on hierarchical, machinelike controls. Flexibility and tight rules do not go together. The more flexible and adaptive an organization is, and that includes government departments, the looser the framework has to be within which people work. But rules exist for a reason: they provide external controls to induce certain behaviours. If these external controls are removed, we have to rely increasingly on internal controls, that is, on shared norms and values, and integrity.

Integrity of Process

Good policy in modern government depends on the personal integrity of the policy-makers, but personal integrity cannot thrive in a corrupt system.

Stephen Carter (1996) has recently provided eight principles that "point toward a politics of integrity" (p. 47). The first is that the nation exists for its people. Our politics and our policies should treat people as ends, not means. The second is that a "politics of integrity is a politics that sets priorities, that does not tell the self-serving lie that every program preferred by a particular movement is of equal value" (p. 48). Third, consistency is important. Carter uses the example of arguments about welfare reform (usually from the right) that claim that government assistance undermines self-reliance. If that is true, then it should also be true of corporate subsidies, but those who make the first argument rarely make the second.

Fourth, a politics of integrity refuses to arbitrarily exclude some citizens with political views that do not meet with the approval of elites. Carter's concern is with various religious groups, and in particular the religious right that have been criticized for trying to push their values on other citizens. The point has broader application, however. As soon as policy actors decide that some group should be excluded from the process because of its views, or its influence, the process itself loses integrity. Fifth, "we must be willing to talk about right and wrong without mentioning the Constitution" (p. 49). Carter is referring to the American constitution, but Canadians have been equally guilty of subsuming policy arguments under the Charter, often making it impossible to discuss issues in anything but terms of rights. Sixth, a politics of integrity must appeal to our higher selves: "we must try to respond to politicians who call us to our highest rather than our lowest selves; in particular, we must respond to politicians who talk of the national interest and our shared obligations, not merely those who promise to enrich us" (p. 50). Seventh, a "politics of integrity is a politics in which all of us are willing to do the hard work of discernment, to test our views to be sure that we are right" (p. 50). We must engage in dialogue, which implies both stating views and listening with care. Finally, we must be prepared to admit that sometimes the other side wins:

> Somebody wins and somebody loses. In practical terms, that means that the people have picked one and rejected the other. Integrity requires us to admit the possibility (indeed, the likelihood) that we lost not because of some shameless manipulation by our villainous opponents, and not because of some failure to get our message across, but because our fellow citizens, a basically rational bunch, considered both our views and those of the other side and decided that they liked the other side's better. (p. 50)

These are not abstract principles. Consider how the 1995 Québec Referendum debate might have been different had they been followed.

There might have been fewer threats, less irritation, and greater willingness to listen.

Integrity of Government

The new public management and a lot of the new policy thinking described in this book is dedicated to making government more businesslike. There is nothing wrong with this, and in some instances, such as quality services and client satisfaction, it is long overdue. However, there is a difference between making government more businesslike, and treating government just like another business. The best businesses recognize that they have public responsibilities, as well as governance responsibilities to their customers, competitors, and employees. But that does not make them governments. The two spheres of government and business are quite distinct, and each should function in ways that are appropriate to its sphere. Government is vital for any civilized society, not simply as an instrument to get things done, but as a public space wherein we fulfil and enjoy our responsibilities and privileges as citizens. The 1996 premiers conference in Jasper is a perfect example of getting it wrong: in order to save $150 000, the leaders of governments allowed themselves to sport company logos and have their event, an event of governance, transformed into a commercial advertising opportunity. Some overlap between sectors is inevitable, but complete cooptation of this sort offends the dignity of government and debases its importance in the eyes of citizens. How can we be expected to respect government when it is "sponsored," just like a little league baseball team?

Several observers have noted that while the emphasis on service-client relations in the new public management thinking holds promise, it is too limited a vision of the full range of responsibilities and rationales of the public sector. Gow (1995), for example, points out that "In considering citizens as clients of the administration, one must wonder about the nature of the relationship as it concerns those who fall under the disciplinary authority of the state, be they prisoners, people in regulated industries or dependents of the state" (p. 558). Doern (1994) makes a similar point: "Bureaucracy seen abstractly as an 'it' serving the customer, 'us' or 'me,' in a new form of franchised 'McState' is not all or even *most* of what democratic governance is about" (p. 92).

Mintzberg (1996) argues that we actually wear four hats in relation to government: customer, client, citizen, and subject. Governments do relatively few things for us as customers, that is, as consumers of goods and services that probably could just as easily be provided through the market. A larger proportion of the services we get from government, such as health care or education, are professional services for which we are clients. But we also relate to government as subjects, in the sense of the duties and obligations that we have to obey, and which, if we do not, will incur the discipline of state authority. Our relationship as citizens is more complex still, embracing both obligations as well as rights. Respecting the integrity of government does not mean that government should do all things, and be all things. What it does mean is respecting the specific nature of government as well as its importance to the exercise of our democratic citizenship. It means preserving the dignity of the public square, in the knowledge that if we characterize government as just another form of business, we risk losing our own character as citizens. A world of customers and clients might be a paradise of consumption and service, but it would not be a democratic commonwealth.

Integrity of Purpose

What is government and public policy ultimately about? What is it for? Both serve citizens in the fulfillment of a good life, and all other policy goals are means to this end. Jobs, for example, are obviously important in creating the foundation for a good life, but policy-makers often confuse means with ends, and seek jobs at all costs. Public policy should not cater to narrow, sectional interests. Nor should it pander to purely material interests. It should keep its eye firmly on its broadest goal—the conditions for a good life for all citizens—and use that as standard for judging specific policy interventions. The ingredients for a good life are not mysterious: health, education, shelter, economic opportunity, respect, civility, and leisure.

The United Nations Development Programme publishes an annual human development index. It ranks countries in terms of "life expectancy, educational attainment and adjusted real income" (United Nations Development Programme 1996). The report argues that the world is in danger of developing gross inequities both within some societies and between groups of countries. It urges a model that concentrates on human development as a first key to economic growth, and one which sees equity as a complement, not a contradiction, to growth.

What policies are needed to realize this new growth-with-equity model? These policies must place people at the centre stage. Furthermore, actions are needed both at the national as well as at the international levels. The Human Development Report 1996 offers a policy framework that has the following components:

At the national level:

- more attention and policy action on the structure and quality of growth to give priority to human development, poverty reduction, employment and long-term sustainability.

- formulation of an equity-based growth strategy—equity in enhancement of capabilities, access to opportunities, especially for women, and inter-generational equity in natural resource management.

- strengthening the links between economic growth and human develop-ment through household activities, government policies and action by vari-ous institutions of civil society.

- faster economic growth in three groups of countries—the low human development ones, especially those of sub-Saharan Africa and the Less Developed Countries (LDCs), the Commonwealth of Independent States (CIS) countries and slow growing countries of Latin America, the Arab States and Asia.

- a political commitment to full employment, backed up by new approaches to expand and improve employment: labor intensive high-growth strate-gies, sustained investments in human capabilities, broader access to land and credit, and encouragement of the informal sector (United Nations Development Programme 1996).

Canada has ranked first overall in the list of countries two years running. In 1995 it ranked sixth in terms of gender equality, but in 1996 was second. There is much to be proud of in this, but it also suggests that if we want to look for indications of "good" public policy, we need not go further than our own backyard. While not perfect, Canadian public policy has helped create the conditions for the best overall standard of living in the world. In our context, good policy is as much a matter of preserving the balance of what we have accomplished in the past, as it is of improving upon it.

FINAL WORDS

I had the good fortune to interview senior policy people from government, NGOs, and think tanks about what constitutes good public policy and what sorts of skills they think the contemporary policy analyst needs. I leave the final words of this book to them.

Analytical Skills

There are certain personal skills, interpersonal skills that you must have. The ability to get along with people and to be attentive to them and understand what they're saying and so on. And there are analytical and technical skills. These are not skills that everyone has in the same proportions. And then there are management and leadership skills that are required to be in the policy game. And then we have all kinds of other things—good communications skills, be able to present things well, and consult, negotiate, facilitate. Because when you're out there, if you're serious about it and you're not just going through an exercise, then it's going to require different sets of skills. Then there's skills inside and then there's skills you have to use outside. And I guess that's one of the reasons why this is a team business. Because if you look at all of the things you're supposed to be able to do, you clearly can't find that in any one person. So you're going to have to put different people together with different skills in order to get the job done.

I think the whole concern with ethics is growing. We did a hundred community studies, and we attempted to have the communities do their own studies. We'd contract with a community health clinic, and they'd hire someone, usually someone from the community. I think it's true in all cases; they want part of the action. That sort of responsibility of the researcher to the community is a responsible approach.

If I'm hiring somebody who's only been working for a few years, I look for someone who's got an advanced course in mathematics or physics, because I look for people who are pretty quantitative and very logical. Anyone who has voluntarily taken grade 12 math and grade 12 physics tells me that I'm dealing with someone who likes to deal with concepts, and can find patterns in things and can make connections.

You need someone who's got a certain amount of political sensibility. There are a lot of people who can make it as a good research analyst, but are never going to make it as policy analysts, because them's the facts, and therefore them's the truth, when that is not the way it is.

Table 8.1 Human Development Report 1996

Human Development Index (HDI) Rank

High	Medium	Low
1 Canada	58 Brazil	127 Cameroon
2 USA	59 Libyan Arab	128 Kenya
3 Japan	Jamahiriya	129 Ghana
4 Netherlands	60 Seychelles	130 Lesotho
5 Norway	61 Belarus	131 Equatorial Guinea
6 Finland	62 Bulgaria	132 São Tomé and
7 France	63 Saudi Arabia	Principe
8 Iceland	64 Ecuador	133 Myanmar
9 Sweden	65 Dominica	134 Pakistan
10 Spain	66 Iran, Islamic Rep. of	135 India
11 Australia	67 Belize	136 Zambia
12 Belgium	68 Estonia	137 Nigeria
13 Austria	69 Algeria	138 Lao People's
14 New Zealand	70 Jordan	Dem. Rep.
15 Switzerland	71 Botswana	139 Comoros
16 United Kingdom	72 Kazakhstan	140 Togo
17 Denmark	73 Saint Vincent	141 Zaire
18 Germany	74 Romania	142 Yemen
19 Ireland	75 Suriname	143 Bangladesh
20 Italy	76 Saint Lucia	144 Tanzania, U. Rep. of
21 Greece	77 Grenada	145 Haiti
22 Hong Kong	78 Tunisia	146 Sudan
23 Cyprus	79 Cuba	147 Côte d'Ivoire
24 Israel	80 Ukraine	148 Central African
25 Barbados	81 Lithuania	Rep.
26 Bahamas	82 Oman	149 Mauritania
27 Luxembourg	83 Korea, Dem.	150 Madagascar
28 Malta	People's Rep. of	151 Nepal
29 Korea, Rep. of	84 Turkey	152 Rwanda
30 Argentina	85 Paraguay	153 Senegal
31 Costa Rica	86 Jamaica	154 Benin
32 Uruguay	87 Dominican Rep.	155 Uganda
33 Chile	88 Samoa (Western)	156 Cambodia
34 Singapore	89 Sri Lanka	157 Malawi
35 Portugal	90 Turkmenistan	158 Liberia
36 Brunei Darussalam	91 Peru	159 Bhutan
37 Czech Rep.	92 Syrian Arab Rep.	160 Guinea
38 Trinidad and Tobago	93 Armenia	161 Guinea-Bissau
39 Bahrain	94 Uzbekistan	162 Gambia
40 Antigua and Barbuda	95 Philippines	163 Chad

Table 8.1   Human Development Report 1996 (cont.)

High	Medium	Low
41 Slovakia	96 Azerbaijan	164 Djibouti
42 United Arab Emirates	97 Lebanon	165 Angola
43 Panama	98 Moldova, Rep. of	166 Burundi
44 Venezuela	99 Kyrgyzstan	167 Mozambique
45 Saint Kitts and Nevis	100 South Africa	168 Ethiopia
46 Hungary	101 Georgia	169 Afghanistan
47 Fiji	102 Indonesia	170 Burkina Faso
48 Mexico	103 Guyana	171 Mali
49 Colombia	104 Albania	172 Somalia
50 Qatar	105 Tajikistan	173 Sierra Leone
51 Kuwait	106 Egypt	174 Niger
52 Thailand	107 Maldives	
53 Malaysia	108 China	
54 Mauritius	109 Iraq	
55 Latvia	110 Swaziland	
56 Poland	111 Bolivia	
57 Russian Federation	112 Guatemala	
	113 Mongolia	
	114 Honduras	
	115 El Salvador	
	116 Namibia	
	117 Nicaragua	
	118 Solomon Islands	
	119 Vanuatu	
	120 Gabon	
	121 Viet Nam	
	122 Cape Verde	
	123 Morocco	
	124 Zimbabwe	
	125 Congo	
	126 Papua New	

Source: United Nations Development Programme (1996).

Facts only take you so far in these things, and behind every average there are lots of people on the outlying ends of your distribution. You need people who think a little bit about that thing, which is the political reality the minister has to deal with all the time.

There will always be a need in government for people who are extremely specialized and narrow, because they are the rowers, and you need lots of rowers to make the ship move. But in order to orchestrate those rowers, and policy-makers are orchestrators, requires somebody with a broad reach. But the ability to be specialized and to understand what the specialists are saying is the broad reach that you're looking for, hiring somebody for a policy shop. They have to have some specialists skills but they also have to have a broad reach. And they can get that in a variety of ways, maybe having had two degrees in different disciplines, say moving from chemistry to economics, or economics to international affairs. Having that kind of interwoven mixtures is what I think makes an ideal policy analyst. As I was saying to a friend the other day, talking about somebody, I said, "She's comfortable with the numbers and yet she understands the broader issues." He said, "Yeah, that's the right person."

Breadth is important; I think that policy analysts should move around departments a lot. That is a problem in government now, there is not a lot of hiring, not a lot of movement now … Once you've got some analytical models, you can start to apply them to almost any problem. And if you only work in one department, you don't necessarily get that degree of confidence or that understanding of how analytical tools can be applied to anything. Or to flip it around a little bit as well, how you can take a common model and by applying some creativity to it, you can mould it to your issue. If you only have the same type of issue, you never had to mould it.

I find that good analysis should allow you to be able to describe what the problem is, in a short, concise way. Long things mean that you really haven't come to a conclusion, as far as I'm concerned. Like you're still fumbling for the answers, you haven't understood the problem. Now there's a deputy minister who has a little thing, he says "Simplify, complicate, simplify." So if somebody comes to you with a problem, he looks at the problem, like parole, it's complicated. "What do you mean it's parole?" So you tell him the issues. Let's simplify what is the problem. So it's like being able to go through that process and come up with something that tells you "I think really this is what it's all about." And to substantiate that in a certain way, knowing full well that there are other viewpoints.

The new skills would be communications, consultations, and team-work. The ability and willingness to work in teams. It's important to get buy-in fairly early on, and to be able to work with people from all across the department, to get their perspective, to get their input, their help, to know how what you're doing is going to affect them. I think there's a lot more of a requirement to do that than there used to be.

One shouldn't forget in all of this the importance of commitment to the higher purpose. People don't join government to make money. And policy work can be hugely frustrating. It's very demanding, it's exhausting, relentless, a lot of time you get nowhere ... you have to have a lot of patience to do it. But above all you really have to want to do it, really feel like you're making a contribution to the nation. It's too easy in policy to be cynical, and look for the easy solution rather than the right solution, to allow yourself to be caught up in the polit-ical agenda or what you think is the political agenda rather than being the objective bureaucrat and saying "This is the problem, this is our assessment of the various options, our recommendation when we look at all of it is this one, and you may not like it, Minister, but that is your judgment to make." There's a higher degree of integrity that's required.

We want people with generic skills. You bring in your specialists on an "as-needed" basis. Because you're into this holistic piece, you're increasingly becoming dependent on experienced people as opposed to less experienced people. When I first started out in the game, there tended to be a lot of people brand new to the area, just kind of play-ing, and it was incremental and you weren't looking across the spec-trum, and you didn't have to have a great depth of knowledge. Fortunately or unfortunately, because we're downsizing so there's a lot of experienced policy analysts around. But once we get through that ... go and look at my policy folks downstairs, they're all between the age of 40 and 55! In five years time I don't know what the hell we're going to do because we don't have anyone coming up.

They need to have incredibly good conceptual skills, because you can't have just vertical thinkers. They need to be superb communicators, because having done the analytical work, which is thorough and detailed, they've got to be able to speak in five minutes sometimes, and get it. I think that's undervalued sometimes. We're a very oral culture here. We write tons of stuff, but that's for other people to read. Decisions ultimately come out of discussion. You're looking for creativity and innovation and not just incremental thinking. The biggest change, though, is that they have to understand management. If you don't understand the doability of it, if you don't understand the implementation of it, and if you don't understand what cost-drivers are driving it, you can't do the policy anymore.

We try to write well, which is very important. We always couch our technical work so that it could be read and understood by someone who knows nothing about it. We are very, very cognizant of political forces. We try to interweave our analysis with a lot of stuff about what's happening with governments and the politics of [the policy field]. There's more to analytics than just saying "Here's the distribution and fifteen different options." Judgment and balance are very much part of our work. The other one is honesty—saying the way things are. We also try to take into account different points of view as fairly as we can. Try to be fair.

It's a way of thinking, an ability to sift the extraneous from the essential, to get to the bottom, to see patterns and connections such as historical or international comparisons. It's the ability to think ahead a few moves, about the consequences downstream. It's the ability to organize information. We are in a situation of total information overload, especially with this Internet thing. Triage is an important sort of thing at the top. What do I need, and where do I get it?

Good Policy Analysis

Good policy analysis is that you have to start with the right question, and that is really, really tough. It has to be comprehensive in analysis but synthesized into chewable decisions. So, you can't get lost in detail, but there has to be a structure and process that give confidence that the detail has indeed been looked at and synthesized into something that a decision can be made on. It has to be tied in to the government agenda in all its parts. You can't lob the grenade in very easily anymore. At the highest level, that's what's going on. At the lowest level, you're still looking for incredibly good writing skills.

We're still a very oral culture, and so in skills, frankly, a lot of it is how it's presented, how it's discussed.

Good policy advice is what it has always been, leaving the politics to elected officials and providing a good range of options as well as consequences of those options with an eye to practicality, feasibility, communication, and implementation, and bringing in things like the implications for national unity.

I think one feature of good policy analysis is balance. We dealt with very volatile issues, and there was a concern on the part of many to be politically correct. But being politically correct sometimes avoids very difficult problems. We needed to have options that were real options. Balance in terms of a balanced perspective is important ... One of the concerns [from the top] right from the outset was to have the full panoply: "Here, don't sort of cut off short of the full range, even if it seems odd to you or outlandish. We want the full spectrum. We'll worry about the costs, and the sensibility and efficiencies and effectiveness later." That really unleashes the creative juices. Once in a while you get one of these far-out ideas that ends up being really cost-effective, or you'll be setting it against a criterion you hadn't thought of. Governments don't unleash the creative talents they have, and when they contract out they're not looking for a lot of creativity.

I look for a few things in good policy analysis. Primarily, it has to be informed, and by that I mean a few things. I mean it commands the available knowledge out there on a problem. It is politically informed about what's feasible and fiscally sustainable. If a policy proposal is not operationally sustainable it isn't going to go anywhere at all. It has to be well-grounded in the economic realities, which is different from the fiscal side. Beyond that, I can say that I find it helpful if a piece of policy analysis can pass four tests. First is the fiscal test. Has the person checked whether there is money to do this, not just now but over the longer term? Second, the policy test. Is this good policy or bad policy in terms of the public interest or what we ultimately want in the long term? Third, the political test. Will it fly, not just with the government and politicians, but with the public? Fourth, there is the federal-provincial test. Anyone that neglects this is going to be in deep trouble.

I was thinking about what would be the top five characteristics of good policy analysis—context would be the first word I would use.

You have to understand the context within which you are trying to make policy and that means you have to try to define what are the parameters, and that is a judgment, there is no right or wrong answer. The second thing is paradoxically, focus, and that too is a judgment. So if you compare policy-making between various countries, dealing with the area of industrial policy you'll find many have defined the context in a different way. That is because there are certain local factors that you have to take into account. But it's very challenging to make that comparison. Then I would say data. You have to decide what data problems there are and then get the data because without data there is no problem, without a problem there is no solution, there is no policy. So data is the third most important thing. Then I guess the fourth most important factor is clarity of the policy. Is it clear? Are the elements clear? And then the fifth one that is important is simplicity. I don't mean simplistic, but I mean simplicity. If a policy is too complex then it can't be followed and will not be implemented successfully. So the most successful policies are the ones that deal with the most complex problems but reduce them to two or three core elements. That is the real challenge in policy-making. And you don't know if you got it right until the history books are written five years down the road.

Good policy analysis these days does involve consultation and understanding where the various interests groups, clients, and other levels of government—what their interests are and what that means. The other piece is coherence. The policy analysis has to situate itself inside the overall context—the context of the government's agenda, the context of the society, and the context of other programs and ways of doing things. Certainly in social policy we're seeing the importance of health policy, of taxation policy, of economic policy. We can't try to do it all ourselves. It's that kind of holistic coherence. I think also that there has to be an element of "do-ability," and reality and staging. Particularly when you're talking about large government programs. There has to be a transition. Policy has to work "out there" be tested "out there" before you can have confidence that it's doable, that it works when it hits the ground. Finally, think about the accountability mechanisms up front. Who's going to be making the decisions? How are they going to be held accountable? How are you going to monitor that they're doing what they said they would do? How are you going to be responsible and responsive to your client group? What do you have built in to make ongoing changes?

Policy-making has to keep an eye to the public interest. It has to find a balance of interests and go beyond the adversarial approach. Good analysis respects the integrity of the policy process. It should be less concerned with substance than with designing processes that build trust and capacity.

Maybe it's going to be captured in the difference between the science of policy-making to the art of policy-making. It's become less scientific, less that there is a set of tools and rules and theories that you can learn and do policy. Now, it's more a practice of working with the affected parties to define the issues, to identify the options, to identify options that are above all practical and doable and are governed by that other set of constraints, fiscal constraints, etc., unity issues. Of course they were always there, it was never the case that you could print money freely, but now they have much more front-end discipline on the development of policy.

To me there are three or four levels of analysis that are now given a lot of weight. One is professional analysis, the kind of thing that economists or sociologists or intergovernmental relations experts will do— you know, you think your way through a problem with the best that the theory and methodology has available with the best data sets and so forth ... So that stuff is kind of a traditional policy function. Secondly, the politics of policy ... the old line between what the minister's offices did and prime minister's offices did, and what bureaucrats did are becoming fuzzier. Certainly for the big files. One of the things that makes a difference is that civil servants know how to do the technical runs which can tell you winners and losers and so forth. There's no way you can go forward with a document on UI changes or old age security changes or whatever without giving your minister the winners and losers business. Thirdly, I think communications. Communications has always been there ... my sense is that it's grown in relative importance. Communications in many, many senses. We did social security reform, but I'm sure it's true of all the finance budgets as well. We had a parliamentary committee hold hearings, we did workbooks which we distributed across the country and got about a hundred thousand back, we had about 200 members of parliament hold town hall meetings, we had about six or eight expert meetings with groups on specialized topics. It's not communications in the sense of writing speeches, it's communications in the sense of trying to build these linkages into various groups who believe

*they have participatory rights. The communications/participation
issues tend to be merged because part of it reflects a belief that it's
hard to make decisions without these groups, and a part of it reflects
a belief that we have to be seen to have done these things even if we're
going to ignore it all at the end . We need to have done enough so that
when we're attacked, we can get up and make speeches about having
talked to this group and met with that group, and done this, and done
that and so forth ... Conceptually, certainly more than twenty years
ago now, there needs to be a part of the policy process that is engaging the citizenry in one way or another. You may be well motivated,
you may be not well motivated, but it's very hard to go to cabinet to
talk about changes without having a long list of groups that you've
engaged and being able to talk about. If you can't do that you'll be
accused of not having done your homework.*

*I am really struck how impatient senior political decision-makers are,
and some of their senior bureaucratic advisors though they may be a
little less so. There's a problem, a new solution is identified, something quite new is tried, and if it doesn't generate results within two
or three years, it's into the trash can and let's find something new.*

*For things that are considered politically tough, analysis on its own
merits, thoughtfulness on its own merits, often is insufficient. You
need some sort of external crisis to galvanize. The point of galvaniza-
tion could be running out of money, or I suppose it could be a constitutional crisis, or foreign policy war, or some sense of being
overwhelmed by international events. But absent that galvanizing
force there's a reluctance, I guess, to take on whatever the embedded
structures are at the moment, the interests behind those structures.
Those interests that have grown accustomed, and so you need a piece
of dynamite in the system to loosen it up.*

*The policy process has got three elements. The first is content. You've
got to know what you're talking about. You've got to have done your
homework. You have to have the analysis, you have to understand the
economics, the sociology, public relations, political climate. So it's
basically having figured it. Figuring out what the question is, figuring out what the dynamics are, what the alternatives are, etc., etc.
The analytical part is absolutely key. The second part is relationships,
and we've come to talk now about our relationships as capital, and we
do reviews of our capital assets ... How many people trust us, how
many people owe us, how many people do we owe, how many allies*

do we have, how broad are our networks? Because when it comes to doing a policy question, you can't all of a sudden create this, you need the capital. I use the capital concept because I've been trying to teach my staff to invest, not to go to people only when you've got a problem. To build relationships and trust and common meaning with a broad enough network, that when we want to do policy work, we can do it. The third thing is process. The quality of process is absolutely essential. The three are all necessary, and none of them are sufficient. You have to be good at all three. Perfect process, if you haven't built up the relationships and trust and whatnot, the process won't happen. If you haven't figured things out, nothing will happen. And if you've got the relationships, and you've figured things out, but you don't do good process, nothing works. You need all three pillars.

Now, what is good policy? ... It should solve the problem. It should create more public good, the public interest should be furthered along. And then you say, well, you have to define what you mean by the public interest, so you're really getting back to good policy, what is your responsibility? We tend to define our responsibility in [this department] as long-term. I tend to think of my children and all the children in their class as the real stakeholders. Because the wise decisions we take now won't affect you and me all that much—it will, but not enormously. It will have a much more profound effect on the next generation and the generation after that. So, I think that good policy is stuff that will make the world a better place for our kids. Bad policy is stuff that gives a short-term gain at their expense.

REFERENCES

Carter, S. L. (1996, July–August). The power of integrity. *Utne Reader*, pp. 47–50.

Doern, G. B. (1994). *The road to better public services: Progress and constraints in five Canadian federal agencies.* Montreal: Institute for Research on Public Policy.

Gow, J. I. (1995). Frauds and victims: Some difficulties in applying the notion of service to the clientele in the public sector. *Canadian Public Administration, 38*(Winter), 557–577.

Koring, P. (1996, August 21). Boyle blames his subordinates. *Globe and Mail*, A1, A4.

Mintzberg, H. (1996, May–June). Managing government, governing management. *Harvard Business Review*, pp. 75–83.

Picard, A. (1996, August 21) Blame me for blood scandal, Bégin says. *Globe and Mail*, A1, A7.

Privy Council Office. (1995). *Third annual report on the public service of Canada* [On-line]. Available: http://info.ic.gc.ca/pco/chap-1e.txt

Tibbetts, J. (1996, August 20). The Premier's Conference, brought to you by …" *Ottawa Citizen*, A1.

United Nations Development Programme. (1996, October 2). *The human development report 1996* [On-line]. Available: http://www.undp. org/undp/news/hdr96.html

Appendix

Interviewees

Below is a list of interviewees for this book. The interviews were conducted between July and October 1996, and most lasted about one hour. I posed several general questions about changes in the policy environment, impacts for analysis, and the characteristics of good policy analysis. Interviews were taped, and it was agreed that I could use the materials on a nonattributable basis.

Ms. Susan Carter
Associate Director
Canadian Council on Social Development

Mr. Kevin Constante
Assistant Deputy Minister, Social Assistance and Employment
Opportunities Division
Ministry of Community and Social Service (Ontario)

Mr. David Hawkes
Former Co-Director, Research
Royal Commission on Aboriginal Peoples

Mr. Jay Illingsworth
Policy Advisor
ABC, Industry Canada

Mr. Arthur Kroeger
Chancellor
Carleton University

Mr. Avrim Lazar
Assistant Deputy Minister
Environment Canada

Mr. Harvey Lazar
Director, Institute of Intergovernmental Relations
Queen's University

Mr. Craig McFadyen
Director, Office of Constitutional Affairs
Ministry of Intergovernmental Affairs (Ontario)

Mr. Simon McInnes
Director, International Science and Technology Policy
Industry Canada

Mr. Jim Mitchell
Senior Partner
Sussex Circle

Mr. Geoffrey Reid
Associate
Centre Track Conflict Resolution

Ms. Sheila Robertson
Policy Advisor
ABC, Industry Canada

Ms. Jan Rush
Assistant Deputy Minister, Policy Coordination
Cabinet Office (Ontario)

Ms. Norine Smith
Assistant Deputy Minister
Human Resources Development Canada

Mr. Norman Steinberg
Director General, Audit and Review Branch
Public Works and Government Services (Canada)

Mr. David Trick
Assistant Deputy Minister, Postsecondary Education Division
Ministry of Education and Training (Ontario)

Mr. Michael Wernick
Senior Advisor, Constitutional Affairs
Privy Council Office (Canada)

Ms. Cynthia Williams
Director-General, Socio-Economic Policy and Programming Branch
Department of Indian Affairs and Northern Development (Canada)

Index

To the owner of this book

We hope that you have enjoyed *Beyond Policy Analysis: Public Issue Management in Turbulent Times* and we would like to know as much about your experiences with this text as you would care to offer. Only through your comments and those of others can we learn how to make this a better text for future readers.

School _____ Your instructor's name _____

Course _____ Was the text required? _____ Recommended? _____

1. What did you like the most about *Beyond Policy Analysis: Public Issue Management in Turbulent Times*?

_____

_____

_____

2. How useful was this text for your course?

_____

_____

_____

3. Do you have any recommendations for ways to improve the next edition of this text?

_____

_____

_____

4. In the space below or in a separate letter, please write any other comments you have about the book. (For example, please feel free to comment on reading level, writing style, terminology, design features, and learning aids.)

_____

_____

_____

_____

Optional

Your name _____ Date _____

May ITP Nelson quote you, either in promotion for *Beyond Policy Analysis: Public Issue Management in Turbulent Times* or in future publishing ventures?

Yes _____ No _____

Thanks!

You can also send your comments to us via e-mail at
college_arts_hum@nelson.com

PLEASE TAPE SHUT. DO NOT STAPLE.

TAPE SHUT

TAPE SHUT

- - - - - - - - - - - FOLD HERE - - - - - - - - - - -

Nelson

MAIL ➤ POSTE

Canada Post Corporation
Société canadienne des postes

Postage paid	Port payé
if mailed in Canada	si posté au Canada
Business Reply	**Réponse d'affaires**

0066102399   01

0066102399-M1K5G4-BR01

ITP NELSON
MARKET AND PRODUCT DEVELOPMENT
PO BOX 60225 STN BRM B
TORONTO ON M7Y 2H1